RECOVERING PAUL'S MOTHER TONGUE

Recovering Paul's Mother Tongue

Language and Theology in Galatians

Susan Eastman

WILLIAM B. EERDMANS PUBLISHING COMPANY
GRAND RAPIDS, MICHIGAN / CAMBRIDGE, U.K.

Published 2007 by

Wm. B. Eerdmans Publishing Co.

2140 Oak Industrial Drive N.E., Grand Rapids, Michigan 49505 /

P.O. Box 163, Cambridge CB3 9PU U.K.

www.eerdmans.com

Printed in the United States of America

12 11 10 09 08 07   7 6 5 4 3 2 1

Library of Congress Cataloging-in-Publication Data

Eastman, Susan Grove, 1952-

    Recovering Paul's mother tongue: language and theology in Galatians /
Susan Eastman.

       p.   cm.

    ISBN 978-0-8028-3165-1 (pbk.: alk. paper)

    1. Bible. N.T. Galatians — Criticism, interpretation, etc.   I. Title.

BS2685.52.E27   2007

227′.406 — dc22

                                2007009969

Excerpts from the lyrics of "Saint of Me" (1997)
by Mick Jagger and Keith Richards are used by permission.

For Eddie, Danny, and Angela

Contents

Contents

Preface

This study is both the fruit of and an attempt to bear witness to what Rowan Williams calls "a moving and expanding network of saving relationship."[1] The instantiation of that network within my own life has included both the church and the academy. The questions that first prompted my intense interest in Paul were generated by pastoral work in a diverse network of Episcopal congregations: Grace Church and Calvary-St. George's in New York City; St. Andrews in Petersburg, Alaska; Prince of Peace in Salem, Oregon; and All Saints in Aliquippa, Pennsylvania. I am grateful to the marvelous folk in each of these churches, who shared their lives and their questions with me. They taught me to ask how Paul's emphasis on crucifixion with Christ and new creation intersects with existing patterns of relationship, identity, and behavior in the lives of individuals and communities. Is genuine change possible in human interaction? How does it happen? How is it sustained and mediated in the life of the community over time?

The pages that follow attempt to wrestle with these questions through engaging with Paul's thorny letter to the Galatians. In that letter, Paul re-preaches the gospel to his recalcitrant converts, urging them to stand fast in embracing the radical change that God has wrought in their midst through the message of faith. As I pondered the character of Paul's proclamation, particularly in the transitional and motivational sections of Galatians 4:12-

---

1. R. Williams, "Incarnation and the Renewal of Community," in *On Christian Theology* (Oxford: Blackwell, 2001), 235-36; repr. from *Theology Wales* (Winter 1998) 24-40.

20 and 4:21-5:1, I came to see its embodied, mimetic, and metaphorical aspects as a clue to the transformative staying power of the gospel. The result is a study of the working relationship between Paul's language and his theology as enacted in the practice of his apostolic ministry.

A few notes on translation are in order. Quotations from the Dead Sea Scrolls are from the translation by Florentino García Martínez.[2] Unless otherwise noted, all other translations are my own. Following the first appearance of key Greek terms I have provided brief parenthetical translations. I have chosen to render the important Pauline term ἀποκάλυψις *(apokalypsis)* as "apocalypse" rather than as "revelation," in order to retain the dynamic and incursive sense of the term instead of limiting it to its visual meaning. In so doing, I follow the influential interpretation of J. Louis Martyn: "The genesis of Paul's apocalyptic — as we see it in Galatians — lies in the apostle's certainty that God has *invaded* the present evil age by sending Christ and his Spirit into it."[3] As we shall see, this apocalyptic context is crucial for understanding Paul's embodied, metaphorical, and mimetic language in Galatians.

The questions generated by years of pastoral work were given room to flourish and grow at Duke University Divinity School, where I wrote the dissertation from which this book developed. In that specific incarnation of "saving relationship," there are several people for whom I remain profoundly grateful. Many years ago Joel Marcus first "saw" me as a biblical scholar, and over the years he encouraged me to pursue further study; I am happy to know him as an old friend and now as a colleague. As teacher and doctoral advisor, Richard Hays always graciously encouraged my work, delighting in mutual exegetical discovery and theological conversation. Mary McClintock Fulkerson introduced me to issues of power and authority in relationship to Pauline imitation. Stanley Hauerwas taught me to ask new and fruitful questions as I read Paul's letters. In more recent years, as I have gone from student to faculty at Duke, many new colleagues have enriched my life and work here, including, in New Testament, Douglas Campbell and Kavin Rowe. Others are too numerous to name here.

Beyond the bounds of Duke, Kathy Grieb read and commented enthusiastically and insightfully on every page I wrote. John Barclay also has

---

2. *The Dead Sea Scrolls Translated* (2nd ed.; Grand Rapids: Eerdmans, 1996).

3. J. Louis Martyn, *Galatians: A New Translation with Introduction and Commentary,* AB 33A (New York: Doubleday, 1997), 99.

been a rigorous and encouraging conversation partner over the years. Special thanks go to Lou and Dorothy Martyn, who early on gave generously of their time and wisdom to help me clarify issues of identity, continuity, and discontinuity in Galatians; my great debt to both of them is apparent in the pages that follow. My debt to the work of Beverly Gaventa will also be apparent, and I am grateful for her gracious collegiality and friendship.

Special thanks are due to Anne Weston of Duke Divinity School, who gave many hours of editorial work, and to my graduate assistant, T. J. Lang, for taking on the tedious task of indexing. Thanks also to Linda Bieze and Jennifer Hoffman of Eerdmans for shepherding the manuscript through the publication process from start to finish.

It was only as I approached the end of writing this book on Paul's "mother tongue" that I realized the extent of my debt to my own mother, Pat Grove. She modeled for me a fascination with language and a love of literature, and she eagerly kept up with my work until her death in 2005. Thus this study of Paul's mimetic and maternal "voice" became, in a particular way, a recovery of my own "mother tongue."

Finally, this book is dedicated to the brightest stars in my constellation of relationships — my husband Eddie, and our children, Danny and Angela. During my years of writing, Danny and Angela grew to young adulthood, developing into their distinct, inimitable, and wonderful selves. They are a joy to us. With considerable personal sacrifice and love, Eddie first encouraged me to return to school, and stood fast through all the changes and uncertainties this new endeavor brought. His faith, humor, and generosity teach me daily the staying power of God's unconditional love.

Abbreviations

Abbreviations

JBL	*Journal of Biblical Literature*
JJS	*Journal of Jewish Studies*
JSNT	*Journal for the Study of the New Testament*
JSNTSup	Journal for the Study of the New Testament Supplements
JSPSup	Journal for the Study of the Pseudepigrapha Supplements
KEK	Kritisch-exegetischer Kommentar über das Neue Testament
LCL	Loeb Classical Library
LEC	Library of Early Christianity
LXX	Septuagint
MT	Masoretic text
NEB	New English Bible
NIB	*New Interpreter's Bible.* Ed. L. E. Keck. 13 vols. Nashville: Abingdon, 1994-2004
NIGTC	New International Greek Testament Commentary
NovT	*Novum Testamentum*
NRSV	New Revised Standard Version
NTS	*New Testament Studies*
OBO	Orbis biblicus et orientalis
OBT	Overtures to Biblical Theology
OTL	Old Testament Library
OTP	*Old Testament Pseudepigrapha.* Ed. J. H. Charlesworth. 2 vols. Garden City, NY: Doubleday, 1983-85
PSB	*Princeton Seminary Bulletin*
RB	*Revue biblique*
RSV	Revised Standard Version
SBLDS	Society of Biblical Literature Dissertation Series
SBLSCS	Society of Biblical Literature Septuagint and Cognate Studies
SBLSP	Society of Biblical Literature Seminar Papers
SBLTT	Society of Biblical Literature Texts and Translations
SNTSMS	Society for New Testament Studies Monograph Series
SP	Sacra pagina
TDNT	*Theological Dictionary of the New Testament.* Ed. G. Kittel and G. Friedrich. Trans. G. W. Bromiley. 10 vols. Grand Rapids: Eerdmans, 1964-76
THKNT	Theologischer Handkommentar zum Neuen Testament
TZ	*Theologische Zeitschrift*
WBC	Word Biblical Commentary
WTJ	*Westminster Theological Journal*
WUNT	Wissenschaftliche Untersuchungen zum Neuen Testament

Chapter One

"The Torturer Became the Mother"

St. Paul the persecutor was a cruel and sinful man,
Jesus hit him with a blinding light and then his life began.
I said ye-e-es.

Mick Jagger and Keith Richards, "Saint of Me" (1997)[1]

But behold all at once the Holy Spirit was sent from heaven, like milk
poured out from Christ's own breasts, and Peter was filled with an abun-
dance of milk. Not long afterwards Saul became Paul, the persecutor be-
came the preacher, the torturer became the mother, the executioner be-
came the nurse, so that you might truly understand that the whole of his
blood was changed into the sweetness of milk, his cruelty into loving
kindness.

Guerric, abbot of Igny (ca. 1157)[2]

1. Mick Jagger and Keith Richards, "Saint of Me," recorded February-June 1997, Ocean Way Recording Studios, Los Angeles, CA. Online: http://www.timeisonourside.com/SOSaint.html.
2. "Second Sermon for Saints Peter and Paul," in *Sermons,* ed. J. Morson and H. Costello, Sources chrétiennes 166 and 202, Série des textes monastiques d'Occident 31 and 43 (Paris: Cerf, 1970-73), 2:384-86; also trans. Monks of Mount St. Bernard Abbey, in Guerric of Igny, *Liturgical Sermons,* Cistercian Fathers series 8 and 32 (Spencer, MA: Cistercian Publications, 1970-71), 2:155. For more examples of maternal imagery used for both Jesus and Paul, see further discussion in C. Walker Bynum, *Jesus as Mother: Studies in the Spirituality of the High Middle Ages* (Berkeley: University of California Press, 1982), 113-29.

D espite the immense temporal and cultural chasm that separates Mick Jagger and Keith Richards of the Rolling Stones from Guerric of Igny, they find common ground in their description of the reversal that defines the course of the apostle Paul's life. Had he heard both descriptions, Paul might well have said, "I couldn't have put it better myself." The change in his life was so great that he described it in terms of death and new life: "I have been crucified with Christ. Nevertheless I live, yet not I but Christ lives in me, and the life I now live, I live by the faithfulness of the Son of God" (Gal 2:20). Clearly, for Paul it was after God's gracious apocalypse (or revelation) of Christ in his own life that, in a profound sense, "his life began." His letter to the Galatians proclaims that death and new life in dramatic language, speaking of deliverance from "the present evil age" (1:4), his "former life in Judaism" (1:13), the turning point of God's apocalypse of his Son in his life (1:16), death to the law and crucifixion with Christ (2:19-20), and a new creation (6:15). Furthermore, Paul expects his converts to experience and display a similar radical change in their own lives, as he reminds them that formerly they were slaves of the elemental spirits of the cosmos, but now they are "sons of God" and "heirs of God" (3:23–4:7). All who belong to Christ belong to the "new creation," in which old identity markers are radically shifted (3:28). In some way Paul sees his own life as exemplary of God's transforming power, exhorting his converts to "become like me" (4:12).

Despite Jagger and Richards's and Guerric's common focus on the change in Paul's life, they diverge in their reaction to that change. For Guerric that reversal is an invitation to his auditors to trust in Paul's message and to embrace a corresponding transformation in their lives. For Jagger and Richards it seems unthinkable; the refrain of their song is, "You'll never make a saint of me," and it reminds us of the existential obstacles to following in Paul's footsteps, if indeed it is possible to do so. The first obstacle is posed by the apostle's emphasis on suffering for the sake of the gospel, raising the question of motivation. This difficulty, of course, is not unique to Paul's life. As Jagger and Richards put it, after Augustine's turn away from "all the special pleasures of doing something wrong," and John the Baptist's martyrdom:

> Could you stand the torture and could you stand the pain,
> Could you put your faith in Jesus when you're burning in the flames?
> I said a yes, oh yes, oh yes,
> You'll never make a saint of me.

Jagger and Richards speak for many when they reject the examples of the martyred saints of the church.[3]

Yet it is not clear that they completely reject those examples of sainthood. Instead, they remain so fascinated and drawn by them that their lyrics carry, not an absolute rejection, but a tortured ambiguity: "I said yes, oh yes, oh yes." They say yes, but at the same time they say no — "You'll never make a saint of me." Here the examples of the saints, beginning with Paul, do have inspirational force, but not enough to move one from admiration to emulation. Therefore the question of motivation becomes also a question of power: whence comes the power that moves one beyond Jagger and Richards's ambiguous *sic et non* to Guerric's unqualified yes — the kind of assent that Paul's own life seems to display?

In addition to the question of motivational force, the dramatic reversal proclaimed by Paul's life and preaching poses a question of durative force. How does one sustain such change over time? This difficulty concerns the intersection of Paul's language of death and new life with the daily lives of individuals and communities — lives that of necessity unfold in at least a somewhat linear fashion.[4] Without some such linearity and continuity, one cannot speak of genuine *transformation,* but only of a continual *replacement* of the "old" by the "new." But without a radical break with the past, one may slip into a kind of determinism, or at the least an evolutionary model of history, that is quite foreign to Paul's apocalyptic convictions. Galatians appears to contain language depicting both linear, "horizontal" narratives and foundational dislocations in those narratives occasioned by the "punctiliar, vertical" inbreaking of the apocalypse of Christ.[5] For this reason Galatians has become somewhat of a battleground between those exegetes who stress discontinuity and radical change as at the heart of Paul's gospel, and others who see in that gospel a model of

3. See in particular Elizabeth Castelli, *Imitating Paul: A Discourse of Power* (Louisville: Westminster/John Knox, 1991).

4. To speak of individual and communal lives over time is to tell a story, and as Douglas Campbell points out, "Narratives, as the unfolding of events and plots in relation to personal actors, tend to presuppose a linear temporal framework." See "The Story of Jesus in Romans and Galatians," in *Narrative Dynamics in Paul: A Critical Assessment,* ed. Bruce W. Longenecker (Louisville: Westminster/John Knox, 2002), 101.

5. For example, Gal 1–2 contains the only "autobiographical" narrative in Paul's Letters, yet it is a narrative of metaphorical death and new life. Paul has died to the law and to the cosmos, yet he also speaks of the fulfillment of the law, and of fulfilling the "law of Christ."

gradual growth.[6] The difficulties are existential as well as exegetical. One may speak of the apocalypse of Christ as a cosmic knife that cuts human history into a "before" and an "after," but where in the lives of individuals and communities does one locate the line between "before" and "after," or in Paul's terms, "present evil age" and "new creation"? How does God's decisive action, the sending of the Son, intersect with and realign the course of human lives over time? As Francis Watson puts it:

> The Pauline gospel announces a definitive, unsurpassable divine incursion into the world — "vertically, from above," in Karl Barth's celebrated phrase — that both establishes the new axis around which the entire world thereafter revolves and discloses the original meaning of the world as determined in the pretemporal counsel of God. So unlimited is the scope of this divine action that it comprehends not only the end but also the beginning — although it takes the highly particular form of an individual human life that reaches its goal not only in death but also in resurrection. The question is whether, for Paul, this life can be presented *both* as the singular divine saving action *and* as a narrative.[7]

In that Paul identifies himself and his converts as "in Christ," the question posed by Watson regarding the life of Jesus applies to the apostle and to the Galatians as well: can these lives be presented *both* as examples of the singular divine saving action *and* as narratives? The focus on divine saving action speaks to the locus and source of transforming and sustaining power; the focus on narrative struggles with the shape of day-to-day human existence.

Paul's Galatian congregations have heard and accepted his initial preaching of Christ. But now they are listening to the preaching of other

---

6. This debate is exemplified by three essays in Jouette M. Bassler, ed., *Pauline Theology*, vol. 1: *Thessalonians, Philippians, Galatians, Philemon* (Minneapolis: Fortress, 1991); James D. G. Dunn, "The Theology of Galatians: The Issue of Covenantal Nomism," 125-46; Beverly R. Gaventa, "The Singularity of the Gospel: A Reading of Galatians," 147-59; and J. Louis Martyn, "Events in Galatia: Modified Covenantal Nomism versus God's Invasion of the Cosmos in the Singular Gospel: A Response to J. D. G. Dunn and B. R. Gaventa," 160-79. The terminology of "linear" and "punctiliar" is coined by Martyn; "the singularity of the gospel" originates with John Schütz, *Paul and the Anatomy of Apostolic Authority*, SNTSMS 26 (Cambridge: Cambridge University Press, 1975), 121.

7. Francis Watson, "Is There a Story in These Texts?" in *Narrative Dynamics in Paul*, 232.

Jewish Christian missionaries. Through circumcision and law observance, these missionaries seem to offer concrete help with the direction and discipline of the Galatians' daily lives, and the Galatians waver in their acceptance of Paul's message. If they are to heed Paul's exhortation, "Stand fast and do not submit again to a yoke of slavery!" they need motivation to join him in his death to the law and to the cosmos, even as that death entails suffering. Further, they need a way to make sense of the struggles in their communal life at the boundary of the present evil age and the new creation, and they need power to persevere in their reliance on the Spirit apart from the law. That is, they need the saving power of God, enacted in the singular cross and resurrection of Christ, to be mediated to and through them over time.

The issue of *motivation* perhaps most exercises those who attempt to preach from Paul's letters, because such preaching must ask what moves people to follow in the footsteps of such a countercultural, counterintuitive, and outrageous apostle. The issue of transforming and sustaining *power* is equally pressing for all who attempt to take seriously Paul's language of radical discontinuity, and at the same time build and nurture a faith community that endures. In the following studies, I shall argue that Paul addresses both of these issues in the central section of his letter, the complex and confusing pericopes of Gal 4:12-20 and 4:21–5:1. The first passage moves from the apostle's reciprocal mimetic appeal, "Become like me, because I also have become like you" (4:12), to his anguished maternal cry, "My little children, with whom I am again in labor until Christ be formed in you!" (4:19). The second passage retells and re-signifies the birth narratives of Ishmael and Isaac through the interpretive lenses of Isa 54:1 and Gal 4:27. The purpose of both passages remains a problematic and debated question in the interpretation of the letter as a whole. In regard to 4:12-20, Hans Dieter Betz remarks, "All commentators point out that the section 4:12-20 presents considerable difficulties. . . . Paul seems to be jumping from one matter to the next, without much consistency of thought."[8] As

---

8. Hans D. Betz, *Galatians: A Commentary on Paul's Letter to the Churches in Galatia,* Hermeneia (Philadelphia: Fortress, 1979), 220. Many remark on the emotional intensity of the passage, with some attributing its difficulty to Paul's passionate outburst, and others recognizing here a rhetorical technique. See, e.g., Albrecht Oepke, *Der Brief des Paulus and die Galater,* THKNT 9 (Berlin: Evangelische Verlagsanstalt, 1960), 140-41; Franz Mussner, *Galaterbrief,* HTKNT 9 (Freiburg: Herder, 1974), 304-5; Ernest D. Burton, *Galatians: A Critical and Exegetical Commentary on the Epistle to the Galatians,* ICC (Edinburgh: T. & T. Clark,

for the allegory in 4:21–5:1, interpretations vary from that of Ernest D. Burton, who calls it an "afterthought," to that of Betz, who sees it as the climax of the *probatio*.[9] Indeed, if 4:12-30 was omitted, the train of thought would flow smoothly from Paul's rebuke of the Galatians for observing the liturgical calendar (4:10), to his warning against circumcision (5:2). Galatians 5:1 would pick up on the warning against slavery to the *stoicheia*, the elemental spirits (4:9). These observations call into question the contribution of the two intervening pericopes — one from experience, one from Scripture, both structured by the language of human relationships — to Paul's repreaching of the gospel.

My thesis is twofold. First, in this difficult section of the letter the apostle communicates to his converts the motivation and power necessary to move them from their wavering *sic et non* to a faith that "stands fast" in its allegiance to Christ alone as the source of their unity and life together. Second, the medium and the message are inseparable: Paul's discourse — packed with familial images, representative, vulnerable and yet authoritative, and above all, marked by personal suffering — demonstrates for his converts the content of the good news.[10] That demonstration has motivational force, drawing his auditors back into a relational matrix with both cosmic and personal dimensions, which in turn mediates the gospel's power to transform and sustain them. Most striking, the apostle's language is replete with maternal imagery — his own "labor pains," the conflict between the slave woman and the free, the claim that "Jerusalem above is free, and she is our mother," and the rejoicing of the barren woman.[11] I call

---

1959), 235; Pierre Bonnard, *L'Épître de Saint Paul aux Galates*, CNT 9 (Neuchâtel: Delachaux et Niestlé, 1972); James D. G. Dunn, *A Commentary on the Epistle to the Galatians*, BNTC (London: Black, 1993), 231.

9. Burton, *Galatians*, 251; Betz, *Galatians*, 238-40.

10. The literature on Paul's use of familial imagery is extensive. See, e.g., Daniel von Allmen, *La Famille de Dieu: La Symbolique familiale dans le paulinisme*, OBO 41 (Göttingen: Vandenhoeck & Ruprecht, 1981); Abraham J. Malherbe, "God's New Family in Thessalonica," in *The Social World of the First Christians: Essays in Honor of Wayne A. Meeks*, ed. L. Michael White and O. Larry Yarbrough (Minneapolis: Fortress, 1995), 116-25; Halvor Moxnes, ed., *Constructing Early Christian Families: Family as Social Reality and Metaphor* (London: Routledge, 1997); E. Elizabeth Johnson, "Apocalyptic Family Values," *Int* 56, 1 (2002): 34-44; Reidar Aasgaard, *My Beloved Brothers and Sisters: Christian Siblingship in Paul* (Edinburgh: T&T Clark, 2004).

11. The maternal imagery has largely been ignored in the secondary literature. Notable exceptions are Mary Callaway, *Sing, O Barren One: A Study in Comparative Midrash*, SBLDS

this mode of communication "mother tongue," and I shall argue that a fresh hearing of Paul's "mother tongue" will illuminate the gospel's power to move, transform, and sustain his auditors in 4:12–5:1. One purpose, therefore, of the following studies is to recapture the positive power of the apostle's familial metaphors, precisely when they are heard as "mother tongue" rather than "father tongue." In the remainder of this chapter I will develop both this heuristic metaphor for the apostle's discourse and the theological stake in the following studies of motivation and staying power in 4:12–5:1.

Recovering Paul's "Mother Tongue"

In a well-known commencement address given at Bryn Mawr College in 1986, Ursula Le Guin describes three different "languages": the "father tongue," the "mother tongue," and the "native tongue."[12] By these metaphorical designations Le Guin does not refer primarily to "men's speech" as distinct from "women's speech," but to different kinds of communication that serve different purposes, whether spoken by men or women.[13] The "father tongue" is the language of dominant power and public discourse, aimed at getting things done. It is the "language of thought that seeks objectivity."[14] Not to be confused with the voice of "reason," which is greater than mere "objectivity," the "essential gesture of the father tongue is not reasoning but distancing — making a gap, a space, between the subject or self and the object or other."[15] Such language is "spoken from above. It goes one way."[16]

The "mother tongue," on the other hand, is "conversation, a word the

91 (Atlanta: Scholars Press, 1986); Beverly R. Gaventa, *Our Mother Saint Paul* (Louisville: Westminster John Knox, 2007); Brigette Kahl, "No Longer Male: Masculinity Struggles behind Galatians 3:28?" *JSNT* 79 (2000): 37-49; and, to a lesser degree, J. Louis Martyn, *Galatians: A New Translation with Introduction and Commentary,* AB 33A (New York: Doubleday, 1997), 426-31.

12. Ursula Le Guin, "Bryn Mawr Commencement Address," *Dancing at the Edge of the World: Thoughts on Words, Women, Places* (New York: Grove Press, 1989), 147-60.

13. Despite this disclaimer, Le Guin does claim that we learn the "mother tongue" primarily from our mothers, and that it is spoken primarily by women and children.

14. Ibid., 148.

15. Ibid.

16. Ibid., 149.

root of which means 'turning together.' The mother tongue is language not as mere communication but as relation, relationship. It connects. It goes two ways, many ways, an exchange, a network. Its power is not in dividing but in binding, not in distancing but in uniting."[17] This "mother tongue" is learned in childhood, often but not always from one's mother.[18] This is the language of emotions and of personal experience, in which subjective, shared self-disclosure is the medium that unites conversation partners. Such language exposes rather than protects the speaker, and therefore it is a fearful enterprise: "People crave objectivity because to be subjective is to be embodied, to be a body, vulnerable, violable."[19] For this reason it is usually spoken in private, in the home: it is not the language of public discourse.

When the private language and the public discourse come together, the result is what Le Guin calls "native tongue." This is the rare "unlearned" language that results from "the marriage of the public discourse and the private experience, making a power, a beautiful thing, the true discourse of reason. This is a wedding and welding back together of the alienated consciousness that I've been calling the father tongue and the undifferentiated engagement that I've been calling the mother tongue."[20] Le Guin's examples of "native tongue" come from music and literature, although it also "can be speeches and science, any use of language when it is spoken, written, read, heard as art."[21] By "art" she apparently means personal experience spoken in public, and both spoken and heard in an embodied way: "I use the words 'literature,' 'art,' in the sense of 'living well, living with skill, grace, energy' — like carrying a basket of bread and smelling it and eating as you go."[22] That is, to be heard fully, the "native tongue" must also be grasped and enacted in one's life, not analyzed at a distance.

---

17. Ibid.

18. Here is part of Le Guin's example of "mother tongue," ibid., 150: "John have you got your umbrella I think it's going to rain. Can you come play with me? If I told you once I told you a hundred times. Things here just aren't the same without Mother, I will now sign your affectionate brother James. Oh what am I going to do? So I said to her I said if he thinks she's going to stand for that but then there's his arthritis poor thing and no work. I love you. I hate you. I hate liver."

19. Ibid., 151.

20. Ibid., 152.

21. Ibid.

22. Ibid., 154.

By way of contrast, Le Guin complains that in creative writing classes, literature "is all taught as if it were a dialect of the father tongue."[23]

Le Guin's metaphors develop and refine the stock metaphor of "mother tongue" as a reference to "native tongue," the first language learned in childhood. For the native speaker, one's mother tongue is richly allusive, idiomatic, the carrier of collective and private memories, inseparable from its cultural history. Mother tongue carries history with it, even while transmuting that history through the medium of experience. For the nonnative speaker, accurate hearing of another's mother tongue is always somewhat elusive and requires sensitivity to both history and experience.

If one turns to Gal 4:12-20 after reading Le Guin's evocative linguistic metaphors, one might recognize in Paul's intensely emotional, experiential, and indeed gendered appeal the apostle's "native tongue." It is notable that Paul does not use abstract terminology such as "theological continuity" to appeal to his converts. Instead, he draws on the power of intimate familial metaphors: father, mother, children, brothers, and sisters. His speech is personal and yet public: aimed at achieving certain results in the Galatians' behavior, yet also aimed at reconciling his relationship with them. Indeed, the reconciliation is fundamental to the desired behavioral change. In the reciprocal call to mutual "likeness" in 4:12, he seeks an ongoing two-way "conversation" — a "turning together" toward Christ. His language is passionate, involved, and intensely personal while also cosmic in scope. As Le Guin astutely remarks, embodiment means vulnerability, and as we shall see, Paul's embodiment and vulnerability in these passages are breathtaking.

Further, as noted above, 4:19 and the subsequent scriptural argument of 4:21–5:1 are replete with maternal metaphors. In the first text, Paul is a mother. Perhaps inspired by his example, in the quotation at the beginning of this chapter Guerric of Igny uses maternal images of the apostle to communicate both reversal and sustenance: "The torturer became the mother, the executioner became the nurse, so that you might truly understand that the whole of his blood was changed into the sweetness of milk, his cruelty into loving kindness."[24] Similarly, Anselm of Canterbury speaks of Paul, as

---

23. Ibid., 153.

24. In Gal 4:19 Paul depicts himself as a mother; in 1 Thess 2:7 he likens himself to a nurse caring for her children. Implicit in Guerric's metaphor is the understanding of female physiology articulated several centuries earlier by Clement of Alexandria; both believe that

well as Jesus, in maternal language: "Fathers you are then by result, mothers by affection; fathers by authority, mothers by kindness; fathers by protection, mothers by compassion."[25]

With a nod to such earlier interpreters of Paul, Beverly Gaventa has suggested that Paul uses maternal imagery in passages that concern his converts' growth and sustenance in the faith, and paternal imagery to speak of their conversion through his preaching.[26] The following chapters will explore and develop Gaventa's claim in depth. But we may note at the outset that the picture emerging from Paul's Letters is more complex than her theory suggests, particularly in regard to Paul's paternal imagery. For example, while her observation certainly holds true for 1 Cor 3:1-2; 4:14-21; and 1 Thess 2:7, it does not take account of 1 Thess 2:11, where Paul's paternal language conveys exhortation and encouragement, not conversion. Indeed, a closer look at the texts reveals a more nuanced pattern of patriarchal imagery: Paul uses γεννάω (to beget) in both masculine and feminine forms to refer to the founding of churches and the conversion of individuals (Gal 4:24; 1 Cor 4:15; Phlm 10), but he uses πατήρ (father) to refer to God as father (1 Cor 1:3; 2 Cor 1:3; Gal 1:3; 4:6; Rom 8:15; Phil 1:2; 4:20; 1 Thess 1:3; Phlm 3) or to his own ongoing responsibility for the care of his converts (1 Thess 2:11).[27] Regarding Paul's use of maternal imagery, the image of protracted labor pains in Gal 4:19 also seems to defy any neat schematization; the punctiliar image of birth suggests conversion rather than growth, but the emphasis on *repeated* labor pains suggests a continuing process of formation.

Despite these caveats, Gaventa's insight points in a promising direction for further investigation of Paul's maternal metaphors in Galatians. In 4:19 the apostle uses maternal imagery of himself; in 4:21–5:1 he joins his converts as a child of "the free woman." If in some way both maternal metaphors contribute to the Galatians' growth and sustenance in the faith,

---

mother's milk is made from the mother's blood. Guerric is not alone in using such maternal imagery of Jesus, the apostles, and church authorities; one need only consider Clement of Alexandria, Anselm of Canterbury, and Bernard of Clairvaux, to name three examples. For extensive discussion see Bynum, *Jesus as Mother*, 113-29.

25. Anselm, prayer 10 to St. Paul, *Opera omnia*, ed. Franciscus S. Schmitt (Edinburgh: T. Nelson, 1940-61), 3:39-41. The translation is from Bynum, *Jesus as Mother*, 114.

26. Gaventa, "Our Mother St. Paul," 34.

27. Martyn has written extensively on γεννάω as Paul's "missioning verb." See *Galatians*, 451-57.

then they also speak directly to the questions of motivation and staying power posed at the beginning of this chapter. The reciprocal mimesis enjoined in 4:12, as well as the apostle's prophetic enactment of his message and the function of his maternal metaphors in 4:19 and 4:21–5:1, will guide the following investigation of his "mother tongue." As an indispensable aspect of his "native tongue," that mother tongue contributes to a peculiar speech that in turn communicates both the transforming power and the durative force of the gospel, thereby motivating the Galatians to adhere to the climactic exhortation of the letter: "Stand fast, and do not submit to a yoke of slavery!" (5:1).

The Staying Power of the Gospel

Paul's concern not only for the conversion but also for the perseverance and growth of his converts is evident elsewhere in his letters. For example, in Phil 1:25 he understands his own call to "remain and continue [μενῶ καὶ παραμενῶ]" with his converts as necessary for their "progress [προκοπὴν] and joy in the faith." That is, the apostle sees himself as a key player in the "good work" that God began in the Philippians and will bring to completion at the day of Jesus Christ (ὅτι ὁ ἐναρξάμενος ἐν ὑμῖν ἔργον ἀγαθὸν ἐπιτελέσει ἄχρι ἡμέρας Χριστοῦ Ἰησοῦ, 1:6). Paul has a specific idea of what such "completion" looks like: abounding in love and discernment, the Philippians will be "pure and blameless for the day of Christ, having been filled with the fruits of righteousness which come through Jesus Christ [πεπληρωμένοι καρπὸν δικαιοσύνης τὸν διὰ Ἰησοῦ Χριστοῦ]" (1:10-11). The same concern for his converts' blamelessness and innocence at the day of Christ surfaces in 2:15-16 (cf. also 1 Thess 3:12-13; 1 Cor 1:8). In Phil 3:12–4:1 Paul defines "those who are mature [τέλειοι]" as those who join with him in pressing forward to the "upward call" of God. The eschatological expectation of judgment and hope of resurrection motivate and warrant the apostle's command to the Philippians, as with affective language he exhorts them: "Therefore, my brothers and sisters, whom I love and long for, my joy and crown, stand firm [στήκετε] in the Lord" (4:1).

One may trace similar motifs in Paul's angry and passionate letter to the Gentile Christian congregations in Galatia as he addresses a specific crisis: other Jewish Christian missionaries have challenged the adequacy of Paul's gospel, telling his converts that they cannot be full members of

God's covenant people without being circumcised (Gal 5:2; 6:12-13).[28] By promoting entrance through circumcision into the family of Abraham, these other missionaries offer to the new Christians a history, a continuity, and a sense of belonging to an embodied, particular institution with its own, albeit countercultural, status. In addition, instruction in the law of Moses can provide the Galatians with a set of practical guidelines for daily life.[29] Paul's proclamation of deliverance from the present evil age, crucifixion with Christ, and life in the Spirit must seem discontinuous and disembodied by comparison, without resources for developing and maintaining a faithful community.

Yet it is precisely the Galatians' unity with Christ and completion in the Spirit that in Paul's view are endangered by the teaching of these other missionaries (see, e.g., 3:3; 5:4). He writes his letter to correct and nurture the Galatians' continuing common life, not to convert them in the first place; his argument builds on the notion that their present means of growth should be consonant with their initial genesis through the message of faith (3:3). Thus, by interpreting the Jewish Christian formula, "Christ gave himself for our sins," as liberation from the present evil age, Paul establishes the context for his repreaching of the gospel: Christ's act of deliverance is the sole power that will bring the Galatians out of slavery to the powers of this age and into the freedom of the new creation (6:15-16).[30] This singular act and its proclamation, apart from the law, have the power

28. The literature about the identity of these other missionaries is extensive. See, e.g., Robert Jewett, "The Agitators and the Galatian Congregation," *NTS* 17, 1 (1971): 198-212; George Howard, *Paul: Crisis in Galatia: A Study in Early Christian Theology*, SNTSMS 35 (Cambridge: Cambridge University Press, 1979), 1-19; Mussner, *Galaterbrief*, 11-29; John Barclay, "Mirror-Reading a Polemical Letter: Galatians as a Test Case," *JSNT* 31 (1987): 73-93; idem, *Obeying the Truth: A Study of Paul's Ethics in Galatians* (Edinburgh: T&T Clark, 1988), 37-74; J. Louis Martyn, "A Law-Observant Mission to Gentiles," *Theological Issues in the Letters of Paul* (Nashville: Abingdon, 1997), 7-36.

29. See Barclay, *Obeying the Truth*, 72: "The introduction of Jewish rites and ceremonies provided a means whereby the Galatians could constantly reinforce their identity as the people of God. . . . The 'works of the law' would perform a crucial social function in preserving the Galatian Christian communities. In the same way the moral directives in the law must have been most welcome to the Galatians." See also Wayne Meeks, "Toward a Social Description of Pauline Christianity," in *Approaches to Ancient Judaism*, ed. William S. Green (Missoula, MT: Scholars Press, 1980), 33; Betz, *Galatians*, 8-9.

30. For the argument that 1:4b, "that he might deliver us from this present evil age," is Paul's explication of the Jewish Christian formula, "who gave himself for our sins," see Martyn, *Galatians*, 88-92, 95-97.

to bring the Galatians from their beginning in the faith to their *telos* (completion) through the power of the Spirit.

For Paul, and perhaps for the other missionaries as well, the means of his converts' beginning in the faith is inseparable from the means of their completion.[31] His driving goal for the Galatians is that Christ take shape in their midst (4:19). He describes the community formed in Christ as one led by the Spirit and bearing the fruit of the Spirit (5:13-25). The end of such fruit bearing is eternal life, sharing in the destiny of Christ whom God raised from the dead (6:8; 1:1). The community characterized by "faith working through love" (5:6), rather than by the divisive works of the law and the flesh, adumbrates the new creation (6:15). On the other hand, the apostle warns the Galatians that if they practice circumcision, they are cut off from Christ; if they practice the works of the flesh, they will not inherit the kingdom of God; if they sow to their own flesh, they will reap corruption (5:4, 21; 6:8).

The contrast between these two futures suggests that the letter concerns the Galatians' movement from beginning to end, from genesis to completion, as Paul explicitly indicates in 3:3. He is not worried that his converts will fail to enter the people of God, because he is convinced that they already belong to God's people: they are children of Abraham because in Christ they are children of God.[32] Paul's concern is rather that when law

31. It may be that here the apostle also is responding to an accusation by the other missionaries, to the effect that Paul's preaching is inadequate, failing to supply his converts with the full requirements and benefits of belonging to the covenant people. For a mirror-reading of Gal 3:3 indicating that the other missionaries taught the Galatians that they would be completed, or "perfected," through law observance, see Oepke, *Galater,* 101; Jewett, "Agitators," 206-7; Martyn, *Galatians,* 289-94; Richard B. Hays, "Galatians," *NIB* 11:252. Dunn (*Galatians,* 155) allows the possibility that 3:3 alludes to language used by the other missionaries, citing Jas 2:22 as an example of Jewish Christian teaching that works "complete" faith. Barclay (*Obeying the Truth,* 39-40), however, cautions against inferring a theology of "perfection" on the basis of one word (ἐπιτελεῖσθε). Whether or not the other missionaries in Galatia taught circumcision on the basis that it was necessary for Paul's converts to be "perfected," clearly Paul sees circumcision as a fleshly act that will sever the Galatians from their completion in the faith (e.g., 5:4).

32. *Pace* E. P. Sanders's influential contention that Galatians answers a very specific historical question: How can Gentiles enter the people of God? See *Paul, the Law, and the Jewish People* (Philadelphia: Fortress, 1983), 19. Although the requirement of circumcision may be the catalyst for the conflict in Galatia, and therefore entrance into the people of God may be the main point at issue for the circumcision mission, in my view Paul does not present it as *his* central concern. The Galatians already are "in," precisely because Christ has come "into"

observance is made the fundamental criterion of Christian existence it will deflect his converts from their true *telos* — the formation of Christ in them (4:19) — resulting in their final harvest of eternal life (6:8). Thus, in Paul's view, the other missionaries' requirement of circumcision is worse than inadequate; it destroys the Galatian congregations and will sabotage both their present fellowship with Christ and one another, and their future hope of righteousness. Paul's response is to remind his converts that the power that can and will bring them to completion is neither law nor the absence of law ("neither circumcision nor uncircumcision"), but the new creative power of God, disclosed and working through Christ. The apostle's arguments about law observance, about relations between Jew and Gentile, about slavery and freedom are addressed out of, and subservient to, this christocentric goal. Thus the letter provides an inside look at Paul's "labor" with his converts until Christ be formed in them and displays his vision of the intersection of the apocalyptic gospel with the daily life of the Christian community.

This proposal is in line with the contention of J. Louis Martyn that in Galatians "Paul has taken as his leading subject not the Law but rather the gospel of Christ and the history that this gospel has created and continues to create. . . . Paul's theological point of departure is . . . the apocalypse of Christ and *the power of that apocalypse to create a history*."[33] The starting point for this "gospel history" is to be found in the advent of Christ. Arguing against a *heilsgeschichtlich* interpretation of Paul that attributes to him an "affirmation of a salvific linearity prior to the advent of Christ," Martyn nonetheless affirms "that Paul understands the gospel to be on a victorious — one can even say linear — march through the world."[34]

Martyn's description of the gospel's victorious, linear "march through the world" explicates a fundamental claim of Paul's gospel preaching: the

---

their lives through faith (3:23-25). Consequently, their preoccupation with entrance requirements is a denial of God's liberating act in Christ and a regression to slavery under the powers of the present evil age (4:9-10). On "entry language" as characteristic of the other Jewish Christian missionaries in Galatia, see especially Martyn, *Galatians*, 348-49. See also Robert H. Gundry, "Grace, Works, and Staying Saved in Paul," *Bib* 66, 1 (1985): 1-38; and Sanders's nuanced reply to Gundry's earlier SBL presentation on the same subject (*Paul, the Law*, 52 n. 20). See also Dunn, "Theology of Galatians," 130. For a critique of both Dunn and Sanders, see Martyn, "Events in Galatia," 167-68 n. 18.

33. Martyn, "Events in Galatia," 164.

34. Ibid., 174.

power that will transform and sustain the Galatians comes solely from God. Martyn describes this central claim in terms of the priority of God's gracious initiative in moving into the sphere of human bondage, rather than human movement into the sphere of God's grace:

> For Paul, the dominant line is the one along which God *has* moved *into the cosmos* in the invasive sending of Christ and in Christ's faithful death for all (note the verbs in 3:23, 24; 4:4, 6, etc.). . . . [T]he difference between human movement into the covenant and God's movement into the cosmos is, in the terms of Galatians, the watershed distinction between religion and ἀποκάλυψις, which is one way of encapsulating the subject of the letter.[35]

One can certainly appreciate Martyn's emphasis on the divine *source* of transforming power in Paul's gospel, and the centrality of that emphasis in Paul's proclamation of the transforming and sustaining power of the gospel over time. The gospel history is a history that reveals this divinely initiated and sustained "line of movement."

Two aspects of Martyn's account, however, hamper further description of what the gospel's "creation of a history" looks like in concrete, historical terms. The first is his distinction between "theological" and "anthropological" continuity. The second is his distinction between divine and human activity. Regarding both distinctions, Martyn's own contribution is somewhat ambiguous. First, while allowing for a "theological continuity" given by God's faithfulness to the promise to Abraham, he emphasizes the notion of "anthropological discontinuity" throughout Galatians. For example, Paul's account of his call displays *only* a radical break between his "former life in Judaism" and his new life in Christ. Again, in the allegory of Gal 4:21–5:1, "continuity is to be found only in *God* and in God's salvific deed, not in the creation of a historical linearity. In a word, Paul's radical reading of the birth stories in Genesis 16–21 is anthropologically discontinuous in order to be theologically continuous."[36]

---

35. Ibid., 168. This direction of the line of movement is what, in Martyn's view (ibid., 167), distinguishes Paul's preaching from that of the other missionaries (whom Martyn dubs "the Teachers"), who "hold that Gentiles *can move*, by Law observance, *into* the covenant community." Here (167-68 n. 18) Martyn critiques Sanders's language of "getting in" and "staying in" as more in line with the Teachers' theology than with Paul's.

36. Ibid., 176. Barclay (*Obeying the Truth*, 104) offers a more nuanced account of the re-

Martyn's argument here is *against Heilsgeschichte* as a prior history into which Christ fits, and *for* the "singularity" of the gospel as a historical event. Nonetheless, when one begins to speak of a history created by the gospel, his further formulation becomes problematic: "one must ask . . . whether . . . the word 'singular' does not necessarily bring with it *an opposition to both 'plural' and 'linear.'*"[37] Again, Martyn qualifies "linear" as referring to "a linear history that begins with Abraham."[38] But questions remain when one attempts to speak of the singular gospel intersecting with the linear lives of individuals and communities. Gospel history may start with the historical crucifixion and resurrection of Jesus of Nazareth, but its starting point in the "histories" of real individuals and communities remains extraordinarily difficult to locate. Similarly, the shifting line between the "present evil age" and the "new creation" remains a matter of debate. Taken by itself, the language of anthropological discontinuity does not provide a way to talk about the intersection of the gospel with real, "linear" human lives. The problem is not with Martyn's rejection of a "pre-Christ linearity," nor with his emphasis on the singularity of the gospel, but rather with the way in which a sharp distinction between "theological" and "anthropological continuity" impedes any further description of the gospel's power to create a history. It is difficult, if not impossible, to speak of the gospel creating a "history" without utilizing language implying anthropological as well as theological continuity. Martyn does not explicitly oppose this possibility, but neither does he facilitate the use of such language.

The difficulty is further exacerbated by a second factor in Martyn's reading of Galatians: his emphatic distinction between divine and human activity. Reading Gal 1:1–2:21, he highlights "Paul's tendency to refer to antinomies, beginning with the venerable one between the actions of hu-

---

lationship between *Heilsgeschichte* and apocalyptic than does Martyn: "Galatians combines apocalyptic motifs with a salvation-historical outlook. Within a consistent apocalyptic framework the past and present are all part of the 'evil age' from which one awaits redemption, and righteousness is only to be found in the coming 'new creation.' In Galatians, however, such radical antitheses are presented side by side with elements of continuity and purposeful history: Abraham was himself justified by faith, the Scriptural promises now reach their fulfilment, the child is coming to his maturity. From one perspective, all of the past has been slavery under 'the elements of the world,' while from another it has provided examples, precedents and prophecies of the gospel."

37. Martyn, "Events in Galatia," 176.
38. Ibid.

man beings and the action of God, and including the application of that fundamental antinomy not only to his own apostolate (1:1) but also — in the form of the human activity of traditioning versus the divine activity of apocalypse — to the gospel itself (1:11-16)."[39] But despite this "venerable" antinomy between divine and human action, a close reading of Galatians complicates such a distinction in regard to Paul's own apostolate. On the one hand, he claims that his call and his gospel came directly from God, not from human beings; that is, he claims divine authority for his preaching. On the other hand, the apostle expects God to work through his own preaching, he himself represents and to some degree embodies the crucified Christ (2:20; 3:1; 4:14), and his goal is that the Galatians do the same. The resulting overlay of subjects renders the distinction between divine and human activity in Paul's own missionary work less clear-cut than a simple reading of 1:1 alone would imply. Similarly, insofar as the apostle labors that Christ be formed in his congregations (4:19) and exhorts them to walk by the Spirit and bear the fruit of the Spirit (5:16, 22-25), he presumes the gracious presence of God working in and through the Galatians' mutual service. Indeed, Martyn himself highlights both the active role of the Spirit in 5:13–6:10 and the active role of the Galatians themselves; they "are far more than mere spectators. Having the Spirit in their hearts, they are soldiers who have been called into military service by the Spirit."[40]

Thus Martyn posits that in the "addressable communities" created by the Spirit, there is an intimate union of divine and human action that at the least demonstrates the "history of the Spirit in the Galatian churches."[41] Yet he also claims that Paul maintains both a time-honored antinomy between divine and human action, and a related distinction between theological and anthropological continuity. Taken together these claims stand in tension with Paul's description of life in the Spirit and complicate any description of "gospel history" in an embodied sense. The question therefore remains whether it is necessary to maintain a complete separation between divine and human activity in order to maintain the centrality of God's gracious initiative in the gospel, or whether such a sep-

39. Ibid., 165.

40. Martyn, *Galatians*, 483. Martyn (535) is careful to delineate a close relationship between the action of the Spirit and that of the Galatians: "Their deeds are first of all the acts of the Spirit (5:22; cf. 4:6), and secondly the acts of themselves as persons into whose hearts the Spirit has made its entrance (5:24)."

41. Ibid., 535.

aration is softened by Paul's assurance of union with Christ. If the latter is the case, then that union also calls into question the necessity of positing anthropological discontinuity "in Christ" in order to maintain the singularity of God's saving act. Implicit in these observations is the further question of whether and how the transforming and sustaining power of the gospel, apart from the law, is mediated over time and made visible in human affairs. Without such visibility, it becomes impossible to describe the history-making intersection of Christ's unique crucifixion and resurrection with the linear narratives of Paul's converts.

Recalling Guerric's gendered description of the reversal in Paul's life, and building on Gaventa's proposal regarding the nurturing function of Paul's maternal metaphors, I suggest that Paul's "mother tongue" provides a distinctive contribution to his communication of the history-making power of the gospel. What is at stake in the following studies of Paul's "mother tongue" is the apostle's display of that power as it is represented in his own life and as it creates a particular kind of community. As we shall see in the next chapter, his mimetic appeal to "become like me" is not unidirectional, but reciprocal. "It goes two ways, many ways, an exchange, a network."[42] As such, it evokes a relational matrix disclosed by the close connections between Paul's own retrospective "history" and that of his converts. That relational matrix, I shall argue, provides both the motivation and the *dynamis* (power) for the Galatians' perseverance in the gospel.

The third chapter traces Paul's mode of proclamation in relation to his identification with the prophetic calls of Jeremiah and Isaiah. While much attention has been paid to Greco-Roman rhetoric as the background for understanding Paul's discourse, the many similarities between his mode of communication and that of the prophets suggest that his "native tongue" must also be heard in concert with his Jewish heritage. Particularly in Jeremiah, one finds an intimate relationship between the prophet's life and message, similar to the apostle's interweaving of testimony and proclamation. To some degree, through this mingling of the medium and the message, the prophet represents both God and the people of God. The result is an experiential appeal that is, like "mother tongue," "embodied . . . a body, vulnerable, violable" and, like "native tongue," both public and personal.[43]

The apostle's vulnerability becomes even more breathtaking in his

42. Le Guin, "Bryn Mawr," 149.
43. Ibid., 151.

self-description as a mother in labor (4:19). Therefore, chapter four builds on the findings of chapter three by investigating Paul's maternal imagery in 4:19, and tracing connections between that imagery and maternal metaphors in both Jeremiah and Isaiah. I shall argue that Paul's "labor" refers to his own continuing suffering as he preaches the gospel, which in turn displays the crucified Christ and replicates God's creative "labor" in bringing forth a new people of God. Drawing on its prophetic roots, the feminine metaphor functions to communicate both motivation and staying power for Paul's auditors.

Chapter five explores the complex maternal metaphors of Paul's "allegory" in 4:21–5:1, through which the apostle turns his converts' focus from their past to their future. That future, already adumbrated in the Gentile churches, is encapsulated in the promise given to the barren woman of Isa 54:1: "Rejoice, O barren woman who does not bear; break forth and shout, you who are not in travail, for the children of the desolate one are many more than the children of the one who has a husband." As in Jewish apocalyptic literature, here the feminine figure associated with the city of Jerusalem functions as a representative picture of transformation and as a lasting refuge for the people of God.[44] The maternal imagery depicts a future that breaks partially into the present in the Spirit-led life of the community, but that also sustains that community's reliance on the Spirit rather than the law, giving it the hope of righteousness (5:5) and the promise of eternal life (6:8).

Chapter six continues the argument of chapter five by developing the characteristics of the two "family systems" represented by the slave woman and the free. These characteristics are displayed in Gal 5–6 in the contrast between attempts to live "under the law" on the one hand, and "by the power of the Spirit" on the other hand. The final chapter offers concluding reflections on the "history" created by Paul's gospel, and its relationship to the apostle's mode of communication as "mother tongue."

---

44. For a sustained discussion of such representative feminine figures in apocalyptic literature, see Edith Humphrey, *The Ladies and the Cities: Transformation and Apocalyptic Identity in Joseph and Aseneth, 4 Ezra, the Apocalypse and the Shepherd of Hermas*, JSPSup 17 (Sheffield: Sheffield Academic Press, 1995). See chapter five below.

A Word about Method

Rather than reconstructing the historical and social setting of Galatians, the following chapters offer a close reading of the selected passages in the context of Galatians and other Pauline letters, and in conversation with Jewish texts. In choosing such conversation partners, I follow Paul's lead in describing his call in terms that echo those of Jeremiah and Isaiah. My hunch is that understanding Paul's "mother tongue" will be enhanced by hearing it in concert with the language of the prophets as well as later Jewish apocalyptic writings.[45] By taking such an approach, I do not want to deny the value of the extensive research that has been done on Paul's use of Greco-Roman rhetoric, but I do want to offer a different angle on reading his peculiar form of discourse.[46]

The question remains whether Paul's Gentile converts heard his language in concert with either the Septuagint or other Jewish sources. Christopher Stanley, for instance, argues strongly against the likelihood that the majority of Paul's auditors understood his biblical allusions.[47] It is certainly difficult if not impossible to say definitively whether Paul's original auditors knew the Septuagint or other Jewish writings well enough to understand all of his allusions. All such arguments remain speculative to some degree; the best we can do is to set some parameters around plausible echoes for a first-century Gentile audience in Galatia. At the same time,

45. This is not to say that Paul's native language was Hebrew; it seems to me that Paul's extensive reliance on the LXX indicates that his native language was Greek, and that he knew the Scriptures of Israel in Greek rather than in Hebrew.

46. The following discussion of Paul's discourse as "mother tongue," insofar as it traces patterns of correspondence between Paul's "story" and those of Christ and of the Galatians, and as it identifies "stories" evoked by his maternal metaphors, bears a family resemblance to narrative readings of Paul's letters. At the same time, "mother tongue" and "narrative" are not identical: narratives, because they tell stories of interaction between characters, usually with dialogue, and because the plot develops along with the characters, would seem necessarily to utilize the relational inflections of "mother tongue." But stories can be told and heard without being embodied in the life of either speaker or listener; indeed, they are routinely transmitted as words on paper without any personal interaction between author and reader. "Mother tongue," on the other hand, requires that the message "take on flesh" in the lives of both speaker and auditor. Furthermore, "mother tongue" is not necessarily narrative: in a discrete conversation one might employ a relational, embodied, metaphorical, gendered mode of discourse without claiming to tell a story.

47. Christopher Stanley, "'Pearls Before Swine': Did Paul's Audiences Understand His Biblical Quotations?" *NovT* 41, 2 (1999): 124-44.

the very fact that reconstructions of the original readers' understanding must remain speculative argues against using such historical models as the primary basis for interpreting the meaning of a text. In this regard the suggestion of Stanley Porter is more helpful: "If one is interested in establishing a given author's use of the Old Testament [or Jewish tradition, in this case], it would appear imperative to orient one's discussion to the language of the author, rather than supposed, reconstructed 'knowledge' of the audience."[48] Close attention to Paul's language demonstrates that whether or not his Gentile converts knew the Septuagint, clearly his *implied* readers do have such knowledge. It seems to me that part of the transforming power of a text is precisely in the dynamic relationship between the implied and the actual readers: Paul's "implied reader" challenges his actual readers to become more knowledgeable about Israel's Scriptures in order to understand what he says. As a recollection of the poetry of T. S. Eliot, or for that matter, the history of biblical interpretation, will demonstrate, richly allusive texts create educated audiences. In any case, since Paul's actual writing is accessible to us, whereas the education and certainly the understanding of his auditors remain a matter of speculation, the present work will be oriented primarily to Paul's language.[49]

A good portion of the language studied in this volume is metaphori-

---

48. Stanley Porter, "The Use of the Old Testament in the New Testament," in *Early Christian Interpretation of the Scriptures of Israel*, ed. Craig Evans and James A. Sanders, JSNTSup 148 (Sheffield: Sheffield Academic Press, 1997), 95.

49. This approach represents a departure from Martyn's insistence that the modern interpreter "take a seat in one of the Galatian congregations, in order — as far as possible — to listen to the letter with Galatian ears" (*Galatians*, 42). Martyn's own work demonstrates the fruitfulness of such an enterprise, but also the pitfalls. As Richard Hays points out, "many of Martyn's proposals remain plausible but they are beyond confirmation or disconfirmation. The spellbinding richness of the imaginative construction can hypnotize unwary readers into believing that somehow we have access to more information than we actually do have" (review of J. Louis Martyn, *Galatians*, *JBL* 119, 2 [2000]: 376). At the same time, my approach is sympathetic to Martyn's wariness toward the use of ancient rhetoric as the basis for interpreting the Letter to the Galatians. Rhetoric persuades "on the basis of various cognitive and emotional elements that are already present in the minds and hearts of his hearers," but Paul's gospel is founded on "something that is not already present in the minds and hearts of his hearers," 146 — that is, God's world-creating act in the crucifixion and resurrection of Christ. In Martyn's view, "the newness of this cosmic good news brings about a newness of rhetoric" (*Galatians*, 22). The present study aims at further understanding Paul's "new" rhetoric; precisely because it is "new," the foundation for understanding it must be sought in Paul's text rather than in the preconceptions and limitations of his original auditors.

cal, so a word about metaphor theory is also in order here. The subject is vast, as demonstrated by a cursory glance at the literature.[50] I shall take as my guide the insightful and constructive analysis of Janet Martin Soskice in *Metaphor and Religious Language*. Soskice's brief definition of metaphor is "that figure of speech whereby we speak about one thing in terms which are seen to be suggestive of another."[51] This definition rejects substitution and emotive theories of metaphor in favor of a precise "interanimation theory" that builds on the work of Ivor A. Richards. That is, metaphors are not a substitution for what could be said directly without metaphors, nor are they simply an emotional appeal. Rather, they are complete utterances that convey one meaning through an "intercourse of thoughts."[52] The underlying meaning is the metaphor's "tenor," while the imagery used to convey that meaning is the "vehicle" of the metaphor. Together, "tenor" and "vehicle" make an irreducible whole.

At stake in Soskice's definition is metaphor's capacity to describe reality, to make truth claims over against a purported distinction between "metaphorical" and "literal truth."[53] By comparing the functions of metaphor in scientific inquiry and in religious language, Soskice further clarifies her point: in both cases the essential, irreducible function of metaphor is to denote reality without exhaustively defining it. Her aim is to "show that models and metaphorical theory terms may, in both the scientific and religious cases, be reality depicting without pretending to be directly descriptive, and by doing so support the Christian's right to make metaphysical claims."[54] For example, in scientific thought, theory-constitutive metaphors may be seen as "representing reality without claiming to be representationally privileged."[55] The metaphysical claims made by reli-

50. Particularly influential accounts of contemporary metaphor theory include Ivor A. Richards, *The Philosophy of Rhetoric* (Oxford: Oxford University Press, 1936); Max Black, "Metaphor," *Models and Metaphors: Studies in Language and Philosophy* (Ithaca: Cornell University Press, 1962), 25-47; Paul Ricoeur, *The Rule of Metaphor: Multi-disciplinary Studies of the Creation of Meaning in Language* (London: Routledge & Kegan Paul, 1978); George Lakoff and Mark Johnson, *Metaphors We Live By* (Chicago: University of Chicago Press, 1980); and Janet M. Soskice, *Metaphor and Religious Language* (1985; repr. Oxford: Clarendon, 2002).

51. Soskice, *Metaphor*, 15.

52. Ibid., 45, quoting Richards, *Philosophy of Rhetoric,* 100-102.

53. The making of such a "false" distinction is at the heart of Soskice's critique of Ricoeur. See Soskice, *Metaphor*, 88.

54. Ibid., 145.

55. Ibid., 132.

gious metaphors are based on experience, and at the same time they utilize images and models that have been embossed and embellished by the community of faith over time. Because this is so, those metaphors grow and communicate intertextually, while at the same time they are grounded in experience.[56] In the ongoing life of metaphors in the church, text and experience continue in mutual interpretation: Christianity's "sacred texts are chronicles of experience, armouries of metaphor, and purveyors of an interpretive tradition."[57]

In many ways Soskice's account of metaphor is evocative of Le Guin's description of "mother tongue" as experiential, irreducible, and in some sense untranslatable. Mother tongue as native language, like metaphor, is a "purveyor of tradition" insofar as it is the bearer of collective memories. Both make truth claims and both claim to describe reality in a way that the language of abstract thought cannot. At the same time, as Soskice argues persuasively, metaphors point beyond themselves to invisible realities. Paul's maternal metaphors, I shall argue, do the same, disclosing the power of God in the midst of weakness and ultimately carrying the Galatians' vision beyond their present conflict to the promise of God's eschatological future.

56. Ibid., 152-54.
57. Ibid., 160.

Chapter Two

"Become Like Me!"
Mimetic Transformations
in Galatians 4:12-20

The notion of imitation presupposes at least two important and related things: a relationship between at least two elements and, within that relationship, the progressive movement of one of those elements to become similar to or the same as the other. This relationship is asymmetrical, for imitation does not involve both elements moving simultaneously toward similarity, but rather one element being fixed and the other transforming itself or being transformed into an approximation of the first.

. . . .

It goes virtually without saying that the very practice of imitation dooms one to failure. One may want to be like the saints, to take on that identity of holiness, but ultimately, those gestures are at best shadowy approximations of the fuller, more complete, indeed perfect gestures of one's models. (Cynicism is not the preferred response to one's inevitable failure, of course; failure becomes the reason to strive still more fervently!)[1]

You'll never make a saint of me.[2]

The wry comments quoted above from Elizabeth Castelli, concerning "the religious formation of generations of Catholic children," may res-

1. Castelli, *Imitating Paul*, 21, 13.
2. Jagger and Richards, "Saint of Me."

onate for many, whether Catholic or Protestant, who have grown up in the church.[3] But whether they accurately reflect either the literary function or practical effects of Paul's imitation language, as Castelli argues, is another matter. To inquire after the "effects" of Paul's injunction to "become like me" would require a historical and sociological investigation that is beyond the focus of this book.[4] This inquiry will be limited to the function within Paul's letter of his first imperative appeal to his Galatian congregations (Gal 4:12): "Become like me, for I also have become like you, brothers and sisters, I beg of you" (Γίνεσθε ὡς ἐγώ, ὅτι κἀγὼ ὡς ὑμεῖς, ἀδελφοί, δέομαι ὑμῶν).

Because the words μίμησις and μιμέομαι do not appear in Galatians, not all scholars have interpreted 4:12 as a mimesis text.[5] While some link the verse with other explicit mimesis texts in the Pauline corpus, others see in it an emotional appeal to a reciprocal relationship. Martyn sets out the presumed antithesis nicely: "Fundamentally, then, Paul speaks not of an

3. Castelli, *Imitating Paul*, 13.

4. See the cogent criticism by Brigette Kahl: "Reading Paul in terms of 'repressive same-ness' and 'coercive universalism,' as, e.g., D. Boyarin . . . and E. Castelli . . . do, would reflect much more the post-Constantine history of Pauline interpretation than Paul himself" ("No Longer Male: Masculinity Struggles behind Galatians 3:28?" *JSNT* 79 [2000]: 45 n. 17).

5. Those who identify Gal 4:12 as an explicit reference to Paul as an example to be imi-tated include Marie-Joseph Lagrange, *St. Paul: Épître aux Galates,* 2nd ed., Études bibliques (1925; repr. Paris: Gabalda, 1950), 110-11; David M. Stanley, "'Become Imitators of Me': The Pauline Conception of Apostolic Tradition," *Bib* 40 (1959): 874-76; Udo Borse, *Der Brief an die Galater,* Regensburger Neues Testament (Regensburg: Pustet, 1984), 149; George Lyons, *Pauline Autobiography: Toward a New Understanding,* SBLDS 73 (Atlanta: Scholars Press, 1985), 165; Benjamin Fiore, *The Function of Personal Example in the Socratic and Pastoral Epistles,* AnBib 105 (Rome: Biblical Institute Press, 1986), 175, 186; Beverly R. Gaventa, "Galatians 1 and 2: Autobiography as Paradigm," *NovT* 28, 4 (1986): 321-22; Frank Matera, *Galatians,* SP (Collegeville, MN: Liturgical Press, 1992), 159; Castelli, *Imitating Paul,* 115-16; Brian Dodd, *Paul's Paradigmatic 'I': Personal Example as Literary Strategy,* JSNTSup 177 (Sheffield: Sheffield Academic Press, 1999), 161-64. Others emphasize the reciprocity and emotional appeal in the text. See, e.g., Martin Luther, *Commentary on the Epistle to the Galatians,* trans. Edwin Sandys (London: Jas. Clarke, 1953), 397-98; Martyn, *Galatians,* 420. Betz (*Galatians,* 222-23) champions a reading of 4:12-18 as part of a literary friendship topos, and explicitly denies any incompatibility between imitation and the friendship topos (222 n. 28). See also Gaventa, "Galatians 1 and 2," 324-26. It is interesting to note that in Betz's ear-lier work he treats 4:12 as an "apostolic command" with no reference to the friendship topos (*Nachfolge und Nachahmung Jesu Christi im Neuen Testament,* BHT 37 [Tübingen: Mohr/ Siebeck, 1967], 152 n. 6). His analysis in that work concurs with that of Wilhelm Michaelis, who excludes 4:12 from a list of imitation texts precisely because of the reciprocity implied by v. 12b ("Μιμέομαι," *TDNT* 4:672 n. 29).

imitation, but of a shared existence, and it is the nature of that shared existence that thus acquires true significance."[6] As the following analysis will show, however, these two interpretive options are not mutually exclusive.[7] Paul does speak of a shared existence, but that shared existence includes both imitation and friendship motifs. At the same time, neither mimesis nor the Greco-Roman topos of friendship adequately accounts for the relational matrix that Paul evokes and promotes in Galatians. In what follows, a brief look at Pauline mimesis texts will demonstrate that the role of 4:12 within the letter is analogous to that of Paul's explicit calls for imitation in his other letters. A more extended analysis of the place of 4:12 within the letter will explore the relational context that grounds Paul's appeal to "become like me."

The explicit Pauline imitation texts are 1 Thess 1:6; 2:14; 1 Cor 4:16; 11:1; and Phil 3:17:

And you became imitators of us and of the Lord, receiving the word in much affliction with joy inspired by the Holy Spirit. (1 Thess 1:6)

For you, brothers and sisters, became imitators of the churches of God in Christ Jesus which are in Judea, because you suffered the same things from your compatriots as they did from the Jews. (1 Thess 2:14)

For though you have countless pedagogues in Christ, you do not have many fathers. For through the gospel I begot you in Christ Jesus. I appeal to you therefore, be imitators of me. (1 Cor 4:15-16)

Just as I try to please everyone in everything, not seeking my own advantage but that of many, that they may be saved. Be imitators of me, as I am of Christ. (1 Cor 10:33–11:1)

---

6. Martyn, *Galatians*, 420.

7. Betz (*Nachfolge,* 169) helpfully discusses the link between imitation and participation: "Analysis of Pauline examples of the terms μιμητής and συμμιμητής indicates that Paul can speak of mimesis in the indicative as well as the imperative and with this concept describes the existence of the believer ἐν Χριστῷ Ἰησοῦ. . . . Thus the indicative use of μιμητής is synonymous with the exclusively indicative use of ἐν Χριστῷ or ἐν κυρίῳ." In my view, links between Paul's participatory and imitative language should be read against the backdrop of representative figures in Judaism who function both as models for the community of faith and as harbingers of its destiny. See, e.g., George Nickelsburg and John J. Collins, eds., *Ideal Figures in Ancient Judaism: Profiles and Paradigms,* SBLSCS 12 (Chico, CA: Scholars Press, 1980).

> Yet whatever gains I had, these I have come to regard as loss because of Christ. . . . I press on toward the goal for the prize of the heavenly call of God in Christ Jesus. Let those of us then who are mature be of the same mind; and if you think differently about anything, this too God will reveal to you. Only let us hold fast to what we have attained. Brothers and sisters, join in imitating me, and observe those who live according to the example you have in us. (Phil 3:7, 14-17)

While each of these verses has distinctive characteristics, they also share certain affinities. Paul consistently uses a form of the verb "to become" (γίνομαι) plus the plural noun "imitators" (μιμηταί) to speak of imitation.[8] In each case the imitation enjoined involves a willingness to suffer for the sake of the gospel, whether that suffering is already being experienced, as in the Thessalonians' case, or it is voluntary self-abnegation, as in Paul's exhortations to the Corinthians and the Philippians. In 1 Thess 1:5-6 and 2:14-16 the Thessalonians have become imitators of Paul and the Judean churches because they proclaim the Word of God in the midst of affliction.[9] Their imitable "downward mobility" reflects the reversal implicit in Christ's humiliation and exaltation. In Phil 3:1-17 that christological foundation is explicit, as it is in 1 Cor 1:18-31. In 1 Cor 4:9-13 Paul's description of the humiliation of the apostles immediately precedes the call to imitation.[10]

In addition to the theme of suffering, these texts convey Paul's concern for the unity and maturity of his congregations. This is particularly the case in 1 Corinthians, where Paul's challenge to imitate his stance of voluntary servanthood follows on his accusation that the Corinthians' factions show them to be still "babes in Christ" (1 Cor 3:1-4). In Phil 3:17 the apostle's exhortation, "Be imitators of me," follows his confession that he is not yet "perfect" (τετελείωμαι) but he presses on — "Let those who are mature be like-minded" (Ὅσοι οὖν τέλειοι, τοῦτο φρονῶμεν). Shortly after Phil 3:17, the apostle urges harmony between Euodia and Syntyche (Phil 4:2-3). Finally, these texts are couched in relational language, whether it be the topos of friendship (Philippians) or the familial metaphors of Paul as "father" (1 Cor 4:14-15; 1 Thess 2:11) or "mother/nurse" (1 Thess 2:7).

In Gal 4:12, although Paul does not use μιμηταί, he does use γίνομαι —

---

8. In Phil 3:17 he uses the related noun, "joint-imitators" (συμμιμηταί).

9. See especially Betz, *Nachfolge*, 143-45.

10. See Dale Martin, *The Corinthian Body* (New Haven: Yale University Press, 1995), 67: "What he calls on them to imitate is his own voluntary acceptance of low status."

"Become like me." The close syntactic parallels with 1 Cor 4:16 and 11:1 — "Become imitators of me" — suggest that Paul's use of γίνομαι in Gal 4:12 also carries the sense of imitation. Such a suggestion carries further weight in light of thematic similarities. As in the explicit imitation texts, so also in Galatians Paul's exemplary self-presentation includes the motifs of suffering for the sake of the gospel, concern for the maturity and unity of his congregations, friendship, and familial language (both maternal and paternal). Based on these common characteristics, it seems reasonable to group 4:12 with the Pauline imitation texts.

At the same time, 4:12 describes a "shared existence" in which the nature of the imitative relationship is transformed by the new apocalyptic situation, which Paul outlines throughout the letter. A consideration of Paul's assertion of mutual "likeness" with his converts *within this apocalyptic framework* leads one to ask what happens to mimetic psychagogy when God's Son is "born of a woman" and crucified, and both the apostle himself and the cosmos are also "crucified with Christ." Such a fundamental reordering of the cosmic hierarchy suggests a corresponding reordering of the mimetic hierarchy. If so, then Paul's vague and confusing exhortation may not simply impose a one-sided and ultimately futile movement from difference to conformity, as Castelli argues. Rather, it may display a different sort of movement and a *transformative* power that upsets rather than supports the status quo. I shall argue that Paul's appeal in 4:12 does indeed invoke such a dramatically altered power relationship between Paul and his converts, because their interaction is embedded in and shaped by the larger contextual relationship between Christ and humanity.[11] Because that larger context describes the sending of God's Son, the crucifixion of the cosmos, and the inauguration of the new creation (6:14-15), it transforms the power structure between Paul and the Galatians such that their interaction is characterized by mimetic reversal and participation. As a result, their relationship itself embodies the content of and the *dynamis* for the imperative "Become like me."

11. This reading is largely consonant with that of Bruce Longenecker in *The Triumph of Abraham's God: The Transformation of Identity in Galatians* (Nashville: Abingdon, 1998), 157-62. Castelli (*Imitating Paul,* 23) might well say that such a reading is a "spiritualizing gesture towards the text," which "reinscribe[s] it unproblematically." Castelli's analysis, however, invites the questions: what *kind* of power relationship is "inscribed" by the text, and what does such an inscription gain for the participants in such a relationship? See further discussion below, chapter three.

Galatians 4:12 in the Context of the Letter

Galatians 4:12-20 comes at a critical juncture in the letter.[12] With its cryptic self-references, it builds on Paul's preceding autobiographical narratives in 1:13–2:21 and brings his theological self-description directly to bear on his relationship with the Galatians. With its references to his former relationship with his converts, it also reminds them of their "story" as it is intertwined with that of the apostle. Further, as the first occurrence of an imperative, this passage anticipates the paraenetic material that will follow in 4:12–6:10, thus explicitly linking both the Galatians' and Paul's "stories" with his exhortation.[13] The passage is both intensely personal and transcendent, beginning with the appeal "Become like *me*" and ending with the desire that Christ be formed among the Galatians. This combination of personal and cosmological elements gathers up the theological and autobiographical strands of the preceding chapters and sets the context for the subsequent exhortations concerning the Galatians' community life.

The passage follows directly upon both Paul's description of the Galatians' apparent turn away from God and back to slavery under the *stoicheia,* and his anguished cry, "I fear for you, lest somehow I have labored among you in vain." Although the disjunctive quality of 4:12-20 has tempted interpreters to neglect these verses as some kind of emotional outburst, the affective language (φοβοῦμαι ὑμᾶς, v. 11; δέομαι ὑμῶν, v. 12) that brackets Paul's appeal to "Become like me" should not obscure the logical sequence here. In vv. 12-20 Paul presents a solution to the dilemma posed by the Galatians' regressive behavior; he points the way forward for

---

12. See discussion in Lyons, *Pauline Autobiography,* 164-65. See also George W. Hansen, *Abraham in Galatians: Epistolary and Rhetorical Contexts,* JSOTSup 29 (Sheffield: Sheffield Academic Press, 1989), 48, who identifies 4:12-20 as "a major turning point in the structure of Galatians," insofar as it signals a change from "rebuke to request," leading up to 5:1-2 as the primary authoritative thrust of the letter.

13. Richard Longenecker, *Galatians,* WBC 41 (Waco: Word, 1990), 189. "Paul evidently wanted to head up all of the hortatory material of 4:12–6:10 by the entreaty, 'Become like me!'" But see Martyn, *Galatians,* 468. Debate continues as to where the paraenetic section of the letter begins. Troels Engberg-Pedersen has rightly questioned the existence of any such distinction between "theology" and "paraenesis" in Paul's thought, arguing that "it is precisely *by* having the crucified Christ revealed to them that Christ-believers *are* brought out of the negative and burdensome state into an 'outwordly' life for God" (*Paul and the Stoics* [Edinburgh: T&T Clark, 2000], 145). Engberg-Pedersen's reading of Paul, however, has the effect of *collapsing* theology into paraenesis or, perhaps more accurately, into anthropology.

the Galatian congregations to regain and maintain an ongoing faithfulness to the gospel.[14] But what exactly is this way forward? In what way are the Galatians to "become like" Paul, and indeed is such a "becoming" even possible? As Gaventa observes, "These are Gentiles who could never duplicate the βίος Paul characterizes in Gal 1:11–2:14, especially because the fulcrum of that βίος is God's action (1:15) — not Paul's."[15] This being the case, what can Paul mean here, and how might his preceding testimony illuminate his appeal to his converts?

The elliptical second clause of this difficult verse, 4:12, points the way forward. The first and second clauses are parallel:

Γίνεσθε ὡς ἐγώ,
ὅτι κἀγὼ ὡς ὑμεῖς

The first difficulty that faces the translator is the absence of the verb in the second clause. The repeated ὡς suggests that γίνομαι should be supplied, although some commentators opt for a form of εἰμί.[16] While either is possible grammatically, since γίνομαι can function as a substitute for εἰμί, γίνομαι is preferable since it preserves the notion of movement implied in the first clause.[17] Paul is calling the Galatians to turn back toward him, because he himself has moved toward them.[18] The use of ὅτι introduces the

---

14. See B. Longenecker, *Triumph*, 158: "The whole of Gal. 4:12-20, then, is enclosed by Paul's understanding of Christian lifestyle in relation to resilient commitment and the blossoming of Christ-likeness within the lives of his followers (4:12a, 19)."

15. Gaventa, "Galatians 1 and 2," 322. See also Barclay, *Obeying the Truth*, 76 n. 1, who notes the limits of Paul's role as a "paradigm," since "most of what Paul recounts is wholly unlike the Galatians' experience."

16. So Burton, *Galatians*, 236. Betz (*Galatians*, 222) argues that the difference is immaterial, because as a gnome the verse is susceptible of multiple meanings. In effect, however, Betz's translation, *"Remain as I am,"* opts for the sense of εἰμί.

17. There is a similar reciprocal movement in Paul's use of γίνομαι in 1 Thess 1:5-6: "You know what we became among you for your sake, and you became imitators of us and of the Lord" (οἴδατε οἷοι ἐγενήθημεν ἐν ὑμῖν δι' ὑμᾶς. Καὶ ὑμεῖς μιμηταὶ ἡμῶν ἐγενήθητε).

18. BAGD, 158-59: "γίνομαι carries the meaning of 'change . . . entering a new condition." Cf. also Dunn, *Galatians*, 232; R. Longenecker, *Galatians*, 189. Burton (*Galatians*, 236) says: "γέγονα corresponds best with γίνεσθε and the actual facts, since the apostle's freedom from law was the result of a becoming, a change of relations," although he also notes that εἰμί matches ἐστέ, supplied after ὑμεῖς. Κἀγώ frequently takes εἰμί as its default verb, as could be the case in 1 Cor 11:1: "Become imitators of me, as I am of Christ [κἀγὼ Χριστοῦ]," although this also could be translated, "as I have become (an imitator) of Christ." Nonetheless, κἀγώ

second clause as the basis for the imperative in the first.[19] Thus we should note that Paul does not say, "just as [καθώς] I have become like you" or "in the same way that I have become like you," but "*because* I have become like you."[20] Paul's choice of words indicates that here his aim is to motivate his converts more than to instruct them in the details of their enjoined "likeness" to him. This observation in turn suggests that, rather than seeking to determine the *content* of Paul's imitative appeal through reference to his own self-description, we should expect to discover the *motive force* of his likeness to his converts.

A further difficulty is presented by the question of tense: does Paul refer to his present, past, or ongoing "likeness" to the Galatians? Here I have opted for the perfect tense, because it captures the temporal ambiguity implied by the absence of the verb and takes account of Paul's recollection in 4:12-20 of his former relationship with his converts.[21] Paul has become like the Galatians in some way in the past, and he remains like them in some way.

But exactly in what way? Is Betz correct in arguing that the main point here is Paul's use of a friendship topos emphasizing reciprocity and equality?[22] Or is Castelli more persuasive when she concludes that the very vagueness of what Paul has become, and what the Galatians are to emulate, is part of Paul's strategy for maintaining power over his converts: "if the moral exhortation is generalized, nonspecific, inexact, then the onus is upon the exhorted one to perform correctly. . . . [I]mprecise exhortations to imitate a model have the dual effect of reinscribing the model's author-

---

sometimes takes the verb of the preceding clause, as indeed it does later in Gal 6:14, where Paul says, "The world has been crucified to me, and I to the world" (ἐμοὶ κόσμος ἐσταύρωται κἀγὼ κόσμῳ). See also 2 Cor 2:10, where "forgive" is implied after κἀγώ in the second clause, picking up on its appearance in the first clause. In order to preserve both the sense in which the Galatians already are "like Paul," and the notion of movement implied by γίνομαι, perhaps the best paraphrase might be: "*Return* to an existence like mine, in relationship with me — that is, return to our shared life in Christ."

19. "Paul then adds the second clause as a reason or incentive to do what he has just said" (Willis P. De Boer, *The Imitation of Paul: An Exegetical Study* [Kampen: Kok, 1962], 191). See also Castelli, *Imitating Paul*, 115.

20. Compare 1 Cor 11:1, where Paul *does* use καθώς. Notably, Paul's object of imitation is different in the two passages; in 1 Cor 11:1 he urges the Corinthians to imitate him in the same way that he imitates Christ.

21. So R. Longenecker, *Galatians*, 189.

22. Betz, *Galatians*, 222.

ity while placing the imitator in the position of perpetual unease as to whether s/he is acting in the proper mimetic fashion."[23] Ironically Castelli's reading opposes that of Betz, although both Betz and Castelli focus on the nature of the relationship implied between Paul and the Galatians, both concentrate on Paul's "rhetorical strategy," and neither reads the verse in an apocalyptic context. Where they differ is in the categorical constructs with which they read the text: Castelli reads 4:12 as a mimesis text, while Betz reads it as part of an appeal based on friendship. Each category brings with it diverse (but not mutually exclusive) assumptions about the nature of the text and therefore about the nature of Paul's relationship with his congregations. Given this categorical confusion, perhaps the best way forward is to join the majority of commentators and attempt to discern the implied content of Paul's affinity with his converts in 4:12b. I will focus on two related aspects of this affinity: first, parallels between the "histories" of Paul and his converts, as told by the apostle; and second, the larger relational matrix disclosed by those histories.

"Chronological" Parallels

Paul's "Story"

One finds the first clue to interpreting the temporal ambiguity of 4:12b in the abundant temporal references in the rest of the letter.[24] Paul frames his autobiographical narrative in a set of contrasts between "formerly" and "now," beginning with his description of his "former [ποτε] manner of life in Judaism," characterized by overflowing zeal for the traditions of his fathers, in which he "persecuted [ἐδίωκον]" the church of God and "progressed [προέκοπτον]" in Judaism (1:13-14). The imperfect verbs indicate an ongoing way of being. In 1:15-16 the temporal marker ὅτε δέ introduces a definite contrast, a punctiliar turning point, as indicated by the aorist εὐδόκησεν ἀποκαλύψαι. The turning from the past is also a turning from human "traditions" toward a calling given only by God's apocalyptic reve-

---

23. Castelli, *Imitating Paul*, 110. Castelli here comments on 1 Cor 4:16, but she later (116) claims that Gal 4:12 "strengthens the argument put forward in relation to 1 Cor 4:16."

24. See extensive discussion in Lyons, *Pauline Autobiography*, 146-52. See also Martyn, *Galatians*, 160, 163-64.

lation, quite apart from "flesh and blood" (1:16). The radical change in Paul's own life, such that "the persecutor is now the proclaimer," displays and vindicates the transformative power of the gospel as the turn of the ages.[25] This transformative power stands in sharp contrast to the law's powerlessness to give life (3:21) and to the weakness and impotence of the *stoicheia* (4:9). As Martyn notes, "Speaking, then, of a sharp contrast between these two periods in his life, does Paul think that they form an analogy to the contrast between the present evil age and the new creation? Some degree of analogy is unmistakable."[26]

Given this sharp contrast, it is tempting to go further and equate the "past," composed of Paul's "former life" and characteristic of "the present evil age," with purely human activity, and Paul's new life in Christ, demonstrating the "new creation," with divine activity. For example, according to George Lyons, the contrast between the past and the present correlates with a contrast between "human" and "God."[27] Nonetheless, such a contrast would be misleading; despite the sharp discontinuities in Paul's life, a close reading of his account of his own calling in grace shows that he does not paint a simple contrast between his former life in Judaism and his present life in Christ. The picture is more complex, as 1:15 demonstrates:

> But when the one (God),
> who set me apart from my mother's womb and called me
> through his grace, was pleased. . . .

> ὅτε δὲ εὐδόκησεν [ὁ θεὸς]
> ὁ ἀφορίσας με ἐκ κοιλίας μητρός μου καὶ καλέσας διὰ τῆς χάριτος
> αὐτοῦ. . . .

The beginning of the sentence announces that something new is coming, and indeed the apocalypse of Jesus Christ "in" Paul is the advent of the

---

25. The phrase comes from Gaventa, "Galatians 1 and 2," 316.

26. Martyn, *Galatians*, 164.

27. Lyons, *Pauline Autobiography*, 152-56. Martyn (*Galatians*, 164), however, qualifies the contrast by noting that in 1:15, "Paul found a witness to God's presuppositionless grace in scripture." See also Stephen Fowl, "Learning to Narrate Our Lives in Christ," in *Theological Exegesis: Essays in Honor of Brevard S. Childs*, ed. Christopher Seitz and Kathryn Greene-McCreight (Grand Rapids: Eerdmans, 1999), 345 n. 18: "Lyons nicely displays the 'formerly-now' contrast in Galatians. He does not, however, recognize that Paul's account of former things has also been transformed through his encounter with Christ."

new creation in his own life.[28] Yet the intervening clause also announces that this new thing is preceded by the prior "setting aside" and "call" of Paul, even from his mother's womb. The parallel construction of the two subclauses links them in time and distinguishes both from the following clause, suggesting that Paul describes his "call" as preceding his birth.[29] As most exegetes note, Paul here echoes both Isa 49:1 and Jer 1:5, setting his own call in the context of earlier prophetic calls. As many also note, God is the subject whose nature is disclosed by the act of "separating out" and "calling" Paul; these very actions are a demonstration of divine grace, which is, in James B. Lightfoot's words, "the sole agency of God as distinct from [Paul's] own efforts."[30] In the same way God's call of Abraham prior to the law demonstrates grace, just as God also called the Galatians by and "in" his grace (1:6).[31]

My purpose here is to explore the way Paul's "chronology" complicates the sharp contrast between two periods in his life. The apostle's "former life in Judaism" is preceded by God's call of him, and it comes to an end with the "apocalypse of Jesus Christ" in and through him. In the same

28. Commentators who translate ἐν as "in" include James B. Lightfoot, *St. Paul's Epistle to the Galatians* (London: MacMillan, 1905), 83; Betz, *Galatians,* 57; Gaventa, "Galatians 1 and 2," 316; Richard Hays, "Christology and Ethics in Galatians: The Law of Christ," *CBQ* 49, 2 (1987): 281; R. Longenecker, *Galatians,* 32. All of these commentators emphasize the notion that Jesus Christ is revealed "in" and "through" the apostle's transformed life. Martyn (*Galatians,* 158) disagrees, preferring "to" as more in line with 1:12. But Martyn's appeal to the parallel ἐν ἐμοί in 1:24 seems to me rather to undermine his argument: the churches in Judea glorify God "in" Paul because they hear of the power of the gospel displayed "in" his life.

29. So also John Barclay, "Paul's Story: Theology as Testimony," in *Narrative Dynamics in Paul: A Critical Assessment,* ed. Bruce Longenecker (Louisville: Westminster John Knox, 2002), 140 n. 22. In Lyons's words, "in the mind of God, at least, his commission predated his birth" (*Pauline Autobiography,* 133-34). *Pace* Betz, *Galatians,* 70; and Lightfoot, *St. Paul's Epistle,* 82, who emphasize "set aside" and "call" as stages. Rather see also Martyn, *Galatians,* 157, who notes the "emphatic parallelism" between setting aside and call in the prophetic traditions; both are functionally equivalent and point to God's grace.

30. Lightfoot, *Galatians,* 82.

31. Regarding the translation of ἐν χάριτι, see the eloquent commentary by Schütz, *Paul and Anatomy,* 117: "God calls ἐν χάριτι, where ἐν is less causal than instrumental, less instrumental than locative, indicating the place 'where' the Galatian Christians were called by God and in which they, as those called, stand." See also Heinrich Schlier, *Der Brief an die Galater,* KEK 7 (Göttingen: Vandenhoeck & Ruprecht, 1949), 12. For a similar use of ἐν in a locative sense, see 1 Cor 7:15, where God calls ἐν εἰρήνῃ, and 1 Thess 4:7, where God calls ἐν ἁγιασμῷ.

way, the giving of the law came after Abraham's call, and the reign of the law came to an end when "faith" came — that is, when Christ came (3:23-24). In Paul's retelling of both his own history and Israel's history, life under the law is bracketed by divine call and divine apocalypse.[32] He does not portray a simple "past" that can be subsumed under the heading "this present evil age" and attributed to human as opposed to divine action. Rather, in a sense Paul narrates two "pasts": his former life in "Judaism" and his identification with Jeremiah and, indeed, with the Servant of Yahweh in being called and set aside from his birth.

This double view of the past means that the apostle's "former life in Judaism" was not simply an instance of "the present evil age" but was rather an "interruption" encompassed by the gracious action of God.[33] There is no time that is outside the sphere of divine sovereignty. As John H. Schütz perceptively puts it,

> ὁ ἀφορίσας με makes it clear that Paul regards both halves of the con-
> trast [between Paul's past and present life] to have been carried out un-
> der the sovereignty of and in loyalty to God. . . . Law is divinely ordained
> and operative until the dramatic break signalled by Jesus' death, inter-
> preted as the provision of grace. . . . Thus there is a formal parallel be-
> tween the autobiography and Paul's understanding of the nature of the
> gospel itself, a parallel underscored by the fact that however sharp the
> antitheses, both halves of the life, of Paul and of all men, are viewed as
> being under God's sovereignty.[34]

Schütz's comments raise sharply the question of divine activity during the parenthetical time of Paul's life in "Judaism." Even while Paul clearly sees that life as one opposed to the people of God, he also may see it as his personal experience of being shut up under sin and the law (3:22-23) until the coming of faith — that is, Christ — in his own life.

Two observations may be deduced from Paul's "testimony" thus far.

32. See Barclay, "Paul's Story," 140: "Paul's life in accordance with the traditions of his ancestors was something of an interlude."

33. It is important to note that Paul qualifies "Judaism" specifically by "overflowing zeal for the traditions of my fathers," in line with the occurrence of Ἰουδαϊσμός in 2 Macc 2:21; 8:1; 14:38; 4 Macc 4:26. That he also qualifies his own call in terms drawn from the prophets demonstrates that he does not consider his break with his "former life" to be a complete break with his Jewish heritage; quite the contrary.

34. Schütz, *Paul and Anatomy*, 133-34.

First, that testimony depicts both a radical discontinuity between different periods in the apostle's life and a profound continuity that derives from his perception of God's sovereignty throughout the whole of his life. Second, the break between "past" and "present" does not correlate with a sharp division between the spheres of divine and human action, as if some aspect or time frame of human existence could be bracketed out of God's purposes.

The Galatians' "Story"

In describing the history of his Galatian converts, Paul also contrasts their *past* life, in which they did not know God, with their *present* (νῦν) life of knowing and being known by God (4:8-9). These verses sum up the series of contrasts that Paul already has set forth: formerly under a pedagogue, now "children of God" (3:25-26); formerly infants and slaves, now children and heirs of God (4:1-7). Here the apostle combines the durative image of growth from infancy to maturity with the punctiliar metaphors of emancipation and adoption, as he appeals to his converts to claim their inheritance of the Spirit. The temporal break between past and present comes "in the fullness of time" with God's sending of the Son and "our" correlative adoption as God's children.[35]

But because the Galatians are "turning back again [ἐπιστρέφετε πάλιν] to the weak and impotent elemental principles," wanting to be their slaves "all over again [πάλιν ἄνωθεν]," Paul also contrasts their *present* apostasy from the gospel with their *former* faithfulness (4:8-11). This comparison becomes explicit in his subsequent remembrance of the close relationship that he formerly enjoyed with his converts, in contrast with his bitter question, "Have I become your enemy by telling you the truth?" (4:16). Thus even as Paul calls them to turn *away* from their pagan past, he calls them to turn *back* to their origin in the message of faith through which they first received the Spirit (3:3-5). His fear that his work among them might be in vain (εἰκῇ) echoes his earlier question (3:4): "Did you suffer so much in vain? If indeed in vain [τοσαῦτα ἐπάθετε εἰκῇ; εἴ γε καὶ εἰκῇ]." So also his reminder in 4:12-15 of their earlier reciprocal relationship echoes his reminder of their earlier experience of the Spirit (3:3-5). The Galatians' present flirtation with the law as taught by the other mis-

---

35. Regarding Paul's shifting pronouns, see Martyn, *Galatians*, 334-36.

sionaries is a detour from their former life in the Spirit; it promises continuity but delivers discontinuity.

Thus Paul narrates the Galatians, like himself, as having two "pasts," although in reverse order from those of the apostle. A chronological mapping of the Galatians' "story" would look like this:

Past I.   Children; slaves to the *stoicheia* (4:3, 8)
Did not know God (4:8)
Gentiles and therefore outside the law

Past II.   Called by grace (1:6)
Received the Spirit by the message of faith (3:3)
Experienced works of power (3:4-5)
Close fellowship with Paul (4:12-15)

Present I.   Children of God (3:26; 4:6)
Abraham's seed (3:29)
Heirs according to promise (3:29; 4:7)
Children of the free woman (4:31)

Present II.   Turning away from the one who called them (1:6)
Foolish and bewitched (3:1)
Turning back to the *stoicheia* and to superstitious
observances (4:9-10)
Pursuing circumcision and rectification through the law
(5:2-4)

"Past I" and "Past II" are clearly sequential, describing the Galatians' life "before" their encounter with the gospel and their initial transforming reception of Paul's preaching. Present I describes the Galatians' current status "in Christ." Their stories converge with that of Paul in the coherent life comprised of their calling in grace and consequent identity as "children of God" (Past II and Present I). This present life in Christ points forward to future inheritance and the hope of righteousness. But their present flirtation with the law (Present II) is a regression to past slavery, consonant with their pagan past, and consequently a turning away from fellowship with Paul (4:16) and from union with Christ (5:4).

A comparison of Paul's retrospective narrations of his past and that of the Galatians demonstrates that they are not strictly parallel, but they do intersect at several significant points.[36] First, in his "former life" Paul lived "under the law"; the Galatians' past also was lived in slavery to oppressive powers, and now at least some of the Galatians are beginning to live "under the law." From his present vantage point "in Christ," Paul narrates his former life in Judaism and the Galatians' former life in paganism synoptically: although in one sense they were distinguished from each other as "Jew" and "Gentile sinner" (2:15), in another sense they were all slaves of the taskmasters who belong to the present age, which is passing away. Thus "we" were confined under the law (3:23); "we" were slaves of the *stoicheia* (4:3).[37]

This shared past in "slavery" gives him a warrant for his present warning against law observance as a return to slavery to "things that are not gods" (4:8-9). He can use the particularity of his own past life under the law as having specific application in the present situation in Galatia. In effect, he says to his converts: "Become as I am now — free from the law. For I also was once as you now want to be — under the law. But through Christ I died to the law that divides Jew and Gentile. I warn you that if you continue in your present course, you sow the seeds of division between you and me, and between each other. The law will not unite us, but divide us. Even now, you're attacking each other!" (5:15). In other words, not only does the law promise continuity but deliver discontinuity; it promises unity but delivers discord. Therefore, as a point of contact between Paul's and the Galatians' life, the law belongs *only* in the past. It is powerless to sustain life, as Paul makes clear by treating it synoptically with the weak and impotent *stoicheia* (4:9).

Second, in a qualified sense Paul became "like" the Galatians by becoming, like a "Gentile sinner," outside the law.[38] A majority of exegetes see here a parallel to Paul's missionary strategy in 1 Cor 9:19-23, where he says that to those outside the law he "became as one outside the law," in order to win them to Christ.[39] Despite the popularity of this comparison, however, there

---

36. See also Barclay, "Paul's Story," 145.

37. See Martyn, *Galatians*, 334-36.

38. See, e.g., Betz, *Galatians*, 223; Gaventa, "Galatians 1 and 2," 321; R. Longenecker, *Galatians*, 189. In Martyn's formulation, "Not observant of the Law when he was among them, Paul became like them in that he could think of himself as a *former* Gentile" (*Galatians*, 420; emphasis added).

39. See, e.g., Betz, *Galatians*, 223; Lightfoot, *Galatians*, 174; Burton, *Galatians*, 236; Schlier, *Galater*, 208; R. Longenecker, *Galatians*, 189.

are two problems with using 1 Cor 9:21 as a parallel for Gal 4:12. (a) If Paul is simply referring to his missionary strategy in converting the Galatians, what in that strategy provides a basis for them to become like him? (b) Commentators who point to 1 Cor 9:21 fail to note the important qualifier that Paul adds to his description of himself as "outside the law": "not being without law towards God, but in the law of Christ." Without delving into the many and vexed questions of exactly what Paul means by "the law of Christ," it seems clear that for Paul, "in Christ," not "without law," is the fundamental identity marker.[40] As Gal 5:6 and 6:15 make clear, "law and not law" is a distinction that belongs to the "present evil age."[41] For example, in 2:15-17 Paul explicitly distinguishes his birth as a Jew from existence as a "Gentile sinner"; it is only in seeking rectification in Christ that he is "found to be a sinner." That is, while being in Christ is incompatible with being under the law, the obverse is not the case for Paul: being outside the law is not the same as being in Christ. In their pagan past, the Galatians were outside the law but they were not thereby in Christ. For this reason, it is accurate but not adequate to say that Paul became like the Galatians by living outside the law, and that this is what he now models for his converts. Rather, he *was* like the Galatians by living in slavery to powers that belong to the present evil age; he *is* like the Galatians only by belonging to Christ.

Thus, third, Paul became and remains as the Galatians have become, only in and through being identified with Christ, in whom they both have died to the dividing law and in whom divisions cease (3:28).[42] Through this mutual sharing in Christ, the separate third person and second person pronouns modulate into the first person plural "we" who receive the promise by faith (3:14), receive adoption (4:5), and are children of promise (4:28) and children of the free woman (4:31).[43] The apostle and his converts share the fact that God called them by his grace prior to the advent of the law in their lives, just as God also called Abraham (1:6, 15; 3:6). At the same time, they do not share the specific calling that Paul describes in 1:15-16, which the apostle is at pains to characterize as unmediated by any human agent, and by which he was "set aside" to preach to the Gentiles. In-

40. For further discussion see Hays, "Christology and Ethics," 268-90.

41. Martyn, *Galatians*, 393 n. 21.

42. B. Longenecker, *Triumph*, 158: "The self-portrait of the Galatians is to be identical to the self-portrait of Paul, with only the figure of Christ appearing within the frame."

43. Martyn, *Galatians*, 336: "Before the advent of Christ humanity was an enslaved monolith; in Christ humanity is becoming a liberated unity."

deed, the Galatians' calling is the fruit of God's revelation to Paul, and he himself was the human agent through which that gracious calling came.

Fourth, there are two "pasts" in Paul's autobiographical narrative, as there are two "pasts" in the Galatians' former existence — a past existence in slavery to the powers of this age and a past that demonstrates God's "presuppositionless" call. Seen from his present perspective, the radical transformation that Paul's life displays is also continuous with the work of God that preceded his birth. As John Barclay has put it, "In truth, the gracious call of God undergirds Paul's whole story and provides the continuity between 'start' and 'finish.'"[44] Bracketed by this continuity of divine purpose, the apostle's life of zeal for "Judaism" looks like an "interruption"; in fact, the apocalypse of Christ "interrupted" the interruption, coming right in the midst of Paul's persecution of the church of God, to bring to fruition the promise implicit in his original calling.[45] The persistent continuity of divine purpose manifest in Paul's life proclaims a promise to the Galatians; insofar as the apostle's autobiographical narrative holds up a mirror to his converts, it tells them two things. (a) The law is not the way to a coherent life over time but rather disrupts the movement from beginning to completion (3:3). (b) Just as God's gracious call and invasive revelation encompassed Paul's life and interrupted his own "detour" under the law, so even now God's gracious activity encompasses their life together and breaks into that life anew through Paul's preaching.

This promissory function of Paul's story carries through the entire pericope to his startling image of himself in labor with the Galatians: the endangered "birth" of the Galatians will come to completion, just as Paul's call from his mother's womb has come to fruition. Chrysostom appeals: "Do you see his parental compassion? Do you see the anguish that is fitting for an apostle? Do you see how he has lamented more bitterly than women giving birth? 'You have ruined the image of God,' he is saying. 'You have lost the kinship, you have exchanged the likeness. You need a rebirth and a reformation. Yet nonetheless I still call the miscarriages and the abortions my children.'"[46]

44. Barclay, "Paul's Story," 140.

45. As Barclay, "Paul's Story," 139 n. 17, notes, the syntax of 1:15-16 "linguistically dramatizes the interruption of the 'I' story by a story set in motion by God."

46. Chrysostom, "Homily on Galatians 4:19," in *Galatians, Ephesians, Philippians*, ed. Mark J. Edwards, ACCS 8 (Downers Grove, IL: InterVarsity Press, 1999), 65. I will return in chapter four to the question of whether Gal 4:19 refers to a "rebirth"; here my interest is in

Finally, there is a significant point of divergence between the apostle's testimony and his picture of the Galatians' present life. Whereas for Paul there is only one present and future life — in Christ — he describes his converts as attempting to live simultaneously in two contrasting modes of existence. The incompatibility of the two accounts of the Galatians' "present life" presents a dilemma.[47] One way to solve this dilemma is to see Paul as presenting his converts with a choice between these two ways of life. Support for this reading comes from the two "futures" contrasted in 5:2 and 5:5. For those who receive circumcision, Christ "will be of no advantage [οὐδὲν ὠφελήσει]" whereas "we wait for the hope of righteousness." On the basis of these verses, Lyons argues that Galatians is a deliberative letter in which Paul "contrasts the past, the present, and the two possible futures," between which his converts must choose: circumcision or freedom in Christ. Lyons continues, "fundamentally the choice of futures amounts to a repetition of their initial encounter with the gospel, i.e., a choice between man and God."[48]

---

the correspondence between the pattern of Paul's life and that of the Galatians. The promissory function of Paul's testimony may be strengthened by reference to his puzzling self-description as a "miscarriage" in 1 Cor 15:8. Observing parallels between Gal 1:15-16 and 1 Cor 15:1-10, George W. E. Nickelsburg has argued that this self-description refers to his persecution of the church, during which he became "an ἔκτρωμα with respect to the purpose for which he was appointed from the womb. In spite of this, God revealed the risen Christ to him and made him what he was intended to be from the womb" ("An Ἔκτρωμα, Though Appointed from the Womb: Paul's Apostolic Self-Description in 1 Corinthians 15 and Galatians 1," in *Christians among Jews and Gentiles*, ed. George W. E. Nickelsburg and George W. MacRae [Philadelphia: Fortress, 1986], 204).

47. The majority of commentators interpret 1:6; 3:1; 4:9-10; 5:2-4; and 6:12 to refer to the danger of a future event (circumcision), not present activity on the part of the Galatians. It is true that 5:2 is in the indicative future, but it is immediately followed by the present tense of 5:3, and the aorist κατηργήθητε ἀπὸ Χριστοῦ of 5:4. The rest of the relevant verses are either present tense (1:6; 4:9-10; 6:12) or aorist (3:1). It seems best to follow Martyn, *Galatians*, 469-70, in seeing 5:2-4 as addressed to two groups in the Galatian churches: those who have been circumcised (5:4), and those who are merely contemplating such an act (5:2). Whether the observers of cultic calendars in 4:9-10 have also been circumcised seems impossible to determine.

48. Lyons, *Pauline Autobiography*, 152. Lyons's language here is reminiscent of the Jewish doctrine of the two ways and seems closer to what Martin C. de Boer has labeled "forensic-apocalyptic eschatology," in which "the emphasis falls on free will and decision" ("Paul and Jewish Apocalyptic Eschatology," in *Apocalyptic and the New Testament: Essays in Honour of J. Louis Martyn*, ed. Joel Marcus and Marion Soards, JSNTSup 24 [Sheffield: JSOT Press, 1989], 181). Martyn (*Galatians*, 304, 324-27) attributes the theology of the two ways to the other missionaries.

But in Paul's view the Galatians' initial encounter with the gospel was no more a matter of "choice" than his own encounter with the apocalypse of God's Son. To the contrary, Paul emphasizes divine initiative and power rather than human decisions.[49] The apostle's depiction of the points of intersection between his and the Galatians' "histories" serves to demonstrate this transforming power of God. There is a "given" quality to these stories, in which God is the chief actor, "setting aside," "calling," "revealing," "sending," "redeeming," "knowing" (1:15-16; 4:4-5, 9). This "givenness" qualifies the tension between the two depictions of the Galatians' present existence — as free children of God on the one hand, and as foolish, bewitched children returning to slavery on the other hand — by the promise of God's faithfulness. It is the embodied, experiential basis for the apostle's confidence that the Galatians will ultimately follow his lead and remain faithful to the gospel (5:10).[50]

The intersections between Paul's story and that of the Galatians illuminate the ways Paul has become like them and they are to become like him.[51] Their interwoven "stories" tell us that they have already "become like" each other, in and only in Christ. But this "likeness" is not an abstract notion; it is embedded in the intensely personal relationship between Paul and his converts. Put another way, for the Galatians the human agent of God's transforming power is now, as at first, the apostle himself, who represents the relational matrix that links his converts' present life in Christ with their origin in the message of the gospel. For this reason, in 4:12-18 he reminds them of their former happy relationship — a relationship that contrasts not only with their present estrangement, but also with the other missionaries' "zeal" for the Galatians.

---

49. Indeed, Lyons elsewhere notes that Paul's "autobiographical remarks" differ from other Hellenistic literature precisely in that he does *not* describe his own "personal choices deciding his character and profession" (*Pauline Autobiography*, 133).

50. See also Martyn, *Galatians*, 468-69; B. Longenecker, *Triumph*, 188.

51. The foil for this pattern of correspondence between Paul's story and his converts is the correspondence between Peter's role in the retrospective drama of 2:11-14, and that of the other missionaries then in Galatia. Peter's separation from the Gentile Christians leads the other Jewish Christians astray from walking in line with the gospel. Paul opposes him as he opposes the Teachers; Peter stands "condemned," just as the Teachers and their followers are in danger of becoming anathema.

Relational Matrix

In 4:13-15 Paul's description of his initial interaction with his converts displays and embodies the mutuality that he enjoins in 4:12. In what follows I will make two proposals. First, the nature of the relationship between the apostle and his converts provides the motivation for the Galatians to "become like" Paul as he has "become like" them, because it mediates the gracious power of God by replicating the sacrificial and liberating movement of Christ into the sphere of human slavery. Second, Paul contrasts his relationship with the Galatians with that of the Teachers by characterizing the latter as conditional, nonreciprocal, and nonsacrificial.

Paul and the Galatians

In contrast to his earlier sharp rebukes, at this point in the letter Paul addresses the Galatians with an affectionate appeal: "I beg of you, my brothers and sisters!"[52] The affective language is of a piece with his immediately preceding "fear" that he has worked among them in vain (4:11), and with his earnest desire to be with them "at once" (ἄρτι) and to "change my voice, because I am perplexed about you" (4:20). As Betz and Martyn have argued, the friendship topos of reciprocity and equality implied by Paul's language in 4:12 extends into his portrayal of their former relationship in vv. 13-14.[53] Paul first came to them in "weakness" and need, and they responded with a generosity that Paul depicts with metaphorical hyperbole: "I bear you witness that, if possible, you would have plucked out your eyes and given them to me!"[54] Such generosity characterizes friendship in the philosophical tradition.[55] Furthermore, Paul's refusal to engage in flattery — his "truth telling," which implicitly contrasts with the Teachers' flirta-

---

52. On the contrast between this affectionate "call to imitation" and Paul's earlier rebuke of his converts, see Gaventa, "Galatians 1 and 2," 322. It is Paul's intervening autobiographical narrative and the way in which it intersects with the Galatians' own story as inaugurated by the grace of God that give him the warrant for his present appeal.

53. Betz, *Galatians*, 222-23; Martyn, *Galatians*, 420.

54. The statement is probably not a reference to a physical condition on the part of the apostle but a hyperbolic statement to indicate extreme devotion. See R. Longenecker, *Galatians*, 193.

55. See Betz, *Galatians*, 221-23, for Greco-Roman references.

tious and manipulative "zeal" in vv. 16-17 — is further evidence of the friendship he claims with his converts.

But Paul's language here goes beyond, and in some ways subverts, that of friendship. When he first came to the Galatians, they received him "as an angel of God, as Christ Jesus." The "truth" that he told them is the "truth of the gospel" (2:5, 14), for which he stood fast against the "false brethren" and later rebuked Peter, just as he also rebuked the Galatians themselves earlier in the letter (1:6). In 4:17-18 Paul shifts to the language of zealous courtship, either between lovers or between young men and their teacher.[56] Finally, by the end of the pericope the Galatians are not only Paul's "brothers and sisters," but his "children" (4:19), implying not equality but the authority of the parent. Paul also refers to his converts as his "children" in 1 Thess 2:7, where he likens himself to a wet nurse, and in 1 Thess 2:11, where he likens himself to a father with his children. In 1 Cor 4:16, which is explicitly an imitation text, he uses paternal language to say he "begot" the Corinthians "in Christ." Here in Gal 4:19 he uses maternal imagery to describe himself as "in labor pains" with the Galatians. The parental imagery, both paternal and maternal, shows that although Paul's relationship with his converts may indeed be reciprocal, it is not thereby simply "equal." Rather, the fraternal mutuality implied by 4:12-15 gives way to the implicit hierarchy of the parent-child relationship in 4:19; the philosophical topos of masculine friendship is transformed into the apocalyptic motif of a woman in labor. It is this unexpected mingling of philosophical and apocalyptic motifs — equality and hierarchy, masculine and feminine imagery, all glued together by language that is both personal and cosmic — that gives the pericope its disjointed and puzzling character.

I suggest that Paul's relationship with his converts cannot be categorized adequately by the language of friendship, erotic courtship, or family structures simply because for Paul the definitive aspect of that relationship is that it exists in, and only in, the new situation inaugurated by the advent of Christ.[57] "In Christ," Paul and his converts participate in a new rela-

---

56. Betz, ibid., 229; Martyn, *Galatians,* 423; Christopher Smith, "Ἐκκλεῖσαι in Galatians 4:17: The Motif of the Excluded Lover as a Metaphor of Manipulation," *CBQ* 58, 3 (1996): 480-99; Lightfoot, *Galatians,* 176-77; R. Longenecker, *Galatians,* 194. Paul's depiction of the other missionaries receives further attention in the next section of this chapter.

57. See, e.g., Johnson, "Apocalyptic Family Values," 36: "It is the quality of the church's life as apocalyptic, that is, as constituted by God's invasive revelation of Christ, that shapes

tional matrix that reconstitutes existing categories of human interaction. Thus, when in 4:12-15 the apostle describes his past encounter with the Galatians, he highlights a mutual self-giving that mirrors Christ's interchange with humanity in 3:13 and 4:4.

The expression "interchange" draws on Morna Hooker's series of articles on "interchange in Christ," in which she identifies a pattern of exchange as central to Paul's understanding of the gospel.[58] The key texts for Hooker are Gal 3:13 and 2 Cor 5:21. In her discussion of Gal 3:13, she notes how it is echoed and expanded by 4:4-5. According to 3:13-14,

> Christ set us free from the curse of the law,
> becoming a curse for us.
> (As it is written, "Cursed be everyone who hangs on a tree.")
> In order that in Christ Jesus the blessing of Abraham might come
>   to the Gentiles,
> in order that we might receive the promise of the Spirit through faith.

In 3:10 Paul already has established the predicament into which Christ enters by becoming a curse: "For whoever is of the works of the law is under a curse." The pattern of exchange is clear: Christ entered the realm of those under a curse, those ἐξ ἔργων νόμου, in order that the Gentiles might receive the blessing of Abraham and that "we" might receive the promise of the Spirit.

Galatians 4:4-5 displays the same pattern of exchange, and the phrases are parallel to 3:13-14.[59] They correspond as follows:

3:13: γενόμενος ὑπὲρ ἡμῶν κατάρα
4:4: γενόμενον ἐκ γυναικός, γενόμενον ὑπὸ νόμον

Paul's language about households and kinship." See also Malherbe, "God's New Family," 123-24; Martyn, *Galatians*, 387.

58. The essays are collected in Morna Hooker, *From Adam to Christ: Essays on Paul* (Cambridge: Cambridge University Press, 1990). See also Nils Dahl, "Form-Critical Observations on Early Christian Preaching," *Jesus in the Memory of the Early Church: Essays* (Minneapolis: Augsburg, 1976); Hays, "Christology and Ethics," 276-83.

59. See Hooker, *From Adam to Christ*, 16. In *The Faith of Jesus Christ: The Narrative Substructure of Galatians 3:1–4:11*, 2nd ed. (Grand Rapids: Eerdmans, 2002), 86-121, Richard B. Hays provides an extensive discussion of the relationship between the two passages. See also Martyn, *Galatians*, 408.

3:13: Χριστὸς ἡμᾶς ἐξηγόρασεν ἐκ τῆς κατάρας τοῦ νόμου
4:5: ἵνα τοὺς ὑπὸ νόμον ἐξαγοράσῃ

3:14: ἵνα εἰς τὰ ἔθνη ἡ εὐλογία τοῦ Ἀβραὰμ γένηται ἐν Χριστῷ
      Ἰησοῦ,
      ἵνα τήν ἐπαγγελίαν τοῦ πνεύματος λάβωμεν διὰ τῆς πίστεως
4:5: ἵνα τὴν υἱοθεσίαν ἀπολάβωμεν

These verses fill out the implications of 3:13 while following the same pattern of exchange: in 3:13 Christ was "born" under the law, while in 4:4 Christ is identified with the human situation in two parallel but not identical phrases — born of a woman, born under the law. Although the second clause would seem to apply only to Jews, the prior clause sets that application within the context of Christ's identification with all humanity. The notoriously shifting pronouns preclude an exact parallel between the two passages, but the logic of exchange is consistent: Christ comes into the human situation in order to effect a change in that situation, such that all receive a new identity "in Christ."[60] In Hooker's pithy sentence, "He who is Son of God was born of a woman in order that those who are born of woman might become sons of God."[61]

In his own "testimony" Paul displays the material content of this new identity. He does this both by suffering persecution and thereby "bodily" proclaiming the crucified Christ, and by breaking down the barriers between "Jew and Gentile" (3:28).[62] Specifically, Paul's own place in relation to the Gentiles, whom he now calls "my brothers and sisters," has been shifted by his "death to the law" and his union with Christ. The movement is explicit in 2:15-18. The pericope begins with the apostle's distinction between his (and Peter's) status as "Jews by nature" rather than "Gentile sinners." But now, being rectified through Christ and not by "works of the law," Paul and his fellow Jewish Christians are "also found to be sinners" in relation to the law. In ch. 3 Paul further breaks down the distinctions be-

---

60. See also Engberg-Pedersen, *Paul and the Stoics,* 143: "Apparently, God aimed to effect a real change in human beings from one concrete state to another. God acted to make an *impact* on human beings." Engberg-Pedersen acknowledges his affinity to Hooker's work (333 n. 29).

61. Hooker, *From Adam to Christ,* 16.

62. I will discuss Paul's "embodied proclamation" of Christ's crucifixion in the next chapter.

tween himself as a Jew and the Gentile Galatians, through the change in *their* "status," which has been effected by the faithfulness of Christ.[63] Through this "faith" they also are now "children of Abraham" and "blessed with faithful Abraham" (3:7-9). They can be sure of this because they have already received the Spirit (3:2-5). Through the apocalyptic act of Christ, who "became a curse for us" (3:13), Jew and Gentile are now included in the "we" who have been set free from the curse of the law and receive the promise of the Spirit (3:13-14). Far from repeating the distinction between Jews and Gentiles set forth in 2:15, the ἡμᾶς, ὑπὲρ ἡμῶν, and λάβωμεν of 3:13-14 all refer to both Jews and Gentiles, demonstrating that the division between them has been overcome by Christ's death.[64]

A similar modulation from an exclusive to an inclusive "we" occurs in 3:22–4:7, under the banner of 3:22: "The Scripture has shut up *all* things [τὰ πάντα] under sin in order that the promise which is through the faithfulness of Jesus Christ might be given to those who believe." In vv. 23-25 the "we" who were imprisoned under the law would appear to be Jews, just as the "we" of 4:3-6 would appear to be Gentiles enslaved by the elemental spirits of the world. But the very fact that Paul includes himself in both categories undermines the distinction between them by acting out the inclusive self-identification of Christ with all humanity in the phrase, "born of a woman" (4:4). Again, it is in light of their new shared status, now not only as "children of Abraham" but as "children of God" (3:26), that the distinction becomes irrelevant. The γάρ of v. 26 links it immediately with the preceding verse: "Now that faith has come *we* are no longer under a pedagogue.

---

63. Without in-depth discussion of the debated interpretation of πίστις Χριστοῦ, I note here simply that I follow the subjective genitive interpretation: it is the faithfulness of Christ that rectifies the human situation, even as it evokes human trust in and loyalty to Christ.

64. See Martyn, *Galatians*, 317. *Pace* Hays, *Faith*, 78 n. 18; Betz, *Galatians*, 148 n. 101. The question is how Gentiles could be under the curse of the law and therefore delivered from it. R. Longenecker (*Galatians*, 121) argues that the phrase here includes Gentiles who have not yet been circumcised. Betz, on the other hand, argues that the Galatian Christians were not under the curse of the law, and would be so only if they became circumcised. The underlying issue is the relationship between slavery to the law and slavery to the elements of the world. In Betz's formulation, "being under the Torah is only another way of being 'under the elements of the world'" (*Galatians*, 148). Martyn's formulation is slightly different: "enslavement under the Law's curse is for Paul the major mark of the fact that, prior to Christ, all human beings stood under the power of the world's elements" (*Galatians*, 317). Martyn (311) builds on his reading of the curse of the law in 3:10 as falling "on both observer and nonobserver" and thereby as universal in application.

For *you* are *all* children of God through [the same] faith, in Christ Jesus." The sudden change of pronouns does not follow logically, for the situation of both "we" and "you" is coterminous — once under a pedagogue, now children of God and, in union with Christ who is Abraham's seed, heirs of the promise (vv. 26-29). Thus the change to "you" serves not to distinguish Gentiles from Jews, but rather to emphasize the inclusion of the Gentile Christians in the Galatian churches. And as v. 29 makes clear, being Abraham's "seed" derives from belonging to Christ, not the reverse.[65]

The pronoun shifts follow the same pattern in 4:5-6. In 4:5 redemption from the law follows immediately upon the predicament of slavery to the *stoicheia* and introduces the purpose clause, "in order that *we* might receive adoption." The subsequent address, "*you* are sons," with its reaffirmation of the presence of the Spirit among the Galatians, repeats 3:26 and serves again to reassure Paul's Gentile converts of their full inclusion in God's people. Thus throughout 2:15–4:7 the pronominal shifts serve to blur distinctions between Jew and Gentile Christian, and between Paul and the Galatians.[66] The particular uses of the second person plural — 3:1-5, 26, 28-29, and 4:6-7 — coupled with the reference in 3:29 to Gentiles receiving the promise of Abraham, reaffirm to the Gentile Galatian Christians that they are partakers of the promises of God solely through Christ, without meeting any legal conditions that the other missionaries might impose.

It is both as part of this new "we" who are constituted by Christ's movement into the human sphere, and as the Paul who lives "by the faithfulness of Christ, who loved me and gave himself for me" (2:20), that Paul makes his appeal to the Galatians in 4:12-20. That is, just as 4:4-5 echoes and amplifies 3:13, so also 4:12 displays in Paul's relationship with the Galatians the same logic of exchange. Christ became as we are, that we — in Christ — might become as he is. Now Paul says to the Galatians, "[In Christ] I became as you are; become as I am [in Christ]." He follows his appeal with a reminder of the way Christ's sacrificial self-giving was embodied in his initial preaching to them, and of the Christlike character of their initial response to him. Indeed, they received him "as Christ Jesus" because

---

65. Martyn, *Galatians*, 306: "The Gentile Christians do not become descendants of Abraham by being incorporated into the Law-observant patriarch or into the line of his plural descendants. . . . They became Abraham's children by being incorporated into Abraham's singular seed, Christ. And that means that their descent from Abraham is secondary to their descent from God that had its genesis in their baptism into Christ (3:26-27)."

66. See Martyn, *Galatians*, 334-36.

in his own person he portrayed in some sense the crucifixion of Christ on their behalf,[67] and they responded in kind. As Bruce W. Longenecker writes, their

> attitude of sincere concern and generosity is (for Paul) not simply a demonstration of friendly devotion and affection, but an attestation of the Galatians' transformation in Christ by the power of God, a testimony to the working of the Spirit of the Son whose own life was marked out by love and self-giving. Their own actions were embodiments of the gospel, manifestations of the Spirit.[68]

Thus in 4:12-15 Paul repreaches to the Galatians the nature of the relationship they already share in Christ. With affective language he invites them back into a shared existence initiated and sustained by the proactive grace of God, which decisively invaded the cosmos through the coming of the Son and which broke into their own former life through Paul's preaching of the Son as he had been revealed in him (1:16; 3:1; 4:14). Just as through their initial calling "in grace," that is, into the sphere of God's graciously operating power, they entered into a relational matrix characterized by a participatory reciprocity with Christ, so now Paul appeals to them in familial terms to remain in that matrix.

His language here, as in his earlier retrospective account, is "ruthlessly personal."[69] That is, the otherwise abstract notion of "interchange in Christ" finds material expression and durative power in the relationships the Galatians share with the apostle and with each other. This is why he desires to be with them now (4:20) and why he subsequently addresses the divisions in their life together (5:13–6:10). It is the personal, concrete nature of the relationship and its historical embodiment that give it motivational force. In twentieth-century sociological terms, the importance of Paul's relationship as a "significant other" for the Galatians might be expressed in Peter Berger's description of "the subjective reality of the world":

---

67. Exactly in what way Christ was first "publicly portrayed as crucified" (προεγράφη ἐσταυρωμένος; 3:1) by Paul to the Galatians is a matter for further exegetical investigation; see below, chapter four.

68. B. Longenecker, *Triumph*, 160.

69. The expression "ruthlessly personal" comes from Schütz, *Paul and Anatomy*, 138.

The world is built up in the consciousness of the individual by conversation with significant others (such as parents, teachers, "peers"). The world is maintained as subjective reality by the same sort of conversation, be it with the same or with new significant others (such as spouses, friends or other associates). If such conversation is disrupted (the spouse dies, the friends disappear, or one comes to leave one's original social milieu), the world begins to totter, to lose its subjective plausibility. In other words, the subjective reality of the world hangs on the thin thread of conversation.[70]

Whether Paul himself would accede to Berger's formulation of "subjective reality," however, is another matter. For even as his language is "ruthlessly personal," it is also "relentlessly mythological."[71] The apostle has been crucified with Christ; now Christ lives "in" him and he lives by Christ's faithfulness (2:20). The cosmos has been crucified to him and he to the cosmos (6:14). The Galatians were formerly slaves to "beings that are by nature not gods"; now they are "children of God" and have "put on Christ" (4:8; 3:26-27). In their new identity in Christ the old social distinctions characteristic of this age carry no further force (3:28). The Galatians' own communities are the site of cosmic warfare between the powers of "the Flesh" and the Spirit (5:17), because they live between the poles of the present evil age and the new creation, the end of one world and the inauguration of the new. The relational matrix of which Paul reminds his converts in 4:12-20 both partakes of this cosmic sphere and becomes visible in their concrete interactions. As an expression of the Galatians' core identity in Christ, together with a reminder that such an identity necessarily issues in sacrificial mutual service, 4:12-20 does indeed anticipate the "hortatory section" of the letter that follows.

---

70. Peter L. Berger, *The Sacred Canopy: Elements of a Sociological Theory of Religion* (Garden City, NY: Doubleday, 1967), 17.

71. The expression "relentlessly mythological" comes from Richard Hays, "Crucified with Christ," *SBLSP* 27 (Missoula, MT: Scholars Press, 1988), 330. See also B. Longenecker, *Triumph*, 26: "Paul frequently evidences the view that people's lives are caught up in a matrix of spiritual forces of one kind or another, whether they be forces for good (e.g., the Spirit, righteousness, grace) or for ill (e.g., the powers of Sin and Death)."

The "Agitators" and the Galatians

While Paul characterizes his relationship with his converts as reciprocal and shaped by Christ's sacrificial involvement in the sphere of human existence, he draws a very different picture of the relationship between the Galatians and the other missionaries. In 4:17, a verse almost as cryptic and oblique as 4:12, Paul abruptly turns his attention to these shadowy teachers who have infiltrated (in his view) his congregations:

ζηλοῦσιν ὑμᾶς οὐ καλῶς ἀλλὰ ἐκκλεῖσαι ὑμᾶς θέλουσιν, ἵνα αὐτοὺς ζηλοῦτε.

They do not seek you for a good purpose, but they want to shut you out, in order that you might seek them.

Even through the lens of Paul's judgmental rhetoric, it is clear that these other missionaries have also invited the Galatian converts into a concrete and historically embodied relationship. Whether they see themselves as supplementing or correcting Paul's preaching of the gospel is difficult to determine with certainty, although obviously Paul himself sees them as opposing his gospel — in his terms they are "the agitators" (οἱ ταράσσοντες; 1:7; 5:10).[72] Since knowledge about them comes only through Paul's highly polemical, and often indirect references to them, it is only possible to make educated guesses concerning their identity and their teaching of the Galatians.[73] Surely they exhorted the Gentile converts to be circumcised and to submit to the Sinaitic law (5:2-3; 6:12-13). It is likely that the law observance they enjoined included observance of the Jewish liturgical calendar (4:10).[74]

---

72. For an argument that the other missionaries saw themselves as supplementing Paul's teaching, see especially Jewett, "Agitators"; Howard, *Paul: Crisis in Galatia*, 1-19; R. Longenecker, *Galatians*, xcv.

73. See Barclay, "Mirror-Reading," 73-93. For a brief history of scholarship on the identity of the other missionaries, see R. Longenecker, *Galatians*, lxxxviii-xcvi.

74. Betz (*Galatians*, 217-18) thinks the calendar observance in 4:10 refers to "*typical* behavior of religiously scrupulous people," and is *not* "typical of Judaism." Barclay, however, is more persuasive when he suggests: "the reason why Paul highlights the Galatians' calendar observance, out of all the manifold 'works of the law', is because he sees here a point of direct comparison with their former pagan worship. Both pagan and Jewish religion involve observing certain sacred 'days' and Paul deliberately chooses such general terms as 'days',

Clues in the text of Galatians, as well as other Second Temple Jewish writings, suggest that Paul's extensive references to the Abraham stories (3:6-29; 4:21-30) are an attempt to "correct" exegesis of those stories on the part of the "agitators."[75] Genesis 17:10-14 would have provided these Jewish Christian teachers with ample scriptural proof for the necessity of circumcision: "Any uncircumcised male who is not circumcised in the flesh of his foreskin shall be cut off from his people; he has broken my covenant." Furthermore, the linkage of circumcision, covenant, and Abraham found here received extensive attention in later Jewish literature.[76] Perhaps most decisive, Abraham was revered as the first proselyte and thus at least by some as the father of proselytes.[77] In teaching the Gentile converts to be circumcised and to keep the law, the agitators could have offered them full membership in the Mosaic covenant and the synagogue fellowship, complete with a set of religious rites, a clear guide for daily behavior, and an acknowledged place in society. In this respect, they may well have appeared to offer much more than Paul. In Barclay's concise summary, "The 'works of the law' would perform a crucial social function in preserving the Galatian Christian communities."[78]

Although the actual teaching and motivation of the other missionaries remain a matter for some speculation, Paul's accusations against them are clear: they are throwing his congregations into confusion (1:7; 5:10), perverting the gospel and preaching a contrary gospel (1:7, 9), "bewitching [casting the evil eye on]" the Galatians (3:1), "compelling" circumcision, and boasting

---

'months' and 'seasons' in order to emphasize the similarities between these two forms of religion: hence he can score a useful polemical point by describing their new Jewish practice as a regression to their former way of life" (*Obeying the Truth*, 63-64).

75. The classic statement of this argument is by C. K. Barrett in "The Allegory of Abraham, Sarah, and Hagar in the Argument of Galatians," *Essays on Paul* (Philadelphia: Westminster, 1982), 154-70. So also Barclay, *Obeying the Truth*, 53-56; Martyn, *Galatians*, 301-6; R. Longenecker, *Galatians*, xcvii, among many.

76. See, e.g., *Jub.* 15:9-14, 26, 33-34; Sir 44:20. *Second Bar.* 57:2 and *Jub.* 16:28 depict Abraham keeping the Mosaic law. See references and discussion in Barclay, *Obeying the Truth*, 54 n. 53. In *Virt.* 212-19, Philo depicts Abraham as the first proselyte, who by virtue of his conversion receives the Spirit (*Philo*, trans. F. H. Colson and G. H. Whitaker, 10 vols., LCL [Cambridge: Harvard University Press, 1929-53], vol. 8). For further discussion see Peder Borgen, *Early Christianity and Hellenistic Judaism* (Edinburgh: T&T Clark, 1996), 262.

77. Barclay, *Obeying the Truth*, 54 n. 55. See also Dieter Georgi, *The Opponents of Paul in Second Corinthians* (Philadelphia: Fortress, 1986), 52-60.

78. Barclay, *Obeying the Truth*, 72. See also Betz, *Galatians*, 8-9.

in the Galatians' "flesh" (6:12-13).[79] Paul also claims that they preach circumcision in order to avoid persecution, in stark contrast to his own willingness to suffer for the "truth of the gospel" (5:11; 6:12).[80] Their embodied identity markers derive from the law; his derive from the cross of Jesus (6:17).

Thus, in Paul's description of the agitators' activities, he paints them as inaugurating a relationship with the Galatians that differs markedly from his own. The contrast is clearest in 6:12-15 and in the passage at hand, 4:12-18. Three observations are pertinent to the distinctive "family identity" enjoined by these other missionaries.[81]

First, the Teachers' requirement of circumcision quite literally inscribes likeness to themselves directly on the Galatians' bodies. This unidirectional movement — "Become like us!" — is the unspoken foil to Paul's contrasting appeal — "because I also have become like you." The other missionaries, at least in Paul's portrayal of them, have not become like the Galatians, nor can they. The requirement of the works of the law, as they understand it, precludes such a reciprocal movement. In contrast to Paul's testimony about the radical change in his own life, which is demonstrated by the shift in his mode of relating to Gentile Christians, there is no indication of such a radical change in the other missionaries' mode of relating to Gentile believers.

Second, whereas the Teachers have not become like the Galatians, they may indeed claim that they sincerely seek the Galatians' good. They share with the Gentile churches the riches of the covenant and the law that, to all appearances, Paul has withheld from his converts. Paul puts it this way: "They zealously court you" (ζηλοῦσιν ὑμᾶς; 4:17). According to his own testimony, Paul's "former life in Judaism" also was characterized by zeal — zeal for "the traditions of my fathers" (1:14; see also Phil 3:6). The connection between zeal and Jewish religious traditions, particularly as distinguishing Jew from Gentile, echoes the famous zeal of Phinehas, as replayed in the zeal of Mattathias (Num 25:6-13; 1 Macc 2:23-26).[82] In 4 Macc 9:23

---

79. On the evil eye in Gal 3:1, see Susan Eastman, "The Evil Eye and the Curse of the Law: Galatians 3:1 Revisited," *JSNT* 83 (2001): 69-87.

80. The historical situation behind these references to "persecution" is difficult, if not impossible, to reconstruct.

81. The helpful term "family identity" comes from Barclay's discussion of the Sarah-Hagar allegory, in *Obeying the Truth,* 92.

82. In 1:14 Paul links προέκοπτον ἐν τῷ Ἰουδαϊσμῷ with περισσοτέρως ζηλωτὴς τῶν πατρικῶν μου παραδόσεων.

and 13:9, two of the few occurrences of μιμέομαι in the LXX, loyalty to the divine law is held up for imitation, accompanied by references to Abraham and family solidarity. However, whereas under Antiochus zeal for the law caused faithful Jews to become *victims* of persecution, the roles are reversed in Paul's telling of his story; his own past zeal caused him to become a *persecutor* of God's people, not a victim (ἐδίωκον τὴν ἐκκλησίαν τοῦ θεοῦ; Gal 1:13; see also Phil 3:6). Similarly, now the other missionaries' zeal is leading them to "persecute," in a sense, the Galatians by "troubling" them and "compelling" them to be circumcised (Gal 1:6; 4:29; 6:12).[83] Paul claims that, rather than indicating a willingness to suffer and a genuine concern for the Galatians, such zeal is an attempt to avoid suffering (6:12). The apostle, on the other hand, aligns himself with his converts by attributing his own experience of persecution to his refusal to preach the law (5:11) — a refusal that is proof of his determination to preserve "the truth of the gospel" on their behalf (2:5).

Thus in 4:17 Paul immediately qualifies the way in which the agitators zealously court the Galatians as "not for good" (οὐ καλῶς). In the subsequent phrase he draws on the imagery of ζηλόω as erotic courtship in order to explain further what he means: "They want to shut you out, so that you will seek them" (ἐκκλεῖσαι ὑμᾶς θέλουσιν, ἵνα αὐτοὺς ζηλοῦτε). That is, the missionaries' gatekeeping requirement of circumcision, through which they exclude the uncircumcised Gentile believers from fellowship with them, is intended to create intensified zeal and yearning for acceptance into full covenant membership.[84] The threat of exclusion gives the Teachers power over the Galatians; indeed, Castelli's description of the

---

83. See Martyn, *Galatians*, 155. Martyn states that "the picture Paul paints of himself prior to his call by God is similar to the picture the Teachers are now presenting of themselves." I would say rather that *Paul* paints similar pictures of his life in Judaism and the Teachers' "Judaistic" zeal. Whether the Teachers presented *themselves* within the tradition of Phinehas and Mattathias is less likely to me; what in that tradition would support or motivate a missionary outreach to Gentiles? B. Longenecker's more cautious assessment is helpful: Paul's double reference to "zeal" "allows for a subtle likening of the pre-Christian Paul to the agitators themselves" (*Triumph*, 28).

84. James D. G. Dunn, "Echoes of Intra-Jewish Polemic in Paul's Letter to the Galatians," *JBL* 112 (1993): 473-76; Martyn, *Galatians*, 422-23; Hays, *Galatians*, 295. Betz (*Galatians*, 229) acknowledges the origin of ζηλόω in "the erotic vocabulary describing the stratagems of the lover to gain control over the beloved," but then focuses on its use here as part of the friendship theme. For extensive discussion of the erotic courtship motif, see further Smith, "'Ἐκκλεῖσαι.'"

pernicious effects of imitation as unidirectional, coercive, and conformist might well be applied to them.

Conclusion

In the first part of this chapter, I traced the "chronological parallels" connecting Paul's retrospective depictions of his own life and that of his converts. Yet a close reading of Paul's testimony also suggests that problems arise when it is understood primarily in simple temporal terms, as delineating discontinuity between "past" and "present," or between "old" and "new." It is not clear just when and where the "past" ends and "new life" begins. Nor is there ever a "past" outside, or prior to, the providential action of God. Paul does not qualify his "crucifixion with Christ" as "I have died to my past life," but as "I have died to the law." Indeed, as his testimony makes clear, his identification with the death of Christ opens the way for him to reconnect with the fundamental action and presence of God in his own "past." In other words, it generates a new way of describing his own history, disrupting old continuities and identity markers, but also creating a new continuity that embraces both the past and the future as "in Christ."

Therefore, in the second part of this chapter, I investigated the "relational matrix" disclosed by the christocentric intersection of the narratives of Paul and his converts. The interweaving of temporal narrative and relational language suggests that the transforming and sustaining power of the gospel is mediated through the shared life of Paul and the Galatians — again, "in Christ." The nature of that shared life is crucial for the apostle, as he contrasts two concrete, imitative patterns of interaction. On the one hand, he describes the relationship that the Teachers seek with the Galatians as embodied through the identity markers of law observance, requiring a unidirectional imitation of themselves and threatening exclusion for those who do not comply with their preaching.[85] He warns that this relationship exists only in the sphere of human abilities: those who follow the Teachers' lead are cutting themselves off from Christ and thus from the power that will sustain their new life in Christ (5:4). They have fallen away

---

85. On the threat of exclusion hanging over the Teachers themselves, articulated in 4:30, see discussion in chapter five below.

from God's first gracious calling of them, and therefore they are severed from their origin in the gospel. Thus the law delivers both discontinuity in the narratives of Paul and his converts, and discord in their relationships with each other and with Christ.

On the other hand, Paul depicts his own relationship with his converts as embodied by the marks of suffering for the sake of the gospel, enacting Christ's sacrificial movement into the sphere of human bondage and creating a reciprocal relationship in which all the participants are moving. The apostle narrates the connections between his converts and himself as already established, such that through their mutual baptism into Christ — and only there — they are already "like" each other. In this relational matrix, none of the players is stationary: Christ moves into the human situation, Paul moves via Christ into the Galatians' sphere, and they move into his. Christ's continued faithfulness is the model of sacrificial service and the *dynamis* that empowers both the interaction between the apostle and the Galatians, and potentially the Galatians' relationships with one another. This dynamic new situation transforms the imitation language in Paul's exhortation to "Become like me, because I have become like you," such that it becomes an appeal for participation in a relationship with both personal and cosmic dimensions, in which there is a pattern of correspondence between Christ, Paul, and the Galatians. It is the transcendent dimension of this relational matrix, precisely as it is enacted in the self-giving apocalypse of Christ, which gives it transformational "staying power."

This chapter began by quoting Castelli's formulation of the imitative relationship as "asymmetrical . . . [involving] one element being fixed and the other transforming itself or being transformed into an approximation of the first." Does this formulation accurately or adequately characterize the relationships between Paul, the Galatians, and Christ? To the contrary, the text points in a different direction: the narrative that leads up to 4:12 tells both the story of Christ's movement into the sphere of those held captive by the powers of this age and the parallel story of the way Paul has been brought to share in that movement into the sphere of the "other," the stranger. Thus the power of the Spirit comes through a fundamental "mimetic reversal" in which Christ becomes like and participates in enslaved humanity, and the apostle "becomes like" the Gentiles whom he now calls "brothers and sisters." To return to, but alter, Castelli's description, here the model moves.

The combination of temporal and relational language in Paul's retrospective narration suggests that the "staying power of the gospel" is mediated by the relational matrix into which both he and his converts have been called. The same thing could be claimed by the other missionaries, however, and the apostle carefully differentiates between the communal life created by their teaching and that created by the gospel he preaches. As the mimetic reversal in Paul's account shows, the key difference is in the direction of what Martyn calls the "line of movement":

> [The Teachers] hold that Gentiles *can move*, by Law observance, *into* the covenant community. For Paul, the dominant line is the one along which God *has* moved *into the cosmos* in the invasive sending of Christ and in Christ's faithful death for all (note the verbs in 3:23, 25; 4:4, 6, etc.). The difference between these two lines of movement is monumental.[86]

To sharpen the point, one may compare Stephen Fowl's formulation of Paul's message:

> for the Galatians to become as Paul is they will have to consider the narrative of Christ's work, which is to occupy the center of their selves. Moreover, *they will have to fit their particular stories into Christ's story* in a manner analogous to the way Paul has embedded his particular story into Christ's in such a way that he no longer lives, but Christ lives in him.[87]

Note that in Fowl's formulation the direction of movement is reversed; the Galatians are to fit their stories into Christ's story. This way of speaking places the burden of change on the Galatians themselves. The difference from Paul's speech is subtle, but crucial. Although the apostle indeed has "narrated his life in Christ," he clearly sees God, not himself, as the author of the narrative. Furthermore, the basic plot in Paul's account traces Christ's movement into the sphere of human bondage, through which Christ's participation in the human "story" catalyzes human participation in Christ's story. This "line of movement" extends, in turn, into the relationship between Paul and his converts, in contrast with that taught by the Teachers. Just as God's movement into the cosmos is a boundary-

---

86. Martyn, "Events in Galatia," 167-68.
87. Fowl, "Learning," 347; emphasis added.

crossing movement into the sphere of enslaved humanity, so Paul's preaching takes the initiative in crossing the boundaries between Jew and Gentile, without requiring that the Gentiles become Jews.

At the same time, precisely because Paul's preaching embodies God's movement into the human sphere, one must question whether the line of movement from God to humanity also necessitates an absolute divide between divine and human activity. We recall that in Martyn's view it apparently does: the Galatians will note "Paul's tendency to refer to antinomies, beginning with the venerable one between the actions of human beings and the action of God. . . . Law observance is merely a *human* activity, whereas what makes for the rectification of human beings is the activity of *God* in Christ's faith."[88] The connection is clear between this antinomy and Martyn's insistence on the direction of movement from God to humanity; rectification is completely God's doing. The issue is one of power: only God has the power to "make right what was wrong."[89] The question remains, however, whether Martyn's formulation might not lead to a kind of docetism, if God's activity does not take shape in some sort of embodied way on an anthropological level within the community of believers.[90] To the contrary, Paul's own testimony, with its mingling of personal and cosmological language, suggests that "in Christ" the absolute distinction between divine and human activity is softened. Yes, only God's gracious movement into the human sphere sustains the continuity to which Paul bears witness. But that divine initiative is not abstract: it takes place in the flesh-and-blood interaction between the apostle and his converts. Paul intends the same gracious movement to be enacted among the Galatians as well, as they "bear one another's burdens, and so fulfill the law of Christ."

Again, comparison with Fowl's work may sharpen the point. Fowl sees Paul's self-characterization in Gal 1–2 as a "precarious" balance between "two potentially competing interests" — "God's grace" and "the specificities of his own life as exemplary." To accomplish such a balance is a

---

88. Martyn, "Events in Galatia," 165.

89. See Martyn, "God's Way of Making Right What Is Wrong," *Theological Issues*, 141-56.

90. For Martyn's own argument against just such a docetic understanding of Christianity, see "Leo Baeck's Reading of Paul," *Theological Issues*, 62-63: "the apocalyptic drama, having been inaugurated by the coming of Christ, has already begun, and it is occurring in the world into which Christ came. True enough, being a genuine apocalyptic drama, it includes suprahuman actors . . . but they do not at all drive the human actors off the stage."

"moral and theological achievement." Fowl cautions that giving too much weight to God's grace risks "obliterating Paul's self," whereas giving too much weight to Paul's example is "to risk the view that Paul's transformation and, hence, his gospel, are the work of his own zeal and self-discipline."[91] Yet the very language of "achievement," with its emphasis on Paul as the acting subject whose life is in some sense in competition with God's grace, does indeed weight the balance in favor of "example." In response, one may ask whether Paul presents God's grace and his own life as "competing interests." Surely he does not. Rather, he presents his life as exemplifying God's grace, such that the power of God works in his life without obliterating his "self" (2:20). Indeed, the power of God frees Paul to be an agent, an acting subject.[92] At issue here is the distinction between divine and human action — a distinction that Paul's language subverts in passages such as 2:20 and 5:16-24.

Thus, while the mingling of temporal and relational language in Paul's preaching to his converts suggests that the staying power of the gospel is mediated through the relationship he shares with them, the mingling of personal and cosmological language further suggests that this relationship has both human and divine participants. The resultant communal life that Paul envisions with his converts is to display the profoundly transformed and transformative "mimetic" relationship that Christ has established with humanity. Because this relationship is inaugurated and characterized by "mimetic reversal," it has profound implications for the usual formula for "Christian imitation" — *imitatio Christi* — in which Christ is the fixed element who is imitated but never equaled, and Christians are to be transformed into Christ's likeness. Transformation into the likeness of Christ is certainly present in Galatians, as 4:19b demonstrates, yet even there Paul maintains the dynamic of Christ's movement into the human situation by speaking of the formation of Christ "in" the Galatian congregations. Thus for Paul this transformation begins with, and is sustained by, a distinctive fundamental relationship in which imitation is grounded and identity is formed. Humanity in its most marginalized and outcast state is the ele-

---

91. Fowl, "Learning," 347.

92. Again, in his response to Baeck, Martyn (*Theological Issues*, 65) upholds human agency within the "apocalyptic drama": "it is in that drama that God is actively freeing the will, thus creating among the Gentiles a liberated community that is able to be addressed by the commandment (1 Cor 7:19). And it is this newly addressable community that is called by God into the apocalyptic warfare for the glorious future of the whole of humanity."

ment toward which God in Christ moves, and whose image Christ assumes. This is the stunning apocalyptic reversal that transforms the mimetic relationship so that all the participants are moving and power is shared. It is this reversal that animates Paul's appeal to his converts, "Become like me, because I also have become like you, I beg of you, my brothers and sisters!"

Chapter Three

Paul among the Prophets

And though my condition was a trial to you, you did not scorn or despise me, but you received me as an angel of God, as Christ Jesus.

Gal 4:14

People crave objectivity because to be subjective is to be embodied, to be a body, vulnerable, violable.[1]

P aul describes his call in prophetic language (1:15-16), and he describes the Galatians' initial reception of him with the parallel phrases, ὡς ἄγγελον θεοῦ and ὡς Χριστὸν Ἰησοῦν (4:14). These depictions of Paul's apostolic calling and relationship with the Galatians are not unrelated, and both yield further understanding of his particular mode of proclamation. At the very least, Paul reminds the Galatians that they first received him as a messenger of the Lord, and indeed as Christ's personal representative.[2] In

---

1. Le Guin, "Bryn Mawr," 151.

2. It seems likely that ἄγγελος means here not simply "messenger," but either designates Paul as an "angel of the Lord," who in the LXX virtually personifies the presence of the Lord (Gen 21:17; Exod 14:19; Judg 13:9), or draws on later Jewish traditions in which the saints on earth have angelic counterparts in heaven. See the discussion in A. J. Goddard and S. A. Cummins, "Ill or Ill-Treated? Conflict and Persecution as the Context of Paul's Original Ministry in Galatia (Galatians 4:12-20)," *JSNT* 52 (1993): 107-10. Betz comments on Gal 4:14: "Therefore, as an apostle Paul is simultaneously a representative of Christ; his appeal

63

chapter four of this study I will investigate the extent of that representative role in Paul's physical presence among the Galatians. Here I will situate Paul's preaching in the context of his identification with the classical prophets, with special attention to Jeremiah.[3] Before we go further, however, it will be helpful to keep in mind a few observations, noted in reading Galatians up to this point.

1. Patterns of correspondence: Paul's "testimony" delineates patterns of correspondence between the "stories" of Paul, the Galatians, and Christ.[4] In particular, the connection between the otherwise divergent lives of Paul and the Galatians is "in Christ." Paul does not explain his "relentlessly mythological" language, nor argue for the correspondence between his life, that of Christ and that of the Galatians; he simply assumes it as fundamental to his testimony. Because now Christ "lives in" Paul and Paul lives by the "faithfulness of the Son of God, who loved me and gave himself for me," because Christ became a curse "for us" and was "born of a woman, born under the law," Paul's actions in relationship to the Galatians emulate the action of Christ in relationship to the human race. Christ "became like" enslaved humanity; "in Christ" Paul "became like" the Galatians.[5]

(παρακαλεῖν) is God's appeal, in him the resurrected Christ speaks and works" (*Nachfolge*, 179). Given Paul's emphasis on his own bearing of Jesus' *stigmata* (6:17), however, it seems more accurate to say the *crucified* Christ speaks and works in him.

3. As noted in chapter one, this chapter represents a departure from current emphases on Greco-Roman rhetoric and society as the background for understanding Paul's discourse and in particular his mimetic language. The literature on Paul's rhetoric and particularly his imitation language within the context of Greco-Roman rhetoric is extensive. See, e.g., Aasgaard, *My Beloved Brothers and Sisters;* Engberg-Pedersen, *Paul and the Stoics;* Betz, *Galatians;* Castelli, *Imitating Paul;* Dodd, *Paul's Paradigmatic 'I';* Fiore, *Function of Personal Example;* John T. Fitzgerald, *Cracks in an Earthen Vessel: An Examination of the Catalogues of Hardships in the Corinthian Correspondence*, SBLDS 99 (Atlanta: Scholars Press, 1988); Gaventa, "Galatians 1 and 2"; Malherbe, "God's New Family"; D. Martin, *Corinthian Body;* Troy Martin, "Apostasy to Paganism: The Rhetorical Stasis of the Galatian Controversy," *JBL* 114 (1995): 437-61; and Michaelis, "Μιμέομαι."

4. Similarly, Andrew T. Lincoln delineates three "levels" of "story" in Paul's Letters: the "underlying story of God's activity in Christ," "the story of Paul and his apostolic mission," and "the stories of the inheritors of Paul's letters," whom Lincoln takes in the first place to be Paul's original auditors, but also today's readers. See "The Stories of Predecessors and Inheritors in Galatians and Romans," in *Narrative Dynamics in Paul*, ed. B. Longenecker, 203.

5. "Correspondence" is not an adequate word to describe the intimate relational matrix displayed in Gal 2:19-20, a relationship that exemplifies the tension between "like" and "different," which is at the heart of the mimetic relationship. For the difficulty of finding an ade-

This mimetic pattern, however, is not limited to *Paul's* representation of Christ and connections with the Galatians. The Galatians themselves have demonstrated a similar correspondence with Christ; in 4:13-14 they "passed the test" posed to them by Paul's bodily condition; in their reception of him as "an angel of God, as Christ himself," they demonstrated their willingness to join him in suffering for the "truth of the gospel." Indeed, perhaps their eager desire to serve is the greatest "miracle" worked among them by the Spirit (3:5). Thus the Galatians' own story, albeit to a lesser degree, "re-presents" the sacrificial love of Christ.

2. Apocalyptic worldview: Paul's temporal and cosmological language, his certainty of divine judgment on the present age, his emphasis on suffering, his implicit correspondence between a divine figure and the faithful community, all have affinities with Hellenistic developments in both Jewish apocalypticism and Wisdom literature.[6] He opens his letter with his own commentary on the early Christian affirmation that Christ "gave himself for our sins," and further interprets that affirmation to mean that Christ's death was to "deliver us out of this present evil age"; he ends his letter with reference to the "new creation."[7] The point of deliverance from the "present evil age" is for Paul the cross of Christ, through which he is crucified to the world and the world to him. In the intervening chapters, the temporal markers emphasize the dramatic difference between the former lives of Paul and his converts and their new life in Christ, even while they affirm God's sovereignty over all time.

---

quate contemporary language to describe Paul's conviction that he and his converts share "real participation in Christ, real possession of the Spirit," see E. P. Sanders, *Paul and Palestinian Judaism: A Comparison of Patterns of Religion* (Minneapolis: Fortress, 1977), 522-23.

6. The thesis linking Wisdom literature and apocalyptic literature was first influentially put forth by Gerhard von Rad, *Old Testament Theology*, 2 vols. (New York: Harper & Row, 1962-65), 2:306. See also Jonathan Z. Smith, "Wisdom and Apocalyptic," in *Religious Syncretism in Antiquity: Essays in Conversation with Geo Widengren*, ed. Birger Pearson (Missoula, MT: Scholars Press, 1975), 154, who traces both Wisdom and apocalyptic to the "paradigmatic thinking" of scribal tradition: "both are essentially scribal phenomena. They both depend on the relentless quest for paradigms." John J. Collins discusses links between apocalypticism and wisdom extensively in *Seers, Sibyls and Sages in Hellenistic-Roman Judaism* (Leiden: Brill, 1997), 317-404.

7. For the argument that 1:4b is a commentary on 1:4a, see Martyn, *Galatians*, 97. The shift implicit in the movement from the first phrase to the second correlates with the distinction that M. C. de Boer draws between "forensic apocalyptic eschatology" and "cosmological apocalyptic eschatology" in "Paul and Jewish Apocalyptic Eschatology," 180-81.

Reviewing Paul's use of ἀποκάλυψις and ἀποκαλύπτω at key points in Galatians (1:12, 15-16; 2:2; 3:23), Martyn notes the interchangeability of "the apocalypse of faith" and "the coming of faith" in 3:23-25. These are parallel with "when the fullness of time came, God sent forth his Son. . . . God sent forth his Spirit into our hearts (4:4, 6)." He concludes, "Paul thus explicates the verb ἀποκαλύπτω with the verbs ἔρχομαι, 'to come [on the scene],' and ἐξαποστέλλω, 'to send [into the scene]' (4:4, 6). . . . The genesis of Paul's apocalyptic — as we see it in Galatians — lies in the apostle's certainty that God has *invaded* the present evil age by sending Christ and his Spirit into it."[8] Paul speaks of the apocalyptic "coming" of Christ in both personal (1:12, 15-16; 2:2; 4:6) and cosmic (3:23; 4:4) contexts, so much so that they seem almost interchangeable: God sent the Son, born into universal human kinship, and God also sent the Spirit into "our hearts, crying Abba! Father!" (4:4, 6). The apostle received the gospel "by apocalypse," which he is at pains to distinguish from human agency, but he also is impelled toward his fellow Christians "by apocalypse" (1:15-16). In this scenario God is the chief actor, who moves into the sphere of human existence, initiating and sustaining a reciprocal movement by the human actors.

3. Centrality of suffering: One of the primary contrasts Paul paints between the Teachers and himself concerns the willingness to suffer persecution for the sake of "the truth of the gospel." His first preaching of the crucified Christ to the Galatians involved suffering occasioned by a "weakness of the flesh" (4:13). Coupled with his later reference to the "stigmata of Jesus," which he bears in his body (6:17), and his earlier reference to the public portrayal of Christ crucified before his converts' eyes (3:1), Paul's language here suggests that he considered his own scars as a sort of billboard of Christ crucified.[9] Whereas the Teachers preach faith as embodied in the identity marker of circumcision, Paul depicts faith as embodied in the

8. Martyn, *Galatians*, 99.

9. See Basil S. Davis, "The Meaning of προεγράφη in the Context of Galatians 3.1," *NTS* 45, 2 (1999): 208: "Paul's claim was that he publicly displayed the crucified Christ in his body, for he bore on his body the stigmata of Christ (Gal 6.17). There is nothing in the context to suggest a tattoo or other religious symbol. The reference is certainly to the marks of the sufferings he endured as an apostle." See also Betz, *Nachfolge*, 152 n. 6; Martyn, *Galatians*, 421; Ernest Baasland, "Persecution: A Neglected Feature in the Letter to the Galatians," *Studia theologica* 38 (1984): 145-46; Goddard and Cummins, "Ill or Ill-Treated?" 93-126. For further discussion of Paul's apostolic suffering, see below, chapter four.

identity marker of "the stigmata of Jesus." Furthermore, he describes the Galatians' past reception of the Spirit and the Spirit's wonder-working power with the word ἐπάθετε (3:4). Moreover, as noted above, Paul reminds his converts of their earlier solidarity with him in his affliction (4:13-15). Through such reminders, Paul seeks to draw them back into fellowship with him in undergoing persecution for the sake of the gospel.

The representational correspondence between Paul, Christ, and the Galatians, the apocalyptic worldview evident throughout the letter, and the centrality of suffering all direct our attention to Paul's identification with the classical prophets of Israel.

Paul among the Prophets

Paul's description of his "call" in Gal 1:15-16 echoes the call of Jeremiah (Jer 1:1-10), and the call of the Servant of the Lord (Isa 49:1-6).[10] Galatians 1:15-16 reads:

> But when the one [God] who set me aside from my mother's womb and called me through his grace was pleased to reveal his son in me, in order that I might preach him among the Gentiles, I did not confer with flesh and blood.

> Ὅτε δὲ εὐδόκησεν [ὁ θεὸς] ὁ ἀφορίσας με ἐκ κοιλίας μητρός μου καὶ καλέσας διὰ τῆς χάριτος αὐτοῦ ἀποκαλύψαι τὸν υἱὸν αὐτοῦ ἐν ἐμοί, ἵνα

---

10. For extended discussion of parallels between Gal 1:15-16 and both Jer 1:1-20 and Isa 49:1, see Karl O. Sandnes, *Paul — One of the Prophets? A Contribution to the Apostle's Self-Understanding*, WUNT 2.43 (Tübingen: Mohr/Siebeck, 1991), 15-18, 62-65. For a review of the secondary literature, see 5-13. With variations, proponents of the view that Paul stands in the tradition of both Isaiah and Jeremiah include Hans Windisch, *Paulus und Christus: Ein biblisch-religionsgeschichtlicher Vergleich*, Untersuchungen zum Neuen Testament 24 (Leipzig: Hinrich, 1934), 137; Bonnard, *Galates*, 30; Lagrange, *Galates*, 13; R. Longenecker, *Galatians*, 30; Matera, *Galatians*, 63; Sam Williams, *Galatians*, Abingdon New Testament Commentaries (Nashville: Abingdon, 1997), 46; Lyons, *Pauline Autobiography*, 133; Dodd, *Paul's Paradigmatic 'I,'* 149-50; Martyn, *Galatians*, 156-57; Johannes Munck, *Paul and the Salvation of Mankind* (Richmond: John Knox, 1959); Jacob M. Myers and Edwin D. Freed, "Is Paul Also among the Prophets?" *Int* 20, 1 (1966): 40-53; Mussner, *Galaterbrief*, 82-83; Borse, *Galater*, 62. Betz (*Galatians*, 69 n. 129) is restrained, acknowledging only that Paul draws on prophetic traditions in his call narrative.

εὐαγγελίζωμαι αὐτὸν ἐν τοῖς <u>ἔθνεσιν</u>, εὐθέως οὐ προσανεθέμην σαρκὶ καὶ αἵματι

Jeremiah's call in Jer 1:5 reads:

Before I formed you in the womb I knew you,
And before you came forth from your mother's womb
    I consecrated you;
I appointed you a prophet to the Gentiles.

πρὸ τοῦ με πλάσαι σε ἐν κοιλίᾳ ἐπίσταμαί σε καὶ πρὸ τοῦ σε ἐξελθεῖν ἐκ <u>μήτρας</u> ἡγίακά σε, <u>προφήτην εἰς ἔθνη</u> τέθεικά σε

In Isa 49:1 the Servant cries out:

Listen to me, islands,
And pay attention, Gentiles.
After a long time it will be established, says the Lord.
From my mother's womb he has called my name.

Ἀκούσατέ μου, νῆσοι, καὶ προσέχετε, ἔθνη· διὰ χρόνου πολλοῦ στήσεται, λέγει κύριος. <u>ἐκ κοιλίας</u> μητρός μου <u>ἐκάλεσεν</u> τὸ ὄνομά μου

Galatians 1:15-16 does not exhibit extensive literary dependence on either of these verses, and it is not necessary to argue for such dependence. But by employing the standard vocabulary of prophetic call narratives, particularly in the context of God's revelation to the Gentiles, here Paul self-consciously places himself within the prophetic tradition.[11] In his presen-

---

11. As R. Longenecker (*Galatians*, 30) observes, "with evident intent," in light of Rom 1:1: Κλητὸς ἀπόστολος ἀφωρισμένος εἰς εὐαγγέλιον θεοῦ. Paul was not alone among first-century Jews in using language from the prophets to describe his call. Josephus also identified himself with Jeremiah in his preaching to Jerusalem and his suffering abuse at the hands of his own people (see *J.W.* 5.375, 391-93; *Ant.* 10.89, 104, 112, 117-18, 125-28). See discussion in Rebecca Gray, *Prophetic Figures in Late Second Temple Jewish Palestine: The Evidence from Josephus* (New York: Oxford University Press, 1993), 70-74; David Daube, "Typology in Josephus," *JJS* 31, 1 (1980): 18-36. In Galatians, however, Paul does not claim to be a prophet in the sense that either Josephus or the first-century sign prophets understood "prophecy" — that is, primarily as prediction of the future. That there were such "prophets" in early Christian circles is indicated by Acts 11:27-28. But Paul's testimony about his "call" serves rather to connect his message and mode of preaching with that of Jeremiah and Isaiah. For discussion of the sign prophets, see further Gray, *Prophetic Figures*, 112-44. For an overview

tation of his apostolic vocation, he shares with the classical prophets two characteristics: he is called by the God of Israel to communicate a specific message, and he is "sent" (ἀποστέλλω) in God's name.[12] Like the prophets who are called "servants [δοῦλοι] of the Lord," Paul calls himself Χριστοῦ δοῦλος (Gal 1:10; see Jer 7:25; 25:4; 33:5; 42:15; 51:4).[13] Like the prophets who persist in proclaiming the divine message, despite its unpopularity, his faithfulness to his calling as Χριστοῦ δοῦλος makes him resist becoming a "people pleaser" (Gal 1:10).

Specifically, the apostle shares with the Servant of the Lord in Isa 49 the distinction of being "called" (καλεῖν) "from my mother's womb" (ἐκ κοιλίας μητρός μου) with a message for the Gentiles (Isa 49:1). Like the Servant, Paul considers the possibility that he has "labored in vain" (εἰς κενόν; Gal 2:2; 4:11; Isa 49:4). But also like the Servant, Paul can claim that God is "glorified" in him (Gal 1:24; Isa 49:3).[14] These corollaries point to Isa 49 as the closest parallel to Paul's call narrative, particularly since he quotes from Isaiah later in the letter (Isa 54:1; Gal 4:27), and since he cites Isaiah so extensively elsewhere in his letters.[15] As will become clear, however, Paul

---

of the extensive traditions about Jeremiah in Second Temple Judaism, see Michael Knowles, *Jeremiah in Matthew's Gospel: The Rejected Prophet Motif in Matthean Redaction*, JSNTSup 68 (Sheffield: Sheffield Academic Press, 1993), 247-64.

12. See extensive discussion in Sandnes, *Paul*, 14-18, 62-65. The relationship between "apostle" and "prophet" through the notion of being "sent" is discussed also by Munck, *Salvation of Mankind*, 15-27; and Windisch, *Paulus und Christus*, 152.

13. Dodd, *Paul's Paradigmatic 'I,'* 149 n. 70, notes the ambiguity of the genitive: "That slaves were property gives support to reading these as genitives of possession. That the prophets were sent in each case supports reading these as subjective genitives, 'the slaves who have come from me'. This same ambiguity exists for 'slave of Christ' in Gal. 1.10."

14. Sandnes, *Paul*, 61-62. See also Barnabas Lindars, *New Testament Apologetic: The Doctrinal Significance of the Old Testament Quotations* (London: SCM, 1961), 223-24; J. Christiaan Beker, *Paul the Apostle: The Triumph of God in Life and Thought* (Philadelphia: Fortress, 1980), 10, 115; Dunn, *Galatians*, 63; Roy E. Ciampa, *The Presence and Function of Scripture in Galatians 1 and 2*, WUNT 2.102 (Tübingen: Mohr/Siebeck, 1998), 111-23.

15. See Sandnes, *Paul*, 62 n. 51, for a convenient list of citations. With regard to the priority of Isaiah, Sandnes (65) concludes, "Paul did not understand his commission in terms of any particular prophet. He describes his call in terms and motifs that are analogous to the call of Isaiah, Jeremiah and the Servant of the Lord. The apostle Paul is, then, as a preacher of the gospel of God's Son a latter day prophet. It comes as no surprise that Isa 49 holds the dominant place, because of his commission to preach the gospel (εὐαγγελίζεσθαι), and the role Judaism attributed to Deutero-Isaiah in defining what an OT prophet was." On the centrality of Isaiah in Jewish tradition, see 35-36, 39-41.

also aligns himself with the tradition of Jeremiah, not only by echoing Jeremiah's prophetic call, but also by the mode of his proclamation in Galatians.[16]

Of course, there are significant differences between Paul and the prophets, because his message is completely centered on the historical figure of Jesus as the Christ. The apostle is a "servant of Christ," who is both the source and content of the message. Therefore, properly speaking, Paul's vocation is specifically to proclaim Christ, just as his goal for his converts is that Christ be formed in them. Nonetheless, for Paul that proclamation of Christ crucified is a revelation of the God who "was pleased to reveal his Son in me" (Gal 1:15-16).[17] In addition, Paul's suffering appears to be somewhat different from that of the prophets: they experience anguish because they must both preach and experience God's judgment and punishment on apostate Israel, whereas Paul suffers in solidarity with the crucified Christ, even as he preaches good news of deliverance from bondage to the powers of this age. His apostolic work is distinct from the preaching of the prophets because, from his perspective, what they proclaimed has now come to pass in the advent of Christ (Rom 1:2-3). The law and the prophets witness to the righteousness of God, which now has been manifested through the faithfulness of Jesus Christ (Rom 3:21-22). Therefore Paul does not call himself a prophet, but he does see his call as continuous with the prophetic tradition and his preaching as continuing and ful-

16. There are three reasons, none of them decisive, why some scholars discount Jer 1:5 as also evoked by Paul's self-description: Jeremiah does not use καλεῖν, he uses ἁγιάζειν rather than ἀφορίζειν, and his statement that God knew him "in the womb" implies election prior to his birth. These difficulties are mitigated by the fact that Jeremiah clearly is commissioned to proclaim a prophetic message, as is Paul. In the LXX, ἀφορίζειν frequently has the sense, "to set aside for consecrated use," and thus can convey the same meaning as ἁγιάζειν (e.g., Exod 19:12-23; 29:27; Lev 20:25-26; 27:21; Ezek 45:1-4). As argued in chapter two, Gal 1:15 can be interpreted to say that Paul also was elected prior to his birth. See Sandnes, *Paul*, 61-64, for review of the literature. For Deutero-Isaiah's use of Jeremiah as a paradigm for both Israel and the Servant, see Benjamin Sommer, *A Prophet Reads Scripture: Allusion in Isaiah 40–66* (Stanford: Stanford University Press, 1998), 61-66.

17. Sandnes, *Paul*, 18. For extensive discussion of the relationship between the revelation of God and the revelation of Christ see also Ulrich Mauser, *Gottesbild und Menschwerdung*, BHT 43 (Tübingen: Mohr/Siebeck, 1971), 122-43. Although he is speaking of Rom 9-11 and not Galatians, Sanders's comment, *Paul, the Law*, 194, is apposite: "it is incredible that [Paul] thought of 'God apart from Christ,' just as it is that he thought of 'Christ apart from God.'"

filling the promises made through the classical prophets. In Karl O. Sandnes's words,

> Paul's identification of the time in which he was acting separated him from the prophets and put them into different epochs of God's plan of salvation. On the other hand . . . the very awareness of proclaiming the eschatological salvation meant an actualization of traditions about eschatological prophets proclaiming the final consolation. We think Paul would have put it this way: The eschatological prophets proclaiming the final comfort in the Last Days are the apostles of Jesus Christ proclaiming the gospel.[18]

Sandnes's comments highlight the affinities between the *message* of the prophets and that of the apostle. In what follows, I will discuss briefly four affinities between the prophetic and apostolic *media* — their respective modes of proclamation — focusing primarily on Jeremiah, with sidelong glances at Hosea, Ezekiel, and the Servant motif in Second Isaiah: (1) the structural interpenetration of "biographical" material and proclamation in Galatians parallels the mode of proclamation of the classical prophets, particularly Jeremiah and Hosea; (2) the patterns of correspondence between God, the preacher, and the people are so close that at times it is difficult to tell who is speaking. As we have seen, such patterns of correspondence also characterize Paul's engagement with the Galatians. Like the prophets, the apostle both speaks and embodies the message in such a way as to become a kind of theophany.[19] (3) For both Paul and the prophets, personal suffering is an integral aspect of their proclamation and their embodiment of the word of the Lord. (4) With regard to God's movement into the realm of human enslavement, divine participation in the anguish of God's people is homologous to the apocalyptic "coming" of Christ into the sphere of human bondage. I will discuss each of these points in turn.

---

18. Sandnes, *Paul,* 244. Sandnes also argues that Paul uses the language of prophetic call narratives to legitimize his apostolic vocation, in defense against charges of being a "false prophet."

19. For the argument that the prophets' embodied proclamation functions as a kind of theophany, see Mauser, *Gottesbild;* idem, "Image of God and Incarnation," *Int* 24, 3 (1970): 336-56; Terence Fretheim, *The Suffering of God: An Old Testament Perspective,* OBT (Philadelphia: Fortress, 1984); Abraham Heschel, *The Prophets,* vol. 1 (repr. New York: Harper & Row, 1969). Unfortunately, Mauser's work has gone virtually unnoticed by Pauline scholars.

The Medium Is the Message

In light of Paul's "testimony" in Gal 1–2, one may trace intriguing parallels between the structures of proclamation in the classical prophets and in Galatians. Nearly two-fifths of the book of Jeremiah is biographical (19:1–20:6; 26:1–29:32; 32:1–45:5), implying an indivisible connection between the prophet's message and his personal history.[20] This intimate connection between the prophet's life and message is certainly not unique to Jeremiah, although it is particularly prominent there.[21] In Hosea as well, the prophet's personal life is profoundly shaped by his message. In Isaiah and Ezekiel the prophets communicate their message through sign-acts.[22] To name a few examples: Isaiah of Jerusalem walks naked and barefoot to signify the captivity of Egypt and Ethiopia (Isa 20:2-4); Jeremiah does not marry, have children, or mourn the dead, in order to display the devastation coming upon Judah (Jer 16:1-5); Hosea's unhappy marriage and unfortunate children are signs of God's relationship with Israel (Hos 1:2–2:23); Ezekiel symbolically acts out the siege and destruction of Jerusalem (Ezek 4–5).

The prophets' physical representation of the message they proclaim is part of their enactment of their calling. Through this enactment, the prophet becomes a sign to the people that God's word is being fulfilled (Ezek 12:6, 11; 24:24, 27). Sometimes the word of God is placed directly into the prophet's mouth at the moment of his call (Ezek 3:1-3; Jer 1:9; 15:16). Consequently, as Terence Fretheim notes, "God calls the prophet to

20. Dale Allison has argued that the same "biographical impulse" can be seen in the development of the Jesus tradition in Matthew: "Our evangelist recognized that many of the sayings passed down under Jesus' name would be liable to grave misunderstanding if they came to be separated from their historical context. . . . Thus, as with the book of Jeremiah, content demanded context. In other words, speech required biography" ("Matthew: Structure, Biographical Impulse, and the *Imitatio Christi*," in *The Four Gospels 1992*, ed. F. Van Segbroeck et al., 3 vols., BETL 100 [Leuven: Leuven University Press, 1992], 3:1213-14).

21. See Timothy Polk, *The Prophetic Persona: Jeremiah and the Language of the Self*, JSOTSup 32 (Sheffield: JSOT Press, 1984), 7: "Nothing distinguishes the book of Jeremiah from earlier works of prophecy quite so much as the attention it devotes to the person of the prophet and the prominence it accords the prophetic 'I', and few things receive more scholarly comment." For a review of the secondary literature, see 7-24.

22. For an investigation of the rhetorical function of nonverbal sign-acts in Jeremiah and Ezekiel, see Kelvin G. Friebel, *Jeremiah's and Ezekiel's Sign-Acts: Rhetorical Nonverbal Communication*, JSNTSup 283 (Sheffield: Sheffield Academic Press, 1999).

take the word received and embody that word from the moment of the call onward."[23]

The same pattern obtains in Galatians, where the apostle's "autobiographical" remarks overlap with his proclamation of the gospel, such that his testimony is interwoven with his preaching. This is particularly evident in Gal 1:11–2:21, but also in the pronominal shifts in Gal 3-4, in the relationship between Paul and his converts in 4:12-15, and in Paul's bearing of the stigmata of Jesus in 6:17. As Gaventa has argued, the apostle presents himself as a paradigm of the gospel.[24] By labeling his scars as "stigmata," he makes his bodily condition a sign of the crucified Christ (6:17). As noted earlier, his testimony, particularly because it mirrors both the Galatians' narrative and the story of Christ, functions as a promise — a prophetic "sign" — that having received the Spirit through the message of faith, the Galatians also will be completed by that same Spirit (3:2-3). To recast Martyn's phrase that the gospel aims "to create a history," Paul's life functions as a sign of the history being created by the gospel.[25] This "history" is both "a new thing," and entirely consonant with the participation of God in the "histories" of the prophets and the people of God.

Who's Talking?

Just as there are patterns of correspondence between the narratives of Paul, the Galatians, and Christ, in the prophets one finds analogous patterns of correspondence between the prophet, the people of God, and God. For example, the sign-acts of Jeremiah clearly embody the present or predicted situation of Israel: Jeremiah's celibacy and childlessness mirror the coming devastation of families, as does his refusal to mourn or to attend festivals (Jer 16:1-9); his purchase of the field at Anathoth signifies the promise of restoration for all of Israel (Jer 32:6-15). Similar observations could be made concerning Ezekiel's sign-acts (Ezek 3:26; 4:1-12; 12:3-6) and the names of Hosea's children (Hos 1:2-11). Furthermore, the prophets' exclamations express the anguish of Israel under judgment, and the joy of restored Israel.[26]

23. Fretheim, *Suffering of God*, 151.
24. Gaventa, "Galatians 1 and 2," 326.
25. Martyn, "Events in Galatia," 164.
26. For example, see Jer 4:5, 8, 31; 14:17, 19-21; 31:18-19. See commentary in Heschel, *Prophets*, 1:119-22.

The prophets also express God's anguish on behalf of Israel — a divine anguish that frequently accompanies divine wrath and punishment. This prophetic enactment of the word of God means that just as the prophet's life and message are woven together, so also the prophet's speech and God's speech are so intertwined as, at times, to be indistinguishable. Again, to quote Fretheim: "In the prophetic materials, while God and 'prophet' (or the name of the prophet) are not interchanged, it is often very difficult, if not impossible, to sort out explicit divine speech from prophetic speech; pronominal references do at times seem to be interchanged, particularly in Jeremiah."[27] Abraham Heschel is more restrained than Fretheim, but Jeremiah's representative function as a prophet remains: "The prophet was fully conscious of his emotional nexus with God. It was at the bidding of God that his compassion and lament were uttered."[28]

Fretheim cites Jer 8:18–9:3 as one example in which both the speech and the anguish of the prophet are indistinguishable from those of God:

> My grief is beyond healing, my heart is sick within me.
> Hark, the cry of the daughter of my people from the length
>   and breadth of the land: "Is the Lord not in Zion? Is her King
>   not in her?"
> Why have they provoked me to anger with their graven images,
>   and with their foreign idols?
> The harvest is past, the summer is ended, and we are not saved.
> For the wound of the daughter of my people is my heart wounded,
>   I mourn, and dismay has taken hold on me.
> Is there no balm in Gilead? Is there no physician there? Why then
>   has the health of the daughter of my people not been restored?

It is not clear who is doing the speaking in this series of questions and complaints. Fretheim suggests that "the passage moves from divine speech (vv. 18-19) to the people (v. 20) to the prophet (8:21–9:1)," but adds, "Yet, it seems best to understand the mourning of God and prophet as so symbiotic that in everything we hear the anguish of both."[29] This understanding is strengthened by the formulaic saying in 9:3 — "says the Lord."

27. Fretheim, *Suffering of God,* 150.
28. Heschel, *Prophets,* 1:119.
29. Fretheim, *Suffering of God,* 160. Fretheim also cites Jer 10:19-20; 13:17-19; and 14:17-18. See also Patrick Miller, "Jeremiah," *NIB* 6:648; J. J. M. Roberts, "The Motif of the Weeping

Jeremiah 4:19 provides another example of mingled prophetic and divine speech: "My anguish, my anguish [τὴν κοιλίαν μου τὴν κοιλίαν μου]! I writhe in pain! Oh, the walls of my heart! My heart is beating wildly; I cannot keep silent; for I hear the sound of the trumpet, the alarm of war."[30] Here the prophet is apparently speaking on behalf of Jerusalem, yet once again his words clearly occur within the context of divine speech, being closely followed by God's complaint: "My people are foolish, they do not know me" (4:22).[31] The prophet's anguished voice and that of God are inseparable. As in Galatians, the language is both "ruthlessly personal" and "relentlessly mythological."

In Isaiah the situation is somewhat different. On the one hand, here the Servant takes up aspects of the prophetic role in representing both God and the people. In Isa 42:7 the Servant leads the blind, as God does in 42:16. In 43:24 God bears Israel's sins, as the Servant will do in 53:4-6. Elsewhere the Servant identifies with Israel as "formed in the womb" (44:1-2; 45:4; 46:1-4; 49:1), as the blind and deaf messenger of the Lord (42:18-19), and as a witness of the Lord (43:10-12; 44:8).[32] On the other hand, in contrast to Jeremiah and

---

God in Jeremiah and Its Background in the Lament Tradition of the Ancient Near East," *Old Testament Essays* 5 (1992): 370-71. *Pace* William McKane, *A Critical and Exegetical Commentary on Jeremiah*, 2 vols., ICC (Edinburgh: T&T Clark, 1986-96), 1:193. Jack R. Lundbom sees this passage as a chiasm distinguished by changes in the speakers, with Jeremiah speaking in vv. 18, 21; the people (represented by Jeremiah) in vv. 19ab and 20; and the Lord in v. 19c. He sees the "I" of vv. 18 and 21 as referring exclusively to Jeremiah himself (*Jeremiah 1-20*, AB 20 [New York: Doubleday, 1999], 529).

30. The Hebrew word that the LXX translates as κοιλία is the plural of מֵעָה, "bowels." In Isa 63:15 and Jer 31:20 it refers to divine mercy. See discussion in Roberts, "Motif of the Weeping God," 368.

31. Fretheim, *Suffering of God*, 160: "It is true that Jeremiah's mourning parallels that of the people (e.g., 4:31), but so does God's." Gerhard von Rad simply sees this as an example of the prophet's "feeling of solidarity with his people in their danger" (*The Message of the Prophets* [New York: Harper & Row, 1968], 165-66). Von Rad's view is that of the majority; see also Lundbom, *Jeremiah*, 350; McKane, *Jeremiah*, 105. Heschel (*Prophets*, 1:119), however, also attributes Jer 4:19-21 to the prophet's "sympathy for Israel," in concert with God's grief on Israel's behalf. So also Miller, *Jeremiah*, 614. Roberts ("Motif of the Weeping God," 368-70) sees God as the only speaker in Jer 4:19-22.

32. The Servant of the Lord is not, properly speaking, a prophet. Nonetheless, there are indications that the Isaianic Servant was sometimes identified with the prophet Isaiah in later Judaism. This is explicit in some of the rabbinic texts. For example, *Pesiq. Rab.* 26:1-2 mentions "Isaiah, of whom it is written 'And now saith the Lord that formed me from the womb'" (Isa 49:5). Identification of Isa 49:1ff. with the prophet Isaiah also occurs in *Midr. Ps.*

Isaiah of Jerusalem, the anonymous author of Deutero-Isaiah remains almost completely unknown to us.[33] Yet there are some notable exceptions: when the prophet does speak in the first person, he identifies at times with the Suffering Servant and at times with guilty Israel. For example, in 50:4-11 the prophet's voice appears to merge with that of the Servant, in phrases that echo the call, suffering, and vindication of Jeremiah (Jer 1:4-10; 20:1-13) and that anticipate the description of the Servant in Isa 53:3-5, 10-12:

> The Lord God has given me the tongue of those who are taught, that I may know how to sustain with a word him that is weary.
> Morning by morning he wakens,
> he wakens my ear to hear as those who are taught.
> The Lord God has opened my ear, and I was not rebellious,
> I turned not backward.
> I gave my back to the smiters, and my cheeks to those who pulled out the beard;
> I hid not my face from shame and spitting.
> For the Lord God helps me; therefore I have not been confounded;
> therefore I have set my face like a flint, and I know that I shall not be put to shame; he who vindicates me is near.
> Who will contend with me? Let us stand up together.
> Who is my adversary? Let him come near to me.
> Behold, the Lord God helps me; who will declare me guilty?[34]

Yet in Isa 53 the anonymous prophet identifies himself not with the Servant, but with the guilty people for whom the Servant suffers (53:4-6). Similarly, 59:9-15 abruptly switches from recounting the sins of Israel in the second (vv. 2-3) and third person (vv. 4-8) to a first person confession

---

9:7; 58:2; and *Sipre Deut.* 3:24. In Isa 50:4 the Servant is given a message, just as Jeremiah is in Jer 1:9. See discussion in Sandnes, *Paul*, 62-63. See also Fretheim, *Suffering of God,* 164; von Rad, *Message of the Prophets,* 221.

33. Von Rad, *Message of the Prophets,* 206: "The messenger himself — a man who would be of the greatest interest to scholars — is completely hidden behind his message."

34. Christopher R. Seitz notes this passage as one in which the author of Deutero-Isaiah "speaks of himself in the first person and as God's servant" ("Isaiah 40–66," *NIB* 6:319). Joseph Blenkinsopp says it "marks a further stage in the disclosure of a prophetic voice and therefore a prophetic presence through the very rare appearance of first-person, self-referential discourse throughout this section of the book" (*Isaiah 40–55,* AB 19A [New York: Doubleday, 2000], 319).

of sin.[35] Thus, although Isa 40–66 does not provide the intensely personal portrayal of the prophet typical of Jeremiah, it does suggest patterns of correspondence between God and the Servant, and between the prophet, the Servant, and the people.[36] These patterns of correspondence point to a relational matrix in which the prophet participates in aspects of the divine life, and God participates in the suffering of his people. Therefore they lead directly to a vocation of suffering on the part of the prophet also.

Prophetic Suffering

For Paul, as for the prophets, suffering is central to the proclamation of God's message. Both the apostle and the prophets suffer in part because they encounter in their communities persecution and opposition to their message. At the same time, both suffer in solidarity with their communities and with the God whose message they preach. Because I will give Paul's suffering in Galatians more attention in the next chapter, here my focus is the prophets: how and to what end do they suffer? Fretheim sketches out three ways in which the prophets suffer: through rejection by God's people, in solidarity with God's people, and on behalf of God's people. In all of these kinds of suffering, because the prophet acts as "embodied word of God" and suffers "as a servant of God," he also "embodies the suffering of God."[37]

First, the prophet is rejected by the people because they reject the word of God, which the prophet speaks. In his life the prophet acts out God's situation. For example, in his marriage Hosea plays the part of God as the "husband" of unfaithful Israel (Hos 1–2).[38] Jeremiah must purchase,

---

35. Stylistically speaking, the pronominal shifts are similar to Paul's notoriously shifting pronouns in Galatians. For the prophet's identification with Israel, see also Isa 63:15-19; 64:5-12. Discussions of the authorship of Isa 40-66 are immaterial to the tradition as Paul received it.

36. In addition, there are similarities between the Servant and Zion. See James Muilenburg, "The Book of Isaiah: Chapters 40-66," *IB* 5:632; Leland E. Wilshire, "The Servant-City: A New Interpretation of the 'Servant of the Lord' in the Servant Songs of Deutero-Isaiah," *JBL* 94 (1975): 356-67; Richsie Abma, *Bonds of Love: Methodic Studies of Prophetic Texts with Marriage Imagery* (Assen: Van Gorcum, 1999), 105-7.

37. Fretheim, *Suffering of God*, 152, 154.

38. Ibid., 155-56; Mauser, "Image of God," passim.

bury, and then wear a linen waistcloth, which becomes spoiled, not only to demonstrate the "spoiling" of Israel through its apostasy, but to experience the way in which God "made the whole house of Judah cling to me, says the Lord, that they might be for me a people, a name, a praise, and a glory, but they would not listen" (Jer 13:11). In Heschel's interpretation: "The prophet must learn to feel for himself God's intimate attachment to Israel; he must not only know about it, but experience it from within. . . . Like Hosea in his marriage experience, Jeremiah must learn the grief of God in having to spoil what is intimately precious to him."[39] In addition, Fretheim suggests that the texts commonly labeled as Jeremiah's "confessions" should be read as expressing divine as well as human dismay over Israel's continued rejection of the message.[40] "The lamenting Jeremiah mirrors before the people the lamenting God."[41]

Second, the prophet suffers in solidarity with God's people. This means that even while the prophet proclaims God's judgment on the people, the prophet also joins the people in suffering the consequences of that judgment. Isaiah of Jerusalem is consumed by weeping (Isa 22:4) and even mourns and writhes like a woman in labor over the devastation of Babylon (Isa 21:3-4). Jeremiah is overcome by grief (Jer 4:19; 8:18–9:1; 10:19-20; 13:17-19; 14:17-18). Ezekiel is commanded to "sigh with breaking heart and bitter grief" (Ezek 21:6).

Third, Fretheim argues that, at least in Ezek 13:4-5; 33:1-9; and 4:4-6, there are intimations of the prophet suffering on behalf of the people. Particularly in the last passage, 4:4-6, where the prophet must symbolically bear the punishment of the house of Israel, there is a "conceptual framework" analogous to that of Isa 53. As noted above, the suffering of the Servant in Isaiah corresponds to the suffering of God, who is burdened by Israel's sins (Isa 43:24).[42]

Because the prophet both speaks for God and through his life and ac-

---

39. Heschel, *Prophets*, 1:117-18.

40. Fretheim, *Suffering of God*, 157-58. Cf. von Rad, *Message of the Prophets*, 172, 174, who says that as "the darkness keeps growing," the confessions show that "the prophet was no longer at one with his office and his tasks." Fretheim's insight is that the prophet's "oneness" with his office and tasks occurs paradoxically in the midst of the darkness and alienation. The texts commonly called the "Confessions" are Jer 11:18-23; 12:1-6; 15:10-12, 15-21; 17:12-18; 18:18-23; 20:7-18.

41. Fretheim, *Suffering of God*, 158.

42. Ibid., 162-65.

tions displays the word of God, the prophet's suffering expresses not only solidarity with Israel but also solidarity with God. The prophet grieves because God grieves; therefore the prophet's sorrow and pain become a word of hope to Israel because they reveal the nature of the God who deals with Israel. "For God to mourn with those who mourn is to enter into their situation; and where God is at work, mourning is not the end."[43] Fretheim's summary is worth quoting at length:

> God is present and active not only in and through what the prophet speaks, but also in what he does and, indeed, in who he is. The prophet's life is an embodiment of the Word of God; the prophet is a vehicle for divine immanence. The prophet's life is thus theomorphic. By so participating in the story of God, his life is shaped into the image and likeness of God. The people thus not only hear the Word of God from the prophet, they *see* the Word enfleshed in their midst. In and through the suffering of the prophet, the people both hear and see God immersed in human experience. Through the prophet, Israel relates not only to a God who speaks, but also to a God who appears. This sequence indicates something of the kind of Word of God with which Israel has to do. It is not a disembodied word; it is a wholly personal word spoken to the whole person.[44]

The question of whether Paul also suffers because of, with, and for the recipients of his message is one that I will take up in depth in the next chapter. But here I may note briefly that Paul also encounters rejection because of the message he has been divinely appointed to proclaim, and he interprets this rejection as a kind of solidarity with the rejected and crucified Lord. Through this solidarity, his experience of persecution manifests the nature of Christ who lives in him (Gal 2:20) and of the God who "apocalypsed his son" in him (1:16). The apostle also suffers on behalf of the Galatians, in that he stands fast for "the truth of the gospel" by refusing to join with those who preach circumcision and thereby avoid being persecuted (2:5; 5:11; 6:12).[45]

---

43. Ibid., 136.

44. Ibid., 165.

45. As noted above, the historical circumstances behind Paul's assertions of persecution are difficult to reconstruct. It is not necessary to determine whether the "false brothers" in 2:4 are identical with, or merely allied with, the other missionaries in Galatia.

God's Participation in the Realm of Human Existence

Finally, one finds in Jeremiah and Isaiah descriptions of divine action that anticipate Paul's use of the word ἀποκαλύπτω in Galatians. In Martyn's words, "Paul thus explicates the verb ἀποκαλύπτω with the verbs ἔρχομαι, 'to come [on the scene],' and ἐξαποστέλλω, 'to send [into the scene],' (4:4, 6). . . . The genesis of Paul's apocalyptic — as we see it in Galatians — lies in the apostle's certainty that God has invaded the present evil age by sending Christ and his Spirit into it."[46] This God who "comes" and "sends" is the God who in Isa 66:18-19 is coming to gather the nations:

> For I know their works and their thoughts, and I am coming to
>   gather all nations [ἔρχομαι συναγαγεῖν πάντα τὰ ἔθνη]
>   and tongues;
> and they shall come and shall see my glory,
> and I will set a sign among them.
> And from them I will send those who are saved to the nations
>   [καὶ ἐξαποστελῶ ἐξ αὐτῶν σεσῳσμένους εἰς τὰ ἔθνη],
> to Tarshish, Put, and Lud, who draw the bow, to Tubal and Javan,
>   to the coastlands afar off, that have not heard my fame or
>   seen my glory;
> and they shall declare my glory among the nations
>   [καὶ ἀναγγελοῦσίν μου τὴν δόξαν ἐν τοῖς ἔθνεσιν].

This is the Lord who reveals his "holy arm" before the nations (ἀποκαλύψει κύριος τὸν βραχίονα αὐτοῦ τὸν ἅγιον ἐνώπιον πάντων τῶν ἐθνῶν; 52:10), and thus the Lord who promises that "my salvation is soon to come, and my mercy to be revealed" (ἤγγισεν γὰρ τὸ σωτήριόν μου παραγίνεσθαι καὶ τὸ ἔλεός μου ἀποκαλυφθῆναι; 56:1). This is also the God whose coming into the sphere of human existence is announced and prefigured by the prophets whom the Lord "sends" (6:8; Jer 1:7; 25:4; 26:5; 33:5; 35:15; Ezek 3:5) both to Israel and to Israel's enemies (Jer 35:15). Even as the prophets are sent bearing the Lord's message of divine judgment and punishment, they also are sent to suffer that punishment along with Israel. Now, says Paul, this divine "coming" and "sending" has come to pass in the Christ who faithfully "became a curse" and "gave himself for our sins, that he might deliver us from the present evil age" (Gal 3:13; 1:4). The Gentiles

---

46. Martyn, *Galatians*, 99.

are being gathered, and Paul himself is sent to the Gentiles to proclaim God's glory.

Although Paul differs from the prophets in his conviction that the coming day of the Lord has been inaugurated in Jesus Christ, the relational matrix in which the prophets live and preach is homologous to that evoked by the apostle's testimony and description of his relationship with his converts. Within this relational matrix, God is the key actor who moves into the sphere of human existence with judgment, suffering, and redemption. The prophets, like the apostle, display in their own lives the message they preach, and they convey thereby divine judgment, compassion, and suffering. At the same time, they share the situation of their auditors; indeed, their solidarity with Israel in its suffering is an essential part of their proclamation. Thus there are patterns of correspondence between the prophet's life and message, the situation of the people of God, and the Lord, even as there are correspondences between Paul's testimony, the Galatians' story, and the story of Christ. The language of Paul and the prophets is both cosmic and personal, limning a mutually participatory interaction in which God is portrayed "anthropomorphically" through the prophet's "theomorphic" actions, emotions, and speech.

Discussion

Paul's description of his prophetic call in terms drawn from Jeremiah and Isaiah, and his willingness to be seen as an "angel of God," provide an important contribution to our hearing of his "native tongue" in his letter to the Galatians. The prophets do not say, "Become like me," but they do, as God's representatives, "become like" the recipients of their message, even as they also portray God's anguish on behalf of the people of God. In addition, this mingling of their actions and their words acts as a powerful stimulus for their auditors to follow their example of faithfulness to God.[47] The patterns of correspondence between the prophet and the people are created by God as the one who comes powerfully on the scene of Israel's his-

---

47. In his study of sign-acts in Jeremiah and Ezekiel, Friebel (*Sign-Acts*, 450) notes the persuasive power of these acts, through emotional impact, threat, and modeling "so as to induce the imitative behavior in the observer." He names, as examples of modeling, Jer 27; Ezek 3:26-27; 21:11, 17; 24:16-17.

tory to judge, punish, suffer, and redeem in the sight of the nations. They also are characterized by the prophets' enactment of the message and by the prophetic representation of the suffering of God and of the people of God. These patterns of correspondence between God, the prophet, and the people of God are homologous to the patterns of correspondence between Christ, the apostle, and his converts. Both Paul and the prophets speak "not only of the participation of God in the appearance of the human, but also in the *history* of the human."[48] The shocking disclosure of the power of God operating through the apparent defeat and vulnerability of the cross is adumbrated by the shocking anthropopathic images of divine grief in the prophets. One finds here the direction of the line of movement from God to humanity and the peculiar mingling of personal and cosmological speech that characterize Paul's embodied proclamation of the gospel. As a peculiar speech that is both personal and public, emotional, physically enacted, vulnerable, and authoritative, this is "native tongue" — "mother tongue" writ large in the public square.

These observations prompt a revisitation of Castelli's claim that Paul's identification with Christ is a coercive, "rhetorical move" that reinforces his own power over his converts. It is true that Paul's representative role, like that of the prophets, does undergird his claims to authority. Castelli's own formulation and evaluation of this authority is harsh:

> because of the superior value which is bestowed upon the model in the mimetic system, the question of authority is foregrounded in the mimetic relationship; the model has authority to which the copy submits. . . . [T]he language of imitation, with its concomitant tension between the drive toward sameness and the inherent hierarchy of the mimetic relationship, masks the will to power which one finds in Pauline discourse.[49]

In other words, the mimetic relationship exists along a vertical spectrum between "same" and "different." The closer one is to the perfect model, the higher one is on the spectrum; the further away, the lower one is on this hierarchical scale. Mimesis moves along this line from differentiation to sameness. Paul's identification with Christ, according to one reading of this model, thus places him in a superior, authoritarian position. Presum-

---

48. Fretheim, *Suffering of God*, 151-52.
49. Castelli, *Imitating Paul*, 86-87.

ably the same might be said of the prophets' presumption to speak for God and their embodiment of the message they proclaim. Such a peculiar mingling of personal and cosmological language thus might function, not as a bridge in the relational matrix shared by the prophet, the people, and God, or by the apostle, the people, and Christ, but rather as a pernicious form of oppression.

Such potential oppression bears witness to what Rowan Williams calls "the almost infinite corruptibility of religious discourse."[50] Williams describes this "corruptibility" in terms that echo, on one level, Castelli's concerns:

> Those who claim to speak in the name of God will always be dangerously (exhilaratingly) close to the claim that in their speech, their active presence, the absent God who is never an existent among others is actually present: a claim of stupendous importance in legitimating any bid for power. Here, it says, is a concrete presence that will tell you what you are. The religious ideologue may say — or seem to be saying — that it is as *his* "other" that you will find your identity (and I do mean "his," given the history of religious hierarchy in most human cultures); and this will effect a definitive closure on what you are entitled to say about yourself. You are required or desired to satisfy the demands mediated by religious law; that is what you are for, and all you are for. . . . What the European Enlightenment revolted against was precisely the sense of having your identity and capacity prescribed by a this-worldly other that claimed other-worldly sanction, claimed a kind of identity with the disinterested perspective of God.[51]

---

50. R. Williams, *Lost Icons*, 162.

51. Ibid., 162-63. Despite the similarities in their analysis of the dangers of religious discourse, Castelli and Williams differ significantly in their constructive proposals. Castelli's critique of "sameness" and valorization of "difference" imply the possible existence and value of nonderivative individuals who exist in some mimesis-free environment, apart from the repressive operations of power. Here power is negative and exclusionary. Williams, on the other hand, immediately qualifies his description of religious discourse with a reference to God's grace and freedom: "the liberty of God challenges any notion that God can be reduced to a simple or tangible sameness with which we negotiate as we do with the other contingent presences in our mental and physical field" (163). Ultimately, Williams's analysis of identity moves in the realm of a gracious relationship characterized by "gift," rather than by "the demands mediated by religious law" (163).

Both Castelli's and Williams's comments express legitimate concerns, suggesting that it would be wise not to speak too quickly or glibly about Paul's "embodiment" of Christ, nor about the prophets' "embodied proclamation" of the divine oracles. It is reasonable to ask where there is anything in Paul's letter that militates *against* this "corruption" of religious discourse. Further reflection on this letter does indeed disclose three countervailing elements in the apostle's discourse.

First, the reversal and movement in the mimetic relationship occasioned by God's participation in the realm of human affairs creates, in the communication of both the apostle and the prophets, a double "mimetic" likeness: they identify with and speak for God, but they also identify with and speak for the people of God. Their position on the spectrum between "same" and "different" is not static but fluid, precisely because it is mandated by God's involvement in human history. Second, as noted in reference to Paul's use of the term ἄγγελος θεοῦ, the apostle does not represent the resurrected, victorious Christ, but Christ crucified, Christ's entry into humanity in its most abject state. In the next chapter I will explore more fully Paul's repeated references to his own experience of "persecution" and his presentation of himself as a re-presentation of Christ crucified. Here I simply raise the question of what either Paul or the prophets gain by their claims to "authority." Jeremiah is constrained by the message he preaches to weep with God and with Jerusalem, to suffer rejection by his own people, and to experience anguish on their behalf. The same is true of the apostle. His exercise of "apostolic authority" *requires* suffering on his part, because only thus can he proclaim in a physical, tactile way the crucified Christ. As Schütz has argued, "Paul specifically subjects the figure of the apostle to the norm of the gospel; there is a clear pattern of subordination."[52] The "power" operating in the apostle's relationships with his converts garners him humiliation and rejection.

Thus, third, the apostle's continued witness to Christ crucified means that the final victory of the eschaton is *not* present directly in and through him. In a sense, rather, he bears witness to a hope that is yet to be fulfilled — "we wait for the hope of righteousness" (Gal 5:5). Insofar as he points toward a *future* hope and a completion yet to be accomplished, he simultaneously bears witness to the imperfection of the status quo, including the state of the present community of faith. One recalls Ernst Käsemann's

52. Schütz, *Paul and Anatomy*, 24.

comments on Rom 8:22-27: the groaning of the Spirit, which Käsemann interprets as glossolalia, is emphatically not "a sign that the Christian community has been translated with Christ into heavenly existence"; to the contrary, "the apostle hears in these things the groans of those who, though called to liberty, still lie tempted and dying and cry to be born again with the new creation."[53]

It is here that the importance of eschatology becomes crucial to an understanding of the kind of power displayed in Paul's relationship with his converts. In a passage worth quoting at length, Schütz discusses the relationship between power and eschatological reservation in the authority structures of the Pauline communities:

> Is Paul's rigorous subordination of everyone and everything to the gospel not really a mask for the subordination of others to himself as an apostle? To answer this we must understand the role played by Paul's eschatological reservation. Power is not a personal attribute because power is essentially an historical force. The central role of the gospel as an interpretation of this power stems from the fact that all Christians have access to power through the gospel. The apostle may preach the gospel, he may thereby make power available, but he does not himself provide it or even control it. . . . All of this makes sense only where power and the gospel are thought of within the milieu of a history moving to fulfillment, where there is still a frontier to cross, a *telos* yet to arrive. The final judgment is the final and unmistakable manifestation of power. . . . This is only to say that in the very nature of the case apostolic authority cannot be final.[54]

Schütz's comments distinguish sharply between the person of the apostle and the source and locus of power — ultimately Paul is not the arbiter of power, but himself remains subject to the final judgment of God. Thus, finally, both Paul's and the prophets' modes of communication may be "embodied" only in a provisional and limited way; that is, in their actions the prophets re-present God's participation in the destiny and suffering of God's people; and in his actions and even in his body, the apostle re-presents Christ's crucifixion and the cruciform shape Christ will assume among his Galatian converts. In so doing, both prophets and apostle point

---

53. Ernst Käsemann, *Perspectives on Paul* (Philadelphia: Fortress, 1982), 134.
54. Schütz, *Paul and Anatomy*, 285.

to a power that lies beyond them, to an eschatological redemption for which they, together with their auditors, wait.

Taken together, these comments suggest that once the twin motifs of suffering and eschatological reservation are lost, then claims to apostolic authority may indeed become subject to Castelli's and Williams's important criticisms. Schütz's insight further raises critical questions about the interpretation of Paul's preaching when the church forgets that "there is still a frontier to cross, a *telos* yet to arrive," and claims its own existence, in and of itself, as the *telos* of God's salvation. Such forgetfulness denies an essential aspect of Paul's message. Rather, the mode of proclamation shared by Paul and the classical prophets necessitates a *partial* "embodiment" of the message and hints at the shape such embodiment will take. In addition, the apostle's rhetoric implies that suffering on the part of his auditors, as well as himself, is necessary in order to make sense of the message of the crucified Christ. Therefore Paul's gospel institutes communities of faith that must remain incomplete and inconclusive, as they await a future eschatological "completion" and remain subordinate to a future judgment.

Recalling from the beginning of this chapter the three characteristics of Paul's retrospective narrative — patterns of correspondence between Christ, the Galatians, and himself; an apocalyptic worldview; and the centrality of suffering — we can recognize similar characteristics in the prophets' mode of proclamation. Insofar as the shared "native tongue" of the apostle and the prophets constitutes communities that remain incomplete as they await God's final judgment and redemption, they limn a "history" that also appears weak and inconclusive. In other words, the partial character of the gospel community of faith prompts further reflection on the nature of any "history" written by and about that community. Such a gospel history promises also to be unfinished and inconclusive, pointing toward a *telos* yet to arrive. One does not see here a victorious *Heilsgeschichte* but a *Heilsgeschichte* that looks like a disaster.[55] Hence questions of the gospel's motivational and sustaining power become more and more pressing; as Jagger and Richards ask,

---

55. Käsemann, *Perspectives on Paul*, 68: "Measured by human criteria, salvation is fundamentally rooted in disaster. That means that the Pauline proclamation of the reality of salvation history is deeply paradoxical."

And could you stand the torture and could you stand the pain?
Could you put your faith in Jesus when you're burning
   in the flames?[56]

It is here that Paul's maternal metaphors come into play in his gospel preaching. They serve to convey a paradoxical blend of suffering, staying power, and apocalyptic hope. As we shall see, the God disclosed by those metaphors is entirely consonant with the God disclosed by the prophets; indeed, recourse to both Isaiah and Jeremiah will help to decode Paul's language. It is striking that the prophets as well as the apostle use familial imagery to depict the relationship between the people of God and their Lord. In the prophets, God is often portrayed as Israel's husband, sometimes as father (e.g., Hos 2:1 LXX; Isa 45:10; 63:16), and a few times as mother (Jer 8:21; Isa 42:14; 45:10; 49:14-15; 66:13).[57] Israel or Jerusalem is portrayed as the mother of her inhabitants and as the divine consort (Isa 50:1-3; 54:1-10; Hos 1–3; Jer 2–3). As noted earlier, in Galatians God is depicted as "father" (Gal 4:2, 5); the Galatians and Paul are "children" (3:29; 4:3-7, 19, 28, 31) and "brothers and sisters" (4:12, 31; 5:13; 6:1); and they share membership in the "household of faith" (6:10).[58] In an explicit appropriation of family imagery from Isaiah, "Jerusalem above" is "mother" (4:26-27; Isa 54:1); significantly, Paul also refers to himself in maternal language at the climax of the passage beginning "Become like me" (Gal 4:19).[59] As

56. Jagger and Richards, "Saint of Me."

57. The secondary literature is extensive; see especially Katheryn P. Darr, *Isaiah's Vision and the Family of God* (Louisville: Westminster John Knox, 1994); Abma, *Bonds of Love.*

58. As noted earlier, some studies have been done on family imagery in Isaiah and some on family imagery in Paul's letters, but little has been done on possible connections between the occurrence of that imagery in the prophets and in Paul. Studies of Paul's family language tend to situate it in the context of Greco-Roman family structures and tend to concentrate on the apostle's paternal and sibling references. See, e.g., Wayne Meeks, *First Urban Christians: The Social World of the Apostle Paul* (New Haven: Yale University Press, 1983); O. Larry Yarbrough, *Not Like the Gentiles: Marriage Rules in the Letters of Paul,* SBLDS 80 (Atlanta: Scholars Press, 1985); Aasgaard, *My Beloved Brothers and Sisters.* Malherbe ("God's New Family," 118) notes the allusion to Hos 2:1 LXX in 2 Cor 6:16-18. See also von Allmen, *Famille de Dieu;* Johnson, "Apocalyptic Family Values."

59. For discussion of maternal imagery in Paul's letters, see Gaventa, *Our Mother St. Paul;* Brigette Kahl, "Der Brief an die Gemeinden in Galatien: Vom Unbehagen der Geschlechter und anderen Problemen des Andersseins," in *Kompendium feministische Bibelauslegung,* ed. Luise Schottroff and Marie-Theres Wacker (Gütersloh: Gütersloher Verlagshaus, 1998), 603-11; idem, "No Longer Male."

suggested in chapter one, these metaphors provide further clues to the nature of the relational matrix that mediates the transforming and durative power of the gospel. Furthermore, the ensuing picture addresses the centrality of suffering and eschatological reservation as characteristic of corporate life "in Christ." In the next two chapters I will investigate these questions by looking at the image of an apostle in labor (4:19) and the story of the barren woman in 4:27/Isa 54:1. The first image displays Paul's suffering as mediating God's transforming power; the second displays the tension between that present suffering and Paul's eschatological hope.

Chapter Four

Galatians 4:19:
A Labor of Divine Love

I thought I heard an angel cry
I thought I saw a teardrop falling from his eye

Jagger and Richards, "Saint of Me"

I n the introductory chapter, the lyrics from Jagger and Richards's song "Saint of Me" raised the question of motivation for following in Paul's footsteps. In chapter three our study of correspondences between Paul's preaching and that of the prophets intensified the same question. A picture of the gospel's power that emphasizes conformity to the cross hardly seems designed to attract many followers, particularly when contrasted with Paul's contention that the other missionaries avoid persecution. Why cast one's lot with a "history" and a "community" that promise suffering? In what is almost a lyrical aside from the driving refrain, "You'll never make a saint of me," Jagger and Richards's own words contain a hint of an answer. The hint is that not only the saints are tortured and "burning in the flame." The suffering extends to the realm of divine existence come down to earth, and perhaps this in turn gives a paradoxical sustenance, motivation, and staying power to those whose lives have been radically touched and changed by Jesus hitting them "with a blinding light." Such will be the argument of this chapter, as we begin to consider the role of maternal metaphors in Paul's "mother tongue."[1] Here the focus will be on the metaphor that pro-

---

1. Paul uses maternal imagery in 1 Thess 2:7; 5:3; 1 Cor 3:1-2; 15:8; Rom 2:22; as well as

vides a stunning climax to the pericope that begins, "Become like me, because I have become like you." It is the cry of an apostle in labor: "My children, with whom I again suffer birth pangs until Christ is formed in you!"

Gaventa describes Gal 4:19, along with Paul's other kinship metaphors, as a "metaphor squared." She draws on contemporary metaphor theory to suggest that the surprise occasioned by such metaphors "forces us to consider things differently," and to "see points of similarity" between apparently dissimilar things.[2] Aristotle's classic definition of metaphor anticipates these comments: "A metaphor is the application of a word that belongs to another thing [ὀνόματος ἀλλοτρίου ἐπιφορά]: either from genus to species or from species to genus or from species to species or by analogy" (*Poetics* 1457b7). In George Kennedy's felicitous summary, "Metaphor is itself a metaphor and literally means 'carrying something from one place to another, transference.'"[3] By importing that which is ἀλλότριος — alien — the metaphor achieves a heightened form of communication that "escapes banality" (*Poetics* 1458a21).

But metaphor is more than ornamental. Such transference of an "alien name" across classificatory boundaries transposes the meanings of words in ways that both rely on and subvert what Paul Ricoeur calls "the logical structure of language."[4] In his study "Between Rhetoric and Poetics," Ricoeur describes the tension between Aristotle's definition of metaphor and the interest in classification that developed in later classical rhetoric:

> Two facts should be noted. First, transposition operates between logical poles. Metaphor occurs in an order already constituted in terms of genus and species, and in a game whose relation rules — subordination,

---

Gal 1:15 and 4:19. He uses paternal imagery in Phlm 10; 1 Cor 4:14; 1 Thess 2:11-12; Phil 2:22; Rom 8:15; Gal 4:6. He refers to his converts as "children" and himself as "parent," without specifying gender in 2 Cor 6:13; 12:14. In addition, in the allegory of Gal 4:21-31, the decisive difference between the sons' freedom and slavery depends on their mother, not their father. For further discussion of the allegory of 4:21-31, see chapter five.

2. Gaventa, *Our Mother*, 4-5, 10-11. See also Soskice, *Metaphor*, 57-58: "The purpose of [the] metaphor is both to cast up and organize a network of associations. A good metaphor . . . [is] a new vision, the birth of a new understanding, a new referential access. A strong metaphor compels new possibilities of vision."

3. Aristotle, *On Rhetoric*, trans. George A. Kennedy (New York: Oxford University Press, 1991), 222 n. 25.

4. Paul Ricouer, "Between Rhetoric and Poetics," in *Essays on Aristotle's Rhetoric*, ed. Amélie O. Rorty (Berkeley and Los Angeles: University of California Press, 1966), 333.

coordination, proportionality or equality of relationships — are already given. Secondly, metaphor consists in a violation of this order and this game. . . . [O]ne simultaneously recognizes and transgresses the logical structure of language.[5]

Thus, says Ricoeur, metaphor is a kind of "categorical transgression, understood as a deviation in relation to a preexisting logical order." On the one hand, such a categorical transgression "destroys an order only to invent a new one." On the other hand, because "metaphor brings learning" (*Rhetoric* 1410b13), it implies the discovery of an underlying similarity between what was previously thought to be disconnected: "the category mistake is nothing but the complement of a logic of discovery. . . . [T]he metaphor bears information because it 'redescribes' reality."[6] Such a "redescription" of reality is at the same time a "discovery" of previously hidden connections. Ricoeur is explicating Aristotle's claim: "the greatest thing is to be metaphorical [μεταφορικὸν εἶναι]. This alone cannot be taken from another, and is a sign of genius [εὐφυΐας], because to use metaphor well is to see similarities [τὸ ὅμοιον θεωρεῖν]" (*Poetics* 1459a3-8). Similarly, in the *Rhetoric* Aristotle says, "metaphors should be transferred from things that are related but not obviously so, as in philosophy, too, it is characteristic of a well-directed mind to observe the likeness even in things very different" (1412a10).

Ricoeur's comments point us in a helpful direction, but they set limits on the potential denotation of metaphors; metaphors can only redescribe an existing reality by pointing out hidden connections — they do not have the power to disclose genuinely new realities. Soskice takes metaphor theory a step farther:

> redescription, however radical, is always *re*-description. The interesting thing about metaphor, or at least about some metaphors, is that they are used not to redescribe but to disclose for the first time. The metaphor has to be used because something new is being talked about. This is Aristotle's "naming that which has no name" and unless we see it, we shall never get away from a comparison theory of metaphor.[7]

Drawing on analogies between religious and scientific metaphors, Soskice argues that both uses of metaphor are based on realist assumptions, and

5. Ibid.
6. Ibid., 334.
7. Soskice, *Metaphor*, 89.

both are essential to genuinely new discoveries of reality. They carry forward such discoveries by providing a way to refer to invisible entities without fully defining them. They thus provide a method of denotation and reference that remains open to correction and further discovery.[8] This capacity to denote without fully defining is of the essence of language about God. In Soskice's eloquent words:

> It is . . . of the utmost importance to keep in mind the distinction, never remote in the writings of Anselm or of Aquinas, between referring to God and defining Him. . . . And, as we have argued, this separation of referring and defining is at the very heart of metaphorical speaking and is what makes it not only possible but necessary that in our stammering after a transcendent God we must speak, for the most part, metaphorically or not at all.[9]

It would be fascinating to explore in depth the convergence between Soskice's claims about metaphor and the use of metaphorical language in apocalyptic literature. Here I simply note that both are concerned with a kind of "seeing" that is a gift, not generally available, and which reveals new things hidden from others. One thinks, for example, of Flannery O'Connor's description of the grotesque in southern fiction, in which the writer looks "for one image that will connect or combine or embody two points; one is a point in the concrete, and the other is a point not visible to the naked eye, but believed in by him firmly, just as real to him, really, as the one that everybody sees." O'Connor continues: "In the novelist's case, prophecy is a matter of seeing near things with their extensions of meaning and thus of seeing far things close up. The prophet is a realist of distances, and it is this kind of realism that you find in the best modern instances of the grotesque."[10] Martyn comments, "you will look a long time before you will find a novelist speaking more clearly [than O'Connor] of the germ of the apocalyptic perspective."[11] This combination of what is

---

8. Ibid., 118-61. One notes in passing how suitable such language is for the forward-looking, incomplete history and community created by the gospel.

9. Ibid., 140.

10. Flannery O'Connor, *Mystery and Manners* (New York: Farrar, Straus & Giroux, 1969), 42, 44.

11. J. Louis Martyn, "From Paul to Flannery O'Connor with the Power of Grace," *Theological Issues*, 290-91.

concrete and "near" with what is invisible and "far-off," yet "real," also characterizes the relational matrix that Paul limns throughout Galatians, described in chapter two as both "ruthlessly personal" and "relentlessly mythological."

Similarly, Paul's confusing self-description in Gal 4:19 connects a known and concrete point — the apostle himself — with an apparently alien and invisible point drawn from prophetic and apocalyptic literature — the pains of a woman in labor.[12] Paul uses metaphorical language to convey an apocalyptic vision of reality. His language works through the combination of, and tension between, what is familiar and what is strange.[13] On the one hand, in order to communicate with Paul's auditors, the metaphor must have a foothold in their experience. That foothold is their experience of the apostle himself; as Paul has reminded them, they know him, they know the manner and occasion of their first encounter with him and his first "hard labor" among them (4:13-14; cf. 4:11). Thus any attempt to understand the "concrete point" of the metaphor requires a close look at the initial encounter between Paul and his converts, as described in 4:13-16.

On the other hand, the "far-off" point of the metaphor redescribes the relationship between Paul and the Galatians in an apocalyptic framework that implicitly expands its horizon. To explore this side of the metaphor, it will be helpful to investigate the background of "labor pains" imagery in prophetic and apocalyptic literature. As we shall see, the very syntax of 4:17-20 directs our attention to both aspects of Paul's metaphor. Therefore,

---

12. These two points refer to one reality, not to different referents, one a "metaphorical truth" and the other a "literal truth." See Soskice, *Metaphor*, 88. By connecting the near point of Paul's and the Galatians' experience with the far-off point of metaphorical labor pains, the metaphor reveals the apocalyptic character of that experience.

13. The same might be said of all metaphorical language about God. In their study of the relationship between biblical conceptions of idolatry and anthropomorphic language about God, Moshe Halbertal and Avishai Margalit comment, "The explanatory power of a metaphor derives from the familiarity of the realm it is drawn from (the realm of human relations), and in the metaphorical process we attempt to extend our understanding beyond the image to the realm it represents. This is the transition from the primary, or representing, realm to the secondary, or represented, realm" (*Idolatry* [Cambridge: Harvard University Press, 1992], 10). In a sense, however, the metaphorical process as described by O'Connor and as operative in apocalyptic literature does not simply "extend our understanding" from the familiar to "the secondary, or represented, realm." Rather, the apocalyptic use of metaphor makes what is "familiar" become strange by casting it in a new light.

three exegetical probes will guide this investigation: the interpretive difficulties of 4:17-20, the concrete meaning of Paul's "labor" in the context of the letter, and the implications of the literary background of ὠδίνω for the interpretation of Gal 4:19.

Questions of Interpretation

The interpretation of 4:17-20 is problematic in two ways. First, the two clauses in 4:19 do not agree in either subject or object. Second, the relationship of 4:19 to both the preceding and subsequent verses is unclear and thus a matter of some debate. As will become clear, attention to both of these problems leads directly to two exegetical probes.

The Syntax of 4:19

The structure of 4:19 may be analyzed in the following way:

	Subject	*Verb*	*Object*
First clause	Paul	ὠδίνω — active	Galatians
Second clause	(Christ)	μορφόω — passive	Christ

While Christ is the grammatical subject of the passive verb in the second clause, it is immediately apparent that the clause leaves unstated the implied subject that is the cause of the action. The implied subject might be Paul himself, in parallel construction with the first clause, so that the apostle means: "with whom I am again in labor until I form Christ among you." Or more plausibly, μορφωθῇ is a divine passive, as Sam Williams argues: "It is rather *God* who is doing the 'forming,' the One who sent his son in the first place (4:6)."[14] The divine passive is characteristic of Paul's letters, and its use in this case seems almost certainly to be the correct interpretation for two reasons.[15] First, although this is the only occurrence of μορφόω in the Pauline corpus, Paul's use elsewhere of the related verbs μεταμορφοῦσθαι and συμμορφοῦσθαι is instructive. In each

---

14. S. Williams, *Galatians,* 123. See also Gaventa, *Our Mother,* 35.
15. For Paul's use of the divine passive, see, e.g., Sanders, *Paul, the Law,* 13 n. 18.

case, the verb is passive, with God as the implied subject, and the goal is formation in the image of Christ. In 2 Cor 3:18 the apostle writes, "we are being changed into his likeness from one degree of glory to another; for this comes from the Lord who is the Spirit." In Phil 3:10 Paul speaks of "being conformed to his death" (συμμορφιζόμενος τῷ θανάτῳ). In Rom 12:2 he exhorts believers not to be conformed to this world but to be transformed by the renewing of their minds. As Gaventa has observed, "While none of these texts refers specifically to the formation *of Christ,* each reflects the conviction that the Christ event issues in a profound shaping and reshaping of human perceptions."[16]

Second, although the LXX does not use μορφόω, many of the occurrences of the synonymous πλάσσω in the prophetic texts refer to God's creative activity in relationship to both Israel and the cosmos (Isa 43:1; 44:2, 21, 24; 29:16; Ps 89:2).[17] God is the one who formed Jeremiah in the womb (Jer 1:5) and the Servant of the Lord in the womb (Isa 49:5), just as God formed Israel in the womb (Isa 44:2, 24). As noted in the previous chapter, Jer 1:5 and Isa 49:1-5 are central to Paul's understanding of his own apostolate. If indeed God is the implied subject of μορφωθῇ in Gal 4:19b, then Paul's activity and God's activity are parallel and interwoven. As argued in chapter three, such an interweaving of divine and prophetic action also characterizes the speech of Jeremiah and Isaiah, and thus is consonant with the apostle's self-identification with the prophetic tradition in 1:15-16.

If God is in the process of forming Christ in the Galatian congregations through Paul's "labor," there are consequences for the nature of the apostle's "labor pains." One possibility is that the parallel clauses suggest God also is in some sense "in labor," but if so, in what sense? Our inquiry will be aided at the outset by considering 4:19 in its immediate context and in the context of the letter as a whole.

The Relationship between 4:19 and 4:17-20

The notoriously difficult v. 19, sandwiched between the repeated references to Paul's desire to be present with the Galatians (vv. 18 and 20), is so striking that it tends to overshadow the surrounding verses. Thus Paul's labor

---

16. Gaventa, *Our Mother,* 35. See also the discussion in Martyn, *Galatians,* 430-31.
17. Burton, *Galatians,* 249.

that Christ "be formed" among the Galatians, rather than his desire to be with them, functions as the climax to the pericope that begins "Become like me." Few verses bristle with more interpretive possibilities than these. Does v. 19 continue the thought of v. 18, or present an abrupt break? Is the δέ of v. 20 connective or adversative? Is v. 19 simply an emotional interruption, or does it relate logically to the repeated παρεῖναι of vv. 18 and 20? If the latter, does it also relate to the contrast between "good" and "bad" zeal in vv. 17-18, and to the implicit contrast between Paul's wish to be present with his converts in v. 20, and the Teachers' wish to shut them out in v. 17?

The interpretive options may be grouped into two broad categories — those that view 4:17-20 as a unit, and those that see 4:19 as an anacoluthon that makes a definitive break from the surrounding verses.[18] Richard Longenecker argues for a break between v. 18 and v. 19 based on an abrupt change in tone; Betz argues for a break on the basis of a shift from the friendship topos to the metaphor of parent and child.[19] Burton, however, maintains that interpreting v. 18 as a reference to the apostle's continued zealous seeking of the Galatians' "good" "best comports with the tone of v. 19 into which he passes from this v[erse] apparently without break in thought."[20]

In my view, Burton's interpretation is the stronger, supported by the repetition of παρεῖναι in vv. 18 and 20, and θέλω in vv. 17 and 20. According to this reading, v. 19 continues the contrast between Paul and the other missionaries: in his "labor" with his converts, he is seeking their good "in a good way," unlike the manipulative courtship that the other missionaries lavish upon the Galatians. His wish to be with them contrasts with the Teachers' wish to exclude them. His labor pains characterize his "zealous courtship" and his desired "presence" in a way that contrasts with the Teachers' exclusionary "zeal" for the Galatians. For that contrast to be effective rhetorically, the Galatians must have an experiential referent for his zealous courtship, his "labor," and his desire to be present with them. These questions lead to the second exegetical probe, the experiential content of Paul's "labor" in his relationship with the Galatians.

---

18. The majority of commentators read v. 19 as an anacoluthon that breaks with v. 18. See Schlier, *Galater*, 151; Mussner, *Galaterbrief*, 312; Betz, *Galatians*, 233; R. Longenecker, *Galatians*, 195. Burton (*Galatians*, 248) and Lightfoot (*Galatians*, 178) read vv. 17-20 as a unit. NRSV and RSV treat v. 19 as a break with v. 18, whereas NEB and JB treat it as a continuation of the previous sentence.

19. R. Longenecker, *Galatians*, 194; Betz, *Galatians*, 233.

20. Burton, *Galatians*, 247.

The Material Content of Paul's "Labor Pains"

I will argue that the Galatians' experiential point of reference for Paul's metaphorical birth pains is the suffering that accompanies his embodied proclamation of the gospel of the crucified Christ.[21] The argument will proceed by means of the following proposals. First, Paul's statement that he is "again" in labor refers to his first preaching of the gospel in Galatia, through which he initially gave birth to the Christian communities there (4:13-15). Second, in his description of that generative event, Paul highlights his "weakness of the flesh," which was a temptation or trial for the Galatians. Therefore, investigating the nature of this "weakness" will illuminate the nature of the experience that the apostle calls "labor pains." In 4:13 "weakness" refers to the physical effects of persecution, the scars of which made Paul's body a "placard" of the crucified Christ (6:17; 3:1). Third, this interpretation is consonant with Paul's link elsewhere in his letters between weakness, proclamation, and the power of God, notably in 1 Thessalonians and the Corinthian correspondence. Finally, this "weakness" describes Christian existence as the arena in which God's power is displayed. Therefore, 4:13-15 as the material referent for Paul's "labor pains" also displays the material sense of "until Christ is formed in you" (4:19b). Christ will be formed in the Galatians when they "become like" Paul by exchanging the marker of circumcision for the brand marks of Jesus — that is, when they join the apostle in suffering for the sake of the gospel.

Labor Pains as the Preaching of the Gospel

Commentators are fairly unanimous in seeing 4:19 as a reference to Paul's founding of the Galatian congregations.[22] The clue to the material content

---

21. See Betz, *Nachfolge*, 173-74: "It is in the concrete events in Paul's life that imitating Christ (μιμεῖσθαι τὸν Χριστόν) and the fellowship of his sufferings (κοινωνία τῶν παθημάτων αὐτοῦ) occur." See also 184-86.

22. Betz, *Galatians*, 234: "Πάλιν ('again') points to the founding of the congregation. In the case of the Galatians' apostasy, the whole act would have to be done again." Betz interprets this as a "rebirth" along the lines of mystery religions. Martyn (*Galatians*, 424), however, says Paul is speaking of the "the image of Christ becoming the real ego of the Galatian communities." In my view, Paul is not talking about a rebirth, but about an extended birth process that is in danger of being aborted by the Teachers.

of Paul's birth pangs is in the word "again" (πάλιν); Paul must repeat something he has done previously. The obvious antecedent for this repetition is in 4:13, where Paul refers to the first time he preached the gospel to the Galatians.[23] The incursions of the other missionaries have made it necessary for Paul to repreach the gospel to his converts, because under the Teachers' influence they are becoming reconformed to the present evil age rather than to Christ.[24]

Elsewhere Paul also depicts his preaching as giving birth to Christian congregations and individuals. In 1 Cor 4:14-15 he begot the Corinthian church; in Philemon he begot Onesimus in the faith. In these verses, however, he uses the verb "to beget" (γεννάω), whereas in Gal 4:19 he uses the verb "to suffer labor pains" (ὠδίνω). Why? The surprisingly scanty scholarly attention given to this question proposes three interrelated answers. (1) Because the "birth" of the Galatian congregations is in danger of being aborted by the Teachers, Paul uses the linear feminine image to describe the continuation of the birth process.[25] (2) Because ὠδίνω in the apocalyptic tradition refers to the anguish that accompanies the coming of the day of the Lord, Paul's use of this image sets the Galatian conflict within an apocalyptic framework.[26] (3) Paul's use of feminine imagery is part of his subversion of the male-female antinomy that, along with the division between Jew and Greek, slave and free, dominates the present evil age (3:28). This is the argument of Brigitte Kahl:

23. The question whether τὸ πρότερον implies one or two visits is immaterial to this discussion. See Burton, *Galatians*, 239-41; Schlier, *Galater*, 148; Mussner, *Galaterbrief*, 307; R. Longenecker, *Galatians*, 190; Betz, *Galatians*, 224 n. 52. It may be that 4:16 refers to an interim visit, as argued by Lightfoot, *Galatians*, 25, 176. As R. Longenecker points out, however, regardless of the number of visits, the important contrast is between Paul's original preaching of the gospel to the Galatians and the present situation.

24. See Martyn, *Galatians*, 430-31.

25. Martyn, *Galatians*, 429; Gaventa, *Our Mother*, 7-8.

26. The connection of ὠδίνω with apocalyptic themes was noted by Timothée Colani, in relationship to Mark 13:8, in *Jésus Christ et les croyances messianiques de son temps* (Strasbourg: Treuttel et Wurtz, 1864), and observed in Paul's Letters by John M. Court, "Paul and the Apocalyptic Pattern," in *Paul and Paulinism: Essays in Honour of C. K. Barrett*, ed. M. D. Hooker and S. G. Wilson (London: SPCK, 1982), 58-59. Proposing that Paul was "revivifying the traditional imagery of childbirth in an eschatological context," Court (58) suggested that the occurrence of ὠδίνω in Gal 4:19 picked up on Isa 54:1, cited in Gal 4:27, as "an echo from one text to the other." See also Gaventa, *Our Mother*, 29-39; Martyn, *Galatians*, 429-30.

the apostolic male, trying to re-shape the Galatian community in the image of Christ, appears as a female him/herself in 4.19. What at first sight seems to be the voice of a patriarchal Pauline rule demanding obedience, in an ironic twist becomes the birth-cry of a woman in labor pains. In the same way, just a few verses before, Paul's apparently "authoritarian" demand to become like him turns out to mean the imitation of "unmanly weakness," which reflects the ultimate weakness of the cross and undermines all the dominance-oriented norms of the honor and shame code both on the individual/social and on a cosmological level (4.12-14).[27]

Kahl's argument is a variation of Martyn's and Gaventa's emphasis on the apocalyptic background of ὠδίνω. Whereas Martyn puts the focus on "the Christ in whom there is neither Jew nor Gentile," Kahl highlights the Christ in whom there is "not male and female."[28] But both see Paul's language as pointing to the formation of the congregation in light of the new creation, one in which old divisions pass away.

Each of these three proposals has merit, and each contributes to an understanding of the "far-off" metaphorical referent for Paul's labor pains. But the question remains: What exactly are these "pains" in the *concrete experience* of Paul and his converts?[29] To rephrase the question, what is so painful about Paul's preaching? Is the apostle simply expressing his anxiety, his mental anguish on behalf of the Galatian congregations, or does he refer to physical suffering? Might other occurrences of ὠδίνω help in answering this question?

Martyn notes that, when used intransitively, the verb refers to severe pain, literally of a woman in labor, and metaphorically of intense emotional or physical suffering. When used transitively, "the verb acquires two

27. Kahl, "No Longer Male," 45-46.

28. Martyn, *Galatians*, 431. Kahl's argument is weakened by the fact that ὠδίνω refers metaphorically to the anguish of soldiers in battle as much as to women in labor. See, e.g., Exod 15:14; Deut 2:25; Ps 47:7 (48:6 ET); Isa 13:8; Jer 27:43 (50:43 ET). Thus Paul's auditors would not necessarily hear his self-description in 4:19 as "female." Kahl is on firmer ground, however, in her depiction of weakness as "unmanly." Weakness was frequently associated with women and effeminate men (1 Pet 3:7; Plutarch, *On Listening to Lectures* 46D). While philosophical psychagogy required knowledge of one's weaknesses, the purpose of such knowledge was to *overcome* weakness rather than to celebrate it.

29. Given that Paul appeals to experience throughout Galatians, and particularly to his shared experience with his converts, it is reasonable to expect that he does so here as well.

foci, first the woman's pains and second the product of those pains, the specific child born in the process."[30] Transitive uses of ὠδίνω are thus rarely metaphorical, and when they are, the object is not concrete.[31] Galatians 4:19 proves to be an exception to these observations, however, because ὠδίνω is both metaphorical and transitive, having a corporate people as its concrete direct object. The question naturally arises whether it also refers to physical pains, as it does in other metaphorical intransitive uses. Obviously, Paul does not physically give birth to his converts, or suffer physical contractions. Nonetheless, there is indeed a concrete referent for his "labor pains."

The "Weakness of the Flesh" in 4:13-14

I suggest that the clue to Paul's material "pains" lies in the circumstances of Paul's initial preaching in Galatia, as described in 4:13-14. The key phrase is δι' ἀσθένειαν τῆς σαρκὸς εὐηγγελισάμην ὑμῖν. The great majority of commentators rightly take διά with the accusative here to express the occasion or cause, rather than the means, of Paul's preaching.[32] Nonetheless, one wonders whether the Galatians themselves would have connected the circumstances of Paul's initial visit and the preaching of a suffering Christ.[33] Also, the great majority of commentators, not to mention translations, rightly read "weakness of the flesh" as some variation of "bodily illness or infirmity."[34] The question is, what kind of infirmity? Speculations as to the nature of Paul's "illness" link it variously to the references to "eyes" in 4:15, or to

---

30. Martyn, *Galatians,* 424.

31. See ibid.

32. Argued by Lightfoot, *Galatians,* 174. So also Burton, *Galatians,* 238; Oepke, *Galater,* 105; Lagrange, *Galates,* 112; Schlier, *Galater,* 148; Mussner, *Galaterbrief,* 307; Betz, *Galatians,* 224; R. Longenecker, *Galatians,* 191.

33. This is the argument of Erhardt Güttgemanns, who claims Paul's "weakness of the flesh" was the means *(Modus)* of his proclamation of the crucified Christ "as epiphany of the crucified one (ἐσταυρωμένος)" (*Der leidende Apostel und sein Herr: Studien zur paulinischen Christologie* [Göttingen: Vandenhoeck & Ruprecht, 1966], 185). See also the discussion in Troy Martin, "Whose Flesh? What Temptation? (Galatians 4.13-14)," *JSNT* 74 (1999): 73-74; Goddard and Cummins, "Ill or Ill-Treated?" 103 n. 29.

34. See the review of the literature in David A. Black, *Paul, Apostle of Weakness: Astheneia and Its Cognates in the Pauline Literature* (New York: Peter Lang, 1984), 73-79; Goddard and Cummins, "Ill or Ill-Treated?" 94-95.

the apostle's "thorn in the flesh" in 2 Cor 12:7.[35] Recognizing the exegetical weaknesses (no pun intended) of these arguments, some recent commentators simply refuse further attempts at definition. Martyn's conclusion is typical: "It is useless to speculate about the nature of Paul's sickness."[36]

Nonetheless, that Paul himself calls attention to this ἀσθένεια τῆς σαρκός, both as the occasion of his preaching and as a trial or temptation for the Galatians, invites speculation as to what the apostle means by it. Again, the πάλιν in 4:19 intensifes the focus on the circumstances of his first encounter with his converts. It is possible, as mentioned above, that "weakness" may refer simply to "sickness." Nonetheless, this interpretation runs up against the difficulty of relating such "sickness" to 4:12b (οὐδέν με ἠδικήσατε) and 4:14 (καὶ τὸν πειρασμὸν ὑμῶν ἐν τῇ σαρκί μου οὐκ ἐξουθενήσατε οὐδὲ ἐξεπτύσατε, ἀλλὰ ὡς ἄγγελον θεοῦ ἐδέξασθέ με, ὡς Χριστὸν Ἰησοῦν). It is unclear why sickness would be an occasion for wrongdoing by the Galatians, or be a πειρασμός for them. One explanation put forth is that the Galatians would view Paul's illness as demonically induced,[37] or even possibly as the result of a curse.[38] Support for this interpretation comes from Paul's use of the *hapax legomenon* ἐκπτύω ("spit out") in 4:14, since spitting was a popular method of defense against demons and the evil eye.[39] Yet even if one accepts such arguments, one still has to ask why Paul would remind the Galatians that his initial preaching to them was a mere by-product of such difficult and negative circumstances.[40]

---

35. See Borse, *Galater*, 151; R. Longenecker, *Galatians*, 191.

36. Martyn, *Galatians*, 420.

37. R. Longenecker, *Galatians*, 191; Martyn, *Galatians*, 421; Oepke, *Galater*, 105-6.

38. Baasland, "Persecution," 145-46; John Elliott, "Paul, the Galatians, and the Evil Eye," *Currents in Theology and Mission* 17, 4 (1990): 262-73.

39. See, e.g., Pliny, *Hist. Nat.* 28.36, 39. Rather than reading ἐκπτύω as a reference to the evil eye, however, I am more persuaded that in Gal 4:14 Paul employs the word pair of ἐκπτύω and ἐξουθενέω. See Goddard and Cummins, "Ill or Ill-Treated?" 105-6. Hays (*Galatians*, 294) notes helpfully that ἐξουθενέω elsewhere occurs in reference to Paul's speech as characterized by his opponents (2 Cor 10:10), to God's choice of "what is low and despised" (1 Cor 1:28), and to the contempt bestowed on Jesus (Mark 9:12; Luke 23:11; Acts 4:11).

40. See Güttgemanns, *Leidende Apostel*, 174: "Is not this 'psychological advertisement,' aided by a reminder of the 'good old days,' actually a fatal compromise by Paul? It would indirectly concede that originally he had no desire to proclaim the gospel to the Galatians, but rather that he founded the congregation only by misfortune, so to speak, as a 'by-product' of an accidental sickness."

Although Paul may mention it simply to highlight the contrast between the Galatians' initial reception and current rejection of him, one suspects it contributes in a more substantive way to his preaching of the gospel.

Some commentators have suggested that the phrase "weakness of the flesh" in 4:13 should be interpreted in connection to its occurrence in Rom 6:19.[41] On this basis, Hermann Binder proposes that the expression refers to human limitations that are the occasion for a demonstration of God's power.[42] Troy Martin follows Jerome in reading Gal 4:13 as "the weakness of *your* flesh," and argues that it should be interpreted in light of the use of σάρξ elsewhere in the letter. According to this proposal, in both Rom 6:19 and Gal 4:13 the phrase simply describes the "pre-gospel condition" of Paul's readers.[43] Any physical referent for "flesh" in v. 13 is lost. Martin must still deal with the clear reference to Paul's physical "flesh" in v. 14, however, and the way in which it presented a trial or temptation to the Galatians. Remarkably, his solution is to posit that in v. 14 Paul refers to his own circumcision, which was initially offensive to the Gentile Galatians: "The Galatians' refusal to circumcise even after their acceptance of circumcision as a necessary requirement of the Christian gospel indicates they did view circumcision much as other non-Jews did. They preferred returning to their paganism rather than submitting to this socially repulsive surgery."[44] Martin's ingenious thesis fails to answer some crucial questions: Why are these same Gentiles now apparently so eager to be circumcised? And why is Paul so upset? In other words, Martin's disembodied and highly "theological" interpretation of 4:13-14 has led him to undercut Paul's theological argument completely.[45]

There is a third possibility: Paul's "weakness of the flesh" refers specifically to the wounds he suffered as a result of persecution. This has been argued forcefully by A. J. Goddard and S. A. Cummins.[46] It also follows the lead of earlier exegetes, notably Chrysostom, Theodore of Mopsuestia, Au-

---

41. T. Martin, "Whose Flesh?" 84-86; Hermann Binder, "Die angebliche Krankheit des Paulus," *TZ* 32 (1976): 1-13.

42. Binder, "Angebliche Krankheit," 6-7, 13.

43. T. Martin, "Whose Flesh?" 78-82.

44. Ibid., 89.

45. T. Martin makes the same argument on rhetorical grounds in "Apostasy to Paganism."

46. Goddard and Cummins, "Ill or Ill-Treated?" passim. See also R. Longenecker, *Galatians*, 191, 299-300; Martyn, *Galatians*, 421; Davis, "Meaning of προεγράφη," 208; Hays, *Galatians*, 293-94.

gustine, Aquinas, and Luther. In Chrysostom's words, "What is he saying? 'I was persecuted, I was flogged, I underwent many near-deaths in preaching to you, and even so you did not despise me.'"[47] In my view, although it remains speculative, this ancient interpretation presents the most compelling and fruitful line of investigation, because it makes the most sense of Paul's other references in Galatians to suffering and persecution, and it is consonant both with the apostle's portrayal of his ministry elsewhere in the Pauline corpus and with his identification with the prophetic tradition.

This interpretation hears Paul's ongoing experience of persecution as part of his solidarity with the crucified Christ who lives in him (2:20).[48] Under the banner of God's revelation of Christ "in" the apostle (1:16), this apostolic solidarity with the indwelling, crucified Christ sets the context for the "public proclamation" of Christ crucified in 3:1.[49] Paul's use of the verb προεγράφη in 3:1 has been interpreted either to mean "vividly depict in word pictures," or "make an authoritative pronouncement."[50] Basil Davis affirms the merits of each interpretation, but notes that as "purely metaphorical" readings they do not account for Paul's emphasis on "the visual element" that "addressed not only the intellect but also the eyes of his au-

---

47. Chrysostom, "Homily on Galatians 4:14," in *Galatians, Ephesians, Philippians,* ed. Mark J. Edwards, ACCS 8 (Downers Grove, IL: InterVarsity Press, 1999), 62. See also Luther, *Galatians,* 400-401.

48. The key texts are Gal 1:16; 2:19–3:4; 4:13-15; 5:11; 6:12-17. In what follows, I rely extensively on the argument of Goddard and Cummins, with one caveat: they posit that 4:12 refers specifically to an earlier shared experience of persecution that accompanied Paul's initial preaching in Galatia. As argued in chapter two, I agree that Paul evokes a shared experience in 4:12, but the content of that shared "experience" is fundamentally existence "in Christ," and only derivatively a willingness to suffer for the sake of the gospel. It is impossible and unnecessary to determine whether the Galatians' "suffering" in 3:4 refers to circumstances attending their initial reception of the gospel or subsequent events.

49. Davis, "Meaning of προεγράφη," 206; Barclay, *Obeying the Truth,* 83. In his comment on 4:14, Martyn (*Galatians,* 421) links 1:16, 6:17, 3:1, and 2:19-21, although he does not do so in his comment on 3:1, which he interprets simply as a vivid public narration of the "punctiliar event" of Jesus' passion and resurrection (283).

50. See references and review of the evidence in Davis, "Meaning of προεγράφη," 202-5. Richard Hays suggests that προεγράφη functions as a "veiled" reference to Scripture's "prefiguration of Christ's crucifixion" by linking it to Scripture's active role in "foreseeing" (προϊδοῦσα) God's justification of the Gentiles (*Echoes of Scripture in the Letters of Paul* [New Haven: Yale University Press, 1989], 107, 213 n. 60). Such a subliminal link may indeed be operative in the letter, but in my view the more immediate connection between the *public* (not subliminal) portrayal of Christ and Paul's preaching is stronger.

dience."[51] Arguing rather that "the key to the interpretation of the verb προγράφω lies in the intimate relationship claimed by Paul between himself and the crucified Christ," Davis concludes that "when 3.1 is read as directly following the preceding verses it becomes quite evident that Paul is describing himself as the canvas upon which the crucified Christ was publicly displayed."[52] This physical display of Christ crucified refers to the physical scars on his body, which he proudly names the "*stigmata* of Jesus" (6:17).

Furthermore, these physical scars are part of Paul's explicit contrast between the Teachers and himself at the climax of the letter in 6:12-17. The other missionaries preach circumcision to avoid persecution (6:12), whereas Paul continues to experience persecution because he refuses to preach circumcision (5:11).[53] The Teachers may glory in the circumcised flesh of the Galatians (6:12-13), but Paul glories in nothing but the cross of Christ that has separated him from the cosmos with its old antinomies (6:14).[54] Galatians 6:17 delivers the coup de grace in Paul's judgment on the other missionaries: they may boast in the old marker of circumcision, which belongs to the cosmos that is passing away, but the only markers that count in the new creation are the physical scars that display solidarity with the crucified Christ.[55]

This network of references to suffering and persecution makes sense of 4:13-15, and particularly of the πειρασμός of 4:14. To hear the gospel from a man who is visibly disfigured and weakened by the experience of

51. Davis, "Meaning of προεγράφη," 205-6.

52. Ibid., 207-8.

53. Regarding the historical background to Paul's references to persecution, Sanders (*Paul, the Law,* 191) proposes that what Paul calls "persecution," his opponents probably thought of as "punishment." While recognizing the difficulties of reconstructing the actual circumstances, he says, "at least some non-Christian Jews persecuted (that is, punished) at least some Christian Jews in some places. The best-attested fact is that Paul himself carried out such persecution. . . . From Galatians (especially 5:11 and 6:12) and from 1 Thess. 2:16, it also appears likely that the issue was circumcision; that is, the admission of Gentiles to the people of God without requiring them to make full proselytization to Judaism."

54. Martyn, *Galatians,* 561.

55. "It is the mark of the cross branded in his body, the proof of his commissioning by the crucified and risen Christ, which enabled Paul to dismiss those troublemakers with their insistence on the lesser mark of circumcision (6.17)" (James D. G. Dunn, *The Theology of Paul's Letter to the Galatians,* New Testament Theology [Cambridge: Cambridge University Press, 1993], 32).

being tortured would surely test the Galatians' faith and tempt them to reject his message. Nonetheless, they "received [him] as an angel of God, as Christ Jesus," implicitly because they saw the message — that is, Christ Jesus — displayed in the messenger. The apostle cannot proclaim his message without enacting it in a concrete way, just as the prophets enacted their message. Thus, when in 4:19 he speaks of going through labor pains "again," his auditors and he both know that his continued proclamation of the circumcision-free gospel entails his continued exposure to persecution (5:11).[56]

"Weakness" in Paul's Letters

The case for interpreting Paul's "weakness" in 4:13 as his embodiment of the crucified Christ gains further support from a review of ἀσθένεια and its cognates elsewhere in Paul's letters.[57] Two key passages will suffice to illustrate the point. First, the evidence from 1 Thess 1:6-8 indicates that early in his ministry Paul saw a connection between proclamation, suffering, and the power of God.[58] Here imitation is linked to suffering: Paul praises the Thessalonians for imitating him by both receiving and proclaiming the word in the midst of affliction. Again in 2:14 he praises them for becoming imitators of the churches of God in Judea, precisely through suffering persecution. It is clear that the context and occasion for their affliction and suffering is eschatological: they live in expectation of the day of the Lord, close at hand and accompanied by destruction "as labor comes upon a

---

56. Cf. Goddard and Cummins, "Ill or Ill-Treated?" 119: "It is likely that the Galatians were all too aware that persecution was a regular by-product of Paul's circumcision-free mission."

57. In addition to the passages discussed, see also 1 Cor 2:1-5; 4:10, 15-16; 9:22; 2 Cor 4:7-12; 6:1-13.

58. See Jerry L. Sumney, "Paul's 'Weakness': An Integral Part of His Conception of Apostleship," *JSNT* 52 (1993): 84: "In 1.4-6 Paul further interprets his suffering as the means through which his message is seen as God's word. His preaching in the midst of persecution demonstrates that God is at work in him and actualizes the meaning of the resurrection in the present through the activity of the Spirit." Unfortunately, it would be more accurate to title his article "Paul's Affliction," in that ἀσθένεια does not appear in the letter. Nonetheless, the point stands. See also Raymond F. Collins, "Paul as Seen through His Own Eyes: A Reflection on the First Letter to the Thessalonians," *Studies on the First Letter to the Thessalonians*, BETL 66 (Leuven: Leuven University Press, 1984), 175-208.

woman with child" (5:3).[59] Affliction is to be expected in these circumstances, as Paul reminds the Thessalonians in 3:4-5, and this affliction is a test of their faith, causing him to fear that his work might be in vain: μή πως ἐπείρασεν ὑμᾶς ὁ πειράζων καὶ εἰς κενὸν γένηται ὁ κόπος ἡμῶν.[60] In Galatians Paul also worries that his work has been vain, and with good cause; like the Thessalonians, the Galatians initially "passed the test" posed by persecution: unlike the Thessalonians, however, now some of them are turning away from the gospel.

The second key text is 2 Cor 11:21-30. Here, as in Gal 4, Paul contrasts his ministry with that of other missionaries. His defense of his apostleship takes the form of a typical list of hardships. As numerous studies have shown, such *peristasis* catalogs were a common philosophical topos, frequently employed to demonstrate one's superior moral character and fortitude.[61] But Paul puts his hardships to an unexpected use: he brackets them with references to his own "weakness" (11:21, 29-30), which thereby becomes the umbrella term for physical suffering and persecution as well as his pastoral anxiety for all the churches. Through these references to his own weakness, Paul describes his hardships in ironic counterpoint to the abusive behavior of the "false apostles" (11:19-20). Again, this contrast between the "true" philosopher, whose life matches his teachings, and the "false" philosopher, who is all talk but no action, is a common topos that Paul uses to his advantage in distinguishing himself from his opponents.[62]

---

59. For the present experience of eschatological distress, see also 1 Cor 7:26-29; Rom 1:18; 8:18; 1 Thess 2:16. First Thessalonians 5:3 may be the first extant reference to the "birth pangs of the Messiah," attested also in *1 En.* 62:4; Mark 13:8; Rev 12:2; 1QH III, 7-10. For the association of labor pains with "the Day of the Lord," see Isa 13:8; Jer 22:23; 30:5-6; 48:41; Hos 13:13; Mic 4:9-10; 5:2. See discussion in Dale Allison, *The End of the Ages Has Come: An Early Interpretation of the Passion and Resurrection of Jesus* (Philadelphia: Fortress, 1985), 5-14, 62-65.

60. See discussion in Goddard and Cummins, "Ill or Ill-Treated?" 104.

61. "The noble man holds his hardships to be his greatest antagonists, and with them he is ever wont to battle day and night, not to win a sprig of parsley as so many goats might do, nor for a bit of wild olive, or of pine, but to win happiness and virtue throughout all the days of his life" (Dio Chrysostom, "The Eighth Discourse: Diogenes, or On Virtue," *Orations*, 8.15-16, trans. J. W. Cohoon and H. Lamar Crosby, 5 vols., LCL [London: Heinemann, 1932-51], 1:384-85). See also Abraham J. Malherbe, *Moral Exhortation: A Greco-Roman Sourcebook*, LEC 4 (Philadelphia: Westminster, 1986), 26-28, 141-42; Fitzgerald, *Cracks*.

62. Fitzgerald (*Cracks*, 77-85) discusses the widespread belief that hardships are the proving ground for manliness and virtue. This view is summed up by Epictetus, *The Dis-*

It is one thing, however, to boast of enduring hardships in order to magnify one's own strength of character and self-control. It is quite another to boast of them in order to magnify one's weakness, particularly when this weakness includes anxiety — hardly a Stoic virtue! As John T. Fitzgerald notes concerning 2 Cor 11:28-30: "Paul's inclusion here of a psychic hardship in his *peristasis* catalogue is most atypical in comparison to other such catalogues. The Stoic typically made a distinction between the body, which alone can suffer injury, and the true self, which is above it (cf. Sen. *Ep.* 65.18-22). Paul, on the contrary, admits to psychic hardship, and yet still boasts of it."[63] Here Fitzgerald points out the uniqueness of the apostle's use of a *peristasis* catalog in 2 Cor 11:21-30 to prove his weakness, rather than to demonstrate his own personal power or self-control.[64] Instead, the list of sufferings demonstrates God's power, just as Paul proclaims in 2 Cor 12:9-10: "I will all the more gladly boast of my weakness, that the power of Christ may rest upon me. For the sake of Christ, then, I am content with weaknesses, insults, hardships, persecutions, and calamities, for when I am weak, then I am strong [ὅταν γὰρ ἀσθενῶ τότε δυνατός εἰμι]." Here, as in 11:21-30, "weakness" is the term Paul uses to designate and sum up his experience of hardships and persecutions, which in turn provide the paradoxical setting for the "signs of an apostle . . . signs and wonders and mighty works" (12:12). The conclusion is that Paul's weakness displays the indwelling Christ who speaks in him (ἐν ἐμοὶ λαλοῦντος Χριστοῦ), who "was crucified in weakness, but lives by the power of God" (13:3-4). Therefore Paul's "weakness" becomes the sign of his true apostleship, in comparison with that of the pseudo-apostles, because it paradoxically reveals the power of God.[65]

In Gal 4:12-20, as in 2 Cor 11:21–13:4, Paul's "weakness" is central to the way he contrasts his ministry with that of the opposing missionaries.

---

courses as Reported by Arrian, the Manual, and Fragments, trans. William A. Oldfather, 2 vols., LCL (Cambridge: Harvard University Press, 1925-28), 1.24.1: "It is difficulties that show what men are."

63. Fitzgerald, *Cracks,* 387 n. 267.

64. Epictetus's dictum that the beginning of philosophy is consciousness of one's own weakness and impotence with reference to the things of real consequence (*Diss.* 2.11.1), stresses the need for self-knowledge in order to overcome one's weaknesses. The philosopher is like a doctor who diagnoses the client's weaknesses in order to prescribe proper treatment. See also *Diss.* 3.23.23-38.

65. See also 2 Cor 10:10-18.

In both passages, this "weakness" becomes grounds for accepting him as one who speaks for Christ. That in 2 Corinthians Paul connects "weakness" with both the endurance of hardship and the demonstration of the indwelling Christ suggests that he may employ ἀσθένεια in a similar way in Gal 4:13.[66] Thematic similarities between Gal 4:13-15 and both 1 Thess 3:4-5 and 2 Cor 11:21-33 further support the interpretation of Paul's "weakness of the flesh" (Gal 4:13) as a reference to a physical condition caused by persecutions and hardships. Through this condition the apostle publicly portrayed the indwelling Christ, and by it the Galatians' faith was tested.

The Cruciform Formation of Christ in Galatians

Paul's embodiment of the sufferings of Christ certainly puts a bite in his appeal in 4:12 to "Become like me [not like the Teachers who avoid persecution]," and thus gives concrete significance to the second half of 4:19: "until Christ be formed in [among] you." In John Koenig's words, "the crucified Christ Paul once preached to the Galatians (3:1) must now be formed in them again. Instead of rejecting the weak apostle, they must become like him (4:12) in allowing their existence to be shaped by the cross (2:20; 6:17)."[67] Martyn specifies this "formation" in terms of crucifixion to the old cosmos and its divisions between Jew and Gentile (6:14). The shape of the pericope supports this interpretation, in that the relationship between the Gentile Galatians and the apostle is a living expression of the cessation of old divisions and the inauguration of the new creation in Christ. Thus, as Martyn puts it,

> The final key to the reading of v 19b is provided, then, by v 12 with its motif of double likeness. For the Galatians to become like Paul will in-

---

66. While some scholars posit that Paul's emphasis on "weakness" stemmed from his experiences in Corinth and Athens, the nexus of proclamation, affliction, and eschatological expectation in 1 Thessalonians suggests that the apostle was thinking along these lines early in his ministry. See Sumney, "Paul's 'Weakness,'" 71-72, for a review of the literature.

67. John T. Koenig, "The Motif of Transformation in the Pauline Epistles: A History of Religious/Exegetical Study" (Ph.D. diss., Union Theological Seminary, New York, 1971), 117. So also D. Stanley, "Become Imitators of Me," 875; Goddard and Cummins, "Ill or Ill-Treated?" 115; Gaventa, *Our Mother,* 6.

volve their being once again parted from conformity to their old cosmos, just as Paul has been parted from conformity to his (6:14). And that in turn means that the Christ who is to be (re-)formed in their congregations is the Christ in whom there is neither Jew nor Gentile (3:28).[68]

I agree with this assessment, but in light of the discussion thus far I also want to emphasize the centrality of suffering as an essential, inevitable corollary of nonconformity to the old cosmos. For the Galatians to become like Paul, they must join him in suffering for the proclamation of the circumcision-free gospel. Paul's message in the vernacular might sound something like this: "You want something to brag about? You want identity markers? I'll give you identity markers! You see these scars? I'm branded for Jesus. Become like me!"

In other words, in the experience of the apostle and his converts, life in this "new creation" inevitably runs up against opposition from the structures and relational patterns of the old cosmos, and therefore entails suffering and persecution. Indeed, as the eschatological background of ὠδίνω implies, this suffering is part of the labor pains that attend the death of the old cosmos and the inauguration of the new creation.[69] Although reconstruction of the historical circumstances remains speculative, Paul reminds the Galatians that they themselves also experienced suffering even as they experienced the powerful working of the Spirit in their midst (3:3-5).[70] Indeed, the repeated questions of 3:3 and 3:4 imply

---

68. Martyn, *Galatians*, 431.

69. See 1 Thess 5:3; Rom 8:22. See below for discussion of the prophetic texts.

70. Most translations and many commentators read ἐπάθετε as "experienced," presumably on the basis of context. See review of the literature in R. Longenecker, *Galatians*, 104. Elsewhere in the Pauline letters and throughout the NT as well as the LXX, however, the verb has the negative sense of "to suffer." Betz (*Galatians*, 134) refers to the word pair μαθεῖν and παθεῖν in order to argue that Paul here uses this established association between experience and learning to remind his listeners of their early experience. Betz fails to notice, however, that the verbs have different subjects in Gal 3:2 and 4; it is not the Galatians but Paul himself who wants to "learn." In addition, in the only other occurrence of this word pair in the New Testament, Heb 5:8, παθεῖν clearly means "to suffer": Jesus "learned obedience through what he suffered." Indeed, Heb 5:8 simply amplifies the theme stated in Heb 2:10 that Jesus was perfected through suffering (διὰ παθημάτων τελειῶσαι). For sustained arguments in favor of reading ἐπάθετε as "suffered," see Baasland, *Persecution*, 139-40; and Goddard and Cummins, "Ill or Ill-Treated?" 119. See also Hays, *Galatians*, 250-51.

that suffering is a part of the new life that they "began with the Spirit." Whatever the circumstances behind Paul's almost offhand remark, there is no implication that suffering is incompatible with the miraculous work of the Spirit among the Galatians. To the contrary, elsewhere in Paul's letters God's power is manifested in the midst of suffering and weakness — why not here? As Paul reminds the Galatians, the message of faith through which they first received the Spirit (3:3) came in the midst of Paul's "weakness of the flesh" (4:13). Goddard and Cummins suggest, "Paul's concern is that the Galatians (once again) become like him (4:12) precisely in this respect: being faithful to Christ in their lives even if this entails co-crucifixion."[71]

I have proposed that the experiential referent for Paul's labor pains in 4:19 is his embodied, cruciform proclamation of the gospel in 4:13-15 — that is, the physical suffering that he endures as a result of preaching the circumcision-free gospel. Now it is possible to suggest an answer to part of the puzzle posed by the syntax of 4:17-20: what is the relationship between Paul's "labor" and his "presence" with the Galatians? If the foregoing analysis is correct, the apostle's argument may run as follows. In contrast to the other missionaries, Paul always zealously seeks the good of his converts. Even now as he writes this letter, he seeks their good by repreaching to them the circumcision-free gospel. This preaching is a part of his apocalyptic "labor." But the labor is incomplete apart from Paul's physical presence, because he communicates the gospel bodily as well as verbally. Therefore he immediately expresses his wish that he could be with them and "change [his] voice." While it is likely that Paul wishes to change his tone of voice, in light of his repeated desire to be present with his converts he may also wish that he could change from the voice of the letter to a physical voice.[72] In the crisis at hand, the letter is not an adequate substitute for his actual presence. Thus, while a yearning to be present is a common epistolary topos, it also reinforces the essentially personal and physical character of Paul's communication of the gospel and his relationship with the Galatians.[73] The implication of a close connection between the messenger and the message recalls the

71. Goddard and Cummins, "Ill or Ill-Treated?" 115. See also R. Collins, "Paul," 192.

72. So Betz, *Galatians*, 236; R. Longenecker, *Galatians*, 196; Hays, *Galatians*, 296. *Pace* Lightfoot, *Galatians*, 179; Burton, *Galatians*, 250; Martyn, *Galatians*, 426.

73. Betz (*Galatians*, 236) discusses the "refinement" of the voice as a technique of persuasion in ancient rhetoric.

close correspondence that Paul sees between Christ and himself, as well as his identification with Jeremiah's suffering embodiment of the prophetic message.

Yet clearly in 4:19 the apostle is doing far more than reiterating his embodied preaching; through the metaphor of labor pains he refers to the eschatological horizon and apocalyptic character of the conflict in Galatia. Richard Hays says that 4:19 "puts the personal appeal of this passage in its proper cosmic context."[74] Paul is reminding the Galatians "what time it is," as well as the high stakes and the true identities of the participants in his "labor." Therefore this investigation now turns from the "point in the concrete" to the "point not visible to the naked eye, but believed in by [the writer] firmly, just as real to him, really, as the one that everybody sees."[75] That is, the investigation turns to the association of ὠδίνω with apocalyptic expectation. Building on Paul's earlier self-identification with the prophetic calls of Jeremiah and the Servant in Isaiah, I will focus on the occurrences of ὠδίνω in those prophetic books.

The Background of ὠδίνω in the Septuagint

Three Proposals

The proposals of Gaventa, Martyn, and Kahl mentioned above provide a useful starting point for further investigation. First, because gestation requires time, the maternal imagery is appropriate for expressing the protracted and repetitive nature of the founding of the Galatian communities. As Martyn puts it: "To picture this decidedly *linear* state of affairs, Paul uses the feminine image."[76] Second, through literary allusion to eschatological texts, ὠδίνω emphasizes the situation in Galatia as the scene of apocalyptic conflict and hope.[77] Finally, Paul's "transgendered labor" expresses the reality of the new creation and the subversion of the old hierar-

---

74. Hays, *Galatians*, 298.

75. O'Connor, *Mystery and Manners*, 42.

76. Martyn, *Galatians*, 429. Gaventa observes: "when Paul uses maternal imagery, the image always requires the elapse of some extended period of time: a woman who is pregnant, after all, is pregnant for a period of time and does not control when her labor will begin" (*Our Mother*, 7).

77. Gaventa, *Our Mother*, 33-34, 37; Martyn, *Galatians*, 429-30.

chical structures of "male and female (3:28)."[78] The third proposal, by Kahl, builds on Gaventa's interest in "bringing the language of maternity out of the footnotes and into the text of Pauline studies."[79]

Before proceeding further, some observations are in order. Neither Gaventa nor Martyn discusses the relationship between the "linear" and "apocalyptic" characteristics of Paul's maternal imagery here in Gal 4:19. This is particularly striking in Martyn's case, because he characterizes God's apocalyptic "invasion" of the cosmos as a "punctiliar" event, occurring precisely at the point of the cross. Furthermore, he contrasts Paul's "punctiliar gospel" with "linear" *heilsgeschichtlich* forms of preaching.[80] Yet here the image of protracted, repeated labor pains communicates both punctiliar and linear images, and is joined with the apocalyptic echoes of ὠδίνω, suggesting that it plays a key role in Paul's assertion that the apocalyptic gospel both engenders and sustains the Christian community over time.[81] If Martyn is indeed correct that Galatians is about the power of the gospel to "create a history," then the apostle's metaphor in 4:19 should shed light on the concrete contours of that "gospel history."[82]

Indeed, clues to the role of ὠδίνω in 4:19 may occur in the prophetic literature to which Gaventa and Martyn have directed our attention. Gaventa cites several passages to make a general conclusion that "Paul's anguish, his travail, is not simply a personal matter or a literary convention having to do with friendship or rebirth but reflects the anguish of the whole created order as it awaits the fulfillment of God's action in Jesus Christ."[83] Martyn focuses tightly on Isa 45:10 as the antecedent for Paul's use of ὠδίνω in Gal 4:19.[84] While agreeing with Martyn that Isa 45:10 provides close similarities to Gal 4:19, I will argue that it is a mistake to limit the semantic field for ὠδίνω to this one text. Rather, it represents a larger textual tradition that also comes into play in Gal 4:19.

---

78. Kahl, "No Longer Male," 43-46.

79. Gaventa, *Our Mother.*

80. Martyn, "Events in Galatia," 160-70, 173.

81. Gaventa claims specifically, "In Galatians 4:19, Paul explicitly applies the image of a woman's birth pangs to his work as apostle in sustaining Christians in the Galatian churches" (*Our Mother,* 8).

82. See discussion in chapter one.

83. Gaventa, *Our Mother,* 34. She (33-34) notes Mic 4:10; Isa 13:6, 8; Jer 6:24; *1 En.* 62:4; *2 Bar.* 56:6; *4 Ezra* 4:42; 1QH III, 7-10; Mark 13:8; Matt 24:8; Rev 12:2; 1 Thess 5:3; Rom 8:22.

84. Martyn, *Galatians,* 426-31.

With regard to Kahl's provocative connection between Paul's "trans-gendered labor" in 4:19 and "not male and female" in 3:28, it is interesting to note that although she explores the identity of the Christ who is formed in the Galatian community, she does not explore the implication of this connection for the identity of the God who does that forming. Again, a closer look at the literary background for ὠδίνω will enhance the picture of the God whom Paul preaches and represents, with the possibility that Paul's maternal labor in 4:19 describes not Paul's representation of a transgendered community, but a transgendered image of God.[85] Finally, while noting that ὠδίνω also occurs in Paul's citation of Isa 54:1 a few verses later in Gal 4:27, none of the commentators explores in depth the contrast between Paul's labor and the miraculous labor-free childbirth of the bar-ren woman in Gal 4:27/Isa 54:1. Discussion of this last observation will be taken up in the next chapter on the allegory of Gal 4:21-31.

There are three other occurrences of ὠδίνω or its cognate noun in Paul's letters: Gal 4:27, as noted above; 1 Thess 5:3 (ἡ ὠδίν); and Rom 8:22. Beyond their common reference to apocalyptic expectation, these passages are rather varied. Although both 1 Thess 5:3 and Rom 8:22 occur in apoca-lyptic contexts, 1 Thess 5:3 refers to the writhing and terror of unbelievers at the unanticipated Day of the Lord, whereas Rom 8:22 refers to the an-guish of the whole created order as it yearns for that day.[86] And Gal 4:27 does not refer to Jerusalem's "labor pains," but rather to the *absence* of such pains. Apparently Paul uses ὠδίνω in a variety of ways, as do the LXX and other texts from Second Temple Judaism.[87]

This variety of usage means that it will be important to attend closely to the immediate context of Gal 4:19, as well as to the contexts of prophetic texts, in order to ascertain Paul's meaning. Following the leads of Gaventa, Martyn, and Kahl, but charting a new course and building on earlier obser-vations about Paul's embodied preaching and identification with the proph-ets, I turn in the next section to the key passages with these questions in mind: Who or what is in labor here? How might this labor contribute to

---

85. See Kahl, "No Longer Male," 46. Kahl's argument would be bolstered by attending to the theophanic aspect of Paul's "labor."

86. For a similar use of ὠδίνω as a metaphor for the anguish of waiting for the new age, see *4 Ezra* 4:40-42.

87. For example, in Deut 2:25 "birth pangs" refers to the fear suffered by Israel's ene-mies; in 1 Sam 4:19, to the physical birth pangs suffered by Phinehas's widow; in Sir 19:11, to the pain of a fool "bursting" to tell a secret.

Paul's overall picture of the relational matrix evoked thus far? How might it strengthen his proclamation of the transformative staying power of the nonnomistic, apocalyptic gospel? How might it motivate his converts to stay the course in their reliance on Christ alone apart from works of the law?

'Ωδίνω *in the Septuagint and Related Literature*

In the metaphorical uses of the verb and its cognate noun, the majority of references are to intense anguish or fear, usually related to the devastation of war.[88] This is a very ancient metaphor, dating back at least to Homer's description of Agamemnon's agony from the wounds of battle (*Iliad* 11.268-72), and it is extremely frequent in the LXX.[89] Sometimes those who suffer thus are Israel's enemies (Exod 15:14; Deut 2:25; Ps 47:7 [48:6 ET]; Isa 13:8; Jer 27:43 [50:43 ET]). More frequently, it is Israel or daughter Zion who suffers anguish under the judgment of the Lord (Jer 6:24; 4:31; 13:21; 22:23; Mic 4:9-10; Nah 2:11). There are also notable instances where the subject of the verb is the prophet (Isa 21:3), or the mingled voice of the prophet and the Lord (Jer 8:21), or clearly the Lord speaking directly (Isa 45:10; 42:14 MT — the LXX has simply ἐκαρτέρησα ὡς ἡ τίκτουσα). In Isa 21:3 the prophet agonizes over the devastation of Babylon; in Jer 8:21 the prophet and the Lord lament together over the fate of Jerusalem; in Isa 42:14 the Lord "gasps and pants like a woman giving birth" while going

---

88. I will leave aside the passages where ὠδίνω refers to physical labor pains (e.g., 1 Sam 4:19; Job 39:1-3; Sir 7:27; 4 Macc 15:7, 16; 16:8).

89. Note also that the Gilgamesh Epic uses the simile of labor pains to characterize the terror of Ishtar in reaction to the deluge:

> The gods cowered like dogs
> Crouched against the outer wall.
> Ishtar cried out like a woman in travail,
> The sweet-voiced mistress of the [gods] moans aloud. . .

("The Epic of Gilgamesh," Tablet 11, ll. 115-17, trans. E. A. Speiser, *ANET*, 94). The intense pain and very real danger accompanying labor were widely dreaded in the ancient world, appearing in both myths and maternity spells. See discussion and examples of the former in Darr, *Isaiah's Vision*, 98-101. For maternity spells, see the uterine spell in *The Greek Magical Papyri in Translation, Including the Demotic Spells*, ed. H. D. Betz (Cambridge: Cambridge University Press, 1986), VII.260-71. Thus Paul's metaphor was well known and vivid for his auditors on many levels, including the danger of miscarriage.

forth "like a warrior" (42:13) to deliver Israel through the Servant.[90] Numerous later texts attest to a widespread and varied association of ὠδίνω with the messianic birth pangs that signal or await the Day of the Lord (e.g., *1 En.* 62:6; 1QH XI.1-13 [III.1-13]; *4 Ezra* 4:42; Mark 13:8/Matt 24:8; Rom 8:22; 1 Thess 5:3; Rev 12:2).

Another set of passages, however, focuses not on the pain itself but on its source — the process of birth. These passages cluster in Hosea and Isaiah.[91] In some cases they speak of a birth process that has been aborted through Israel's idolatry. For instance, in Hos 9:10-14 the judgment for apostasy is that Ephraim will be childless; indeed, the prophet says, "Give them a childless womb and withered breasts" (9:14). In 13:13 Ephraim is an unwise child (οὐ φρόνιμος) who comes to the point of birth but refuses to be born. In Isa 37:3 Hezekiah reacts to the threats of the Assyrian emissary by describing Israel's situation as one of a woman in labor who lacks strength to bring children to birth: ἥκει ἡ ὠδὶν τῇ τικτούσῃ, ἰσχὺν δὲ οὐκ ἔχει τοῦ τεκεῖν.

The apocalyptic counterpoint to texts about labor without birth is to be found in passages that announce birth without labor. There are two such texts in Isaiah, the first of which Paul cites in Gal 4:27: Isa 54:1 and 66:7-9. Like Isa 49:21, these texts develop the motif of the barren mother who miraculously becomes the mother of a multitude.[92] Because these texts will receive extensive attention in the next chapter, I will not discuss them here. Finally, in Isa 45:10 God is named directly as both father and mother, the one who begets and the one who labors, and who in so doing demonstrates divine sovereignty and creative power.[93] These texts from

90. There is another small group of texts that refer to the "birth pains of death" (2 Sam 22:6; Ps 17:5 [18:4 ET]; Ps 114:3 [116:3 ET]).

91. In addition, Mic 4:9-10, while referring to Zion's intense pain *in* exile, appears to use childbirth itself as a metaphor for divine deliverance *from* exile. The text of 1QH XI, 7-10 (III, 7-10) describes the Teacher of Righteousness giving birth to the community within the context of eschatological motifs such as earthquake and flood (12-14). See discussion in Allison, *End of the Ages*, 8-10.

92. See Hays, *Echoes of Scripture*, 119-20.

93. The author of 1QH XVII, 35-36 also characterizes God with maternal as well as paternal language:

> Because you are a father to all the sons of your truth.
> In them you rejoice,
> like one full of gentleness for her child,
> and like a wet-nurse,
> you clutch to your breast all your creatures.

Isaiah use the metaphor of miraculous birth to emphasize God's power and faithfulness over against human weakness.[94] While God is named explicitly as father and mother in Isa 45:10, God is also implicitly the creative power behind the miraculous births in the other passages: Sarah may "labor," but it is God who "multiplies" (51:2); the barren woman, Jerusalem, cannot explain the source of her many children (49:21); she gives birth even before she labors, because the power to give birth comes from the God who is sovereign over both barrenness and fecundity (66:9).

Ὠδίνω *in Galatians 4:19*

This brief survey of texts employing ὠδίν or ὠδίνω raises two questions. First, in these passages there are a variety of subjects who suffer "labor pains"; with whom does Paul identify in Gal 4:19 when he refers to himself as suffering labor pains? Second, does Paul have in mind primarily the general sense of ὠδίνω as "suffer intense anguish," or its specific usage as an image of the birth process, or both? The scholarly proposals at the beginning of this section answer these questions in rather different ways. Gaventa's interpretation emphasizes apocalyptic anguish and sees Paul identifying with the anguish of creation as it waits for the Day of the Lord.[95] Martyn, arguing that "consciously or unconsciously" Paul drew on Isa 45:10, interprets ὠδίνω as birth imagery that refers to God's action in creating a corporate people.[96] The implication of this interpretation, which Martyn does not develop, is that Paul identifies with God's "labor" rather than that of Israel and/or the cosmos. Kahl does not take up the meaning of "labor pains" per se, but suggests that Paul's maternal self-reference models and anticipates the new eschatological community in Christ, in which gender-related social hierarchies are erased.[97] In her interpretation the focus is not on ὠδίνω as anguish or as the birth process, but simply as a feminine image through which Paul represents the new community of those "in Christ."

---

94. Von Rad, *Message of the Prophets*, 232: "On the one side is the world of flesh and the transience of everything in it; on the other, the word of Yahweh, the only thing creative and productive of blessing (Isa. 40.6-8; 45.10f)."

95. Gaventa, *Our Mother*, 33.

96. Martyn, *Galatians*, 428-29.

97. Kahl, "No Longer Male," 44-46.

Of these three proposals, by far the most closely argued is Martyn's exploration of Isa 45:10. He begins by identifying four points of comparison between Isa 45:10 and Gal 4:19: in each verse ὠδίνω is metaphorical (in Isa 45:10 it refers to "a deed of God"); in each verse the verb has a direct object; the verb naturally requires a feminine subject, but in Gal 4:19 a man (Paul) is the subject of ὠδίνω, and in Isa 45:10 God, referred to as masculine in Isa 45:1, is the subject; and the direct object — the child born — is a corporate people.[98]

Martyn further observes that Isaiah's combination of the masculine metaphor of "begetting" (γεννάω) and the feminine metaphor of "giving birth" (ὠδίνω) is similar to Paul's use of both verbs, although not in the same text, to refer to his founding of Christian churches (e.g., 1 Cor 4:14-15; 1 Thess 2:11). Finally, Paul's familiarity with Isa 45 is evident from his citations of that text in 1 Cor 14:25; Rom 9:20 (Isa 45:9); and Rom 14:11.[99]

Drawing on these observations, Martyn comes to conclusions similar to those of Gaventa: Paul uses the feminine image in order to describe the ongoing nature of the "formation" of Christ among the Galatians, and he uses the apocalyptic image to situate his conflict with the Teachers in the context of apocalyptic struggle: "He . . . sees in the Teachers' persecuting activity an instance of the last-ditch effort by which God's enemies hope to thwart the eschatological redemption of the elect."[100]

Martyn's arguments are in many ways compelling, particularly in their close attention to the structure of the metaphor in both texts. The emphasis on divine activity brought in by allusion to Isa 45:10, and the placement of the Galatian situation within the context of cosmic conflict, exhibit close affinity with Paul's argument in Galatians. Nonetheless, for three reasons it is still not certain that one can trace Paul's allusive use of ὠδίνω to this particular text, rather than to a more general motif. First, *pace* Martyn, it is not clear that in Isa 45:9-13 the object of God's labor is the corporate people of Israel. The context gives a defense of God's choice of Cyrus as the instrument through which Israel will be delivered. The challenge of Isa 45:11, "Will you question me about my children?" is answered by v. 13, "I have aroused Cyrus in righteousness."

---

98. Martyn, *Galatians,* 428. Muilenburg ("Book of Isaiah," 473) simply sees here "the birth throes of a new creation," without specifying the content of that new creation.

99. Martyn, *Galatians,* 428-29.

100. Ibid., 430.

Therefore it may well be that in this passage God's creative "labor" brings forth not a corporate people but the unique divine means of fulfilling the promise of redemption.[101]

Second, in the context of Isa 45:10, ὠδινήσεις does not express an "association between apocalyptic expectation and the anguish of childbirth."[102] While it certainly expresses expectation, it does not express anguish at all, but rather God's creative power. Isaiah 45:9-11 is God's retort to those who question the divine plan:[103]

> Woe to you who strive with your maker,
>> earthen vessels with the potter! . . .
> Woe to anyone who says to a father, "What are you begetting?"
>> Or to a woman, "With what are you in labor?"
> Thus says the Lord, the Holy One of Israel,
>> And its maker [LXX "the maker of the things to come"]

In this context, the description of God as father and mother amplifies the power and authority of God as cosmic creator (Isa 45:7-8, 12), issuing in God's freedom to deliver Israel from bondage through a completely new, alien means — the foreigner, Cyrus of Persia. The LXX highlights this connection by changing "its maker" in v. 11 to "the maker of the things to come [τὰ ἐπερχόμενα]." As the creator of heaven and earth, God is also the Lord of the future, who makes "new things spring forth" (42:9). This second observation supports the first: the birth imagery of 45:10 invokes God's power to make a new creation and to work redemption in a new way.

Third, although such imagery would certainly contribute to Paul's proclamation in Galatians, Isa 45:10 remains inadequate as an intertextual echo for Gal 4:19, because it does not account for Paul's reference to himself as the one who is in labor. In Isa 45:10 God is the only actor; in Gal 4:19 *Paul* suffers "labor pains" and *God* "forms" Christ in the Galatian congre-

---

101. Seitz comments: "The work of God's hands whom Israel is not to question is Cyrus. God's freedom to form, and reform Israel, has its counterpart — unexpected or unwelcome though it be — in God's conception of Cyrus and rousing of him to action on Israel's behalf" (*Isaiah 40–66*, 400).

102. Gaventa, *Our Mother*, 33; Martyn, *Galatians*, 429.

103. Claus Westermann, *Isaiah 40–66: A Commentary*, OTL (Philadelphia: Westminster, 1969), 165. See also John McKenzie, *Second Isaiah*, AB 20 (Garden City, NY: Doubleday, 1968), 77-79.

gations.[104] If, as argued above, the material referent for Paul's labor pains is the physical suffering that accompanies his preaching, there is a further distinction between Gal 4:19 and Isa 45:10: in the Isaiah passage ὠδίνω does not carry the sense of "intense pain," but only of creative power. Without denying that God's creative power works implicitly in and through Paul's labor pains, I would say that any investigation of the prophetic background of the apostle's labor must take into account both the dual agency of Gal 4:19 and the apostle's suffering. As I argued in chapter three, there is precedent for such a dual agency in both the classical prophets and later apocalyptic texts. For this reason, it seems best to see Paul's use of ὠδίνω as drawing on a broader literary tradition, including but not limited to Isa 45:10.

A review of the findings thus far will aid further inquiry: In Paul's telling of his own "history" and that of the Galatians, he depicts patterns of correspondence between the Galatians, himself, and Christ. Because Christ "lives in" him, and because his movement into the sphere of the Galatians mirrors Christ's movement into the human sphere, his story converges with that of his converts "in Christ."

Next, Paul identifies himself with the calls of Jeremiah, who embodies the message he proclaims, and the Isaianic Servant, who, modeled after Jeremiah, both identifies with and suffers for the people. These prophetic figures speak in solidarity with both the recipients of their message and its source, God. This embodiment and solidarity entail suffering that is itself a kind of theophany.

Finally, the material, experiential referent for the metaphor of birth pangs in Gal 4:19 is Paul's embodied proclamation of the crucified Christ through which he first engendered the Galatian churches.

These observations, together with the foregoing survey of prophetic texts, may shed light on my earlier two questions and aid in evaluating the scholarly proposals of Gaventa, Kahl, and Martyn. To repeat the questions: There is a variety of subjects who experience labor pains in the textual tradition; with whom does Paul identify himself in Gal 4:19? Does the metaphor refer primarily to intense anguish, or to the birth process, or to

---

104. Von Allmen overstates the case, however, when he says, "In the newly created community, it is Paul, not God, who is at the same time the 'father' who begets and educates, and the 'mother' who bears and cherishes the newborn Christians" (*Famille de Dieu*, 288). Rather, Paul does not here distinguish between his "labor" and the power of God working through him.

both? How do the proposals of Gaventa, Kahl, and Martyn answer these questions?

According to the first interpretive option, represented by Gaventa, Paul represents the anguish of all creation as it waits for the Day of the Lord. The difficulty with this proposal is that it is hard to see how such a representation would contribute to Paul's concerns in the letter as a whole. Given the convergence between the suffering of Zion and the suffering of creation (e.g., Jer 4:23-31), and the frequent use of ὠδίν and ὠδίνω to refer to the anguish of Zion, one might modify this proposal to say that Paul identifies himself with the anguish of God's people as they wait for the day of redemption.[105] In Gal 4:19, however, the people of God are the object, not the subject, of ὠδίνω. Indeed, despite Paul's references to past suffering on the part of his converts (3:4), there is little in the text to indicate that in the current situation the Galatians see themselves as suffering.[106] Furthermore, the references to "present Jerusalem" and "Jerusalem above" (4:25-26) render such an identification problematic. It would hardly advance Paul's argument if he identified himself with "present Jerusalem." On the other hand, "Jerusalem above" miraculously has children *without* suffering labor pains. Therefore it seems that Paul's "labor" does not represent solidarity with either the anguish of unredeemed creation in general or the people of God in particular.

The second interpretive proposal, represented by Kahl, is that Paul's maternal self-description models the eschatological community as shaped by "the meaning of sex/gender-unity in Gal. 3.28 and in Galatians as a whole."[107] It is weakened by the fact that it lacks precedence in the texts in which the metaphor of labor pains occurs. Furthermore, it does not expand upon the meanings of this metaphor either as a reference to intense suffering or to the birth process.

The third interpretive option, implied by Martyn, still seems to be the most fruitful, but with the following modification: Paul's "labor" represents God's "labor," both as intense anguish on behalf of God's people and as cre-

---

105. For this interpretation of Rom 8:22-23 see Susan Eastman, "Whose Apocalypse? The Identity of the Sons of God in Romans 8:19," *JBL* 121, 2 (2002): 263-77.

106. Paul's accusation against the Teachers as "harassing" the Galatians reflects his judgment on the situation, not necessarily that of the Galatians themselves (1:7; 5:10, 12). The case is similar in 2 Cor 11:19-20, where Paul chides the Corinthians for allowing the pseudo-apostles to enslave and abuse them.

107. Kahl, "No Longer Male," 43.

ative power bringing the new creation to birth. As the foregoing analysis of Paul's "weakness" has suggested, the suffering and the power go together. This convergence of suffering and power is central to Paul's contrast between his gospel and the preaching mission of the other missionaries, because it is central to his representation of the God who acts through the crucified Christ. Enlarging the echo chamber for "hearing" ὠδίνω, one finds in the image of a woman in labor a similar convergence of prophetic and divine suffering in Jer 8:18–9:3, and of divine suffering and creative power in Isa 42:10-17.

In the previous chapter I discussed Jer 8:13–9:3 as an example of Jeremiah's mingling of divine and human speech:

> My joy is gone, grief is upon me, my heart is sick,
> Hark, the cry of my poor people from far and wide in the land.
> For the hurt of my poor people I am hurt,
> I mourn, and dismay has taken hold of me.
>
> (Jer 8:18-19, 21)

As noted above, this pericope is bracketed by the formula, "Thus says the Lord" (8:17; 9:3). It is all the more striking, therefore, to find that the LXX version of 8:21 reads:

> For the destruction of the daughter of my people I have been darkened: in my perplexity pangs have seized upon me as of a woman in labor.
>
> ἐπὶ συντρίμματι θυγατρὸς λαοῦ μου ἐσκοτώθην· ἐν ἀπορίᾳ κατίσχυσάν με ὠδῖνες ὡς τικτούσης

It is impossible to distinguish between the prophet's voice and that of God. Rather, the prophet's "labor pains" mirror God's intense pains on behalf of God's people, even as they suffer divine judgment. Here the focus of the metaphor is not on childbirth per se, but completely on the intense pain and empathy of the prophet and God together with Jerusalem. Similarly, Paul's suffering manifests the suffering of Christ, as it portrays to the Galatians the depth of God's compassion and therefore the certainty of God's faithfulness.

The meaning of the metaphor shifts in the two passages from Isaiah, where it signifies some aspect of giving birth. As discussed above, Isa 45:10 emphasizes the creative power of God as the one who both "begets" and "gives birth," with no reference to anguish. In 42:13-16 (LXX) divine anguish and divine power come together in a dramatic convergence of the images of God as warrior and as mother:[108]

> The Lord God of hosts shall go forth, and crush the battle;
>> he shall stir up jealousy, and shall shout mightily against
>>> his enemies.
> I have been silent: shall I also always be silent and forbear?
>> I have endured like a woman in labor
>> [ἐκαρτέρησα ὡς ἡ τίκτουσα];
>> I will amaze and wither at the same time.
> I will make desolate mountains and hills, and will dry up all their
>> grass; and I will make the rivers islands, and dry up the pools.
> And I will bring the blind by a way that they knew not,
>> and I will cause them to tread paths that they have not known:
> I will turn darkness into light for them, and crooked things
>> into straight. These things will I do, and will not forsake them.

Heschel calls 42:14 "the boldest figure used by any prophet" and sees in the image of God as a woman in labor the intensity of divine suffering and the extent of divine solidarity with Israel's affliction.[109] In its immediate context, however, the sense of the image surpasses "solidarity with affliction"; it is that of a woman whose pregnancy has gone on too long, who cannot hold back the child anymore, but must burst forth with awesome creative activity. This activity is the majestic power of God, reshaping the face of the earth:

---

108. On this convergence of images, see especially Katheryn P. Darr, "Like Warrior, like Woman: Destruction and Deliverance in Isaiah 42:10-17," *CBQ* 49, 4 (1987): 560-71. Working from the Hebrew text, Darr (571) argues that Isaiah uses the simile of "like a woman in labor" to emphasize the "awesome, havoc-wreaking" power of God's "breath." She contends that the simile applies only to God's desiccating breath in Isa 42:15, however, and not to the redemption of those who are blind, in v. 16. In my view this interpretation reads the verse in isolation from the larger context. For views interpreting the simile of divine "labor" as creative and not simply destructive, see Muilenburg, "Book of Isaiah," 473; Phyllis Trible, *God and the Rhetoric of Sexuality*, OBT (Philadelphia: Fortress, 1978), 64; James Smart, *History and Theology in Second Isaiah: A Commentary on Isaiah 35, 40–66* (Philadelphia: Westminster, 1965), 89; Mayer Gruber, "The Motherhood of God in Second Isaiah," *RB* 90 (1983): 354-55.

109. Heschel, *Prophets*, 1:151.

> See, the former things have come to pass,
> > and new things I now declare;
> Before they spring forth,[110] I tell you of them. . . .
> I have endured like a woman in labor;
> I will amaze and wither at the same time.
> I will make desolate mountains and hills, and will dry up all their
> > grass;
> and I will make the rivers islands, and dry up the pools. (42:9, 14b-15)

Thus in 42:14 the image of God as a travailing mother serves double duty, evoking both the anguish of apocalyptic warfare and devastation, and divine action that is destructive and creative on a cosmic scale. This double assurance of God's power and empathy gives certainty to the promise of divine renewal, even in the midst of destruction.[111] The time for birth is at hand — who can restrain the creative power of God?[112]

Paul at the same time tells the Galatians that the time for birth is at hand. His own "labor" would be futile did not the creative power of God stand behind it and work through it. Given his own "embodied proclamation" of the crucified Christ, it seems wisest to see that the bold metaphor of Gal 4:19 draws on a rich textual tradition that includes Jer 8:21, Isa 42:14, and Isa 45:10. The apostle's cry reminds the Galatians that his labor is also God's labor, and that God is the one who has power to bring from conception to birth, from beginning to completion. Furthermore, this creative power cannot be divorced from the suffering of God and its embodiment in the apostle's missionary preaching.

---

110. The LXX for "spring forth" is ἀνατεῖλαι, which in classical usage could refer metaphorically to childbirth. See H. G. Liddell and R. Scott, *Intermediate Greek-English Lexicon* (repr. Oxford: Clarendon, 1997), 63.

111. Isaiah elsewhere also uses the feminine image to convey this certainty about God's love and faithfulness toward Israel: "But Zion said, 'The Lord has forsaken me, my Lord has forgotten me.' Can a woman forget her sucking child, that she should have no compassion on the son of her womb? Even these may forget, yet I will not forget you" (Isa 49:14-15). Von Rad says concerning these passages, "As Deutero-Isaiah entices and woos the heart of Israel, hardened by excessive suffering, he uses terms which expose the heart of his God almost shamefully. . . . To be sure, Yahweh kept silent when the enemy exulted over his people. Yet, how he had to restrain himself and hide his pain (Isa. 42.14)!" (*Message of the Prophets*, 217).

112. For the link between childbirth and timing, see also Hos 13:13. The Galatians' regressive behavior is similar to that of Ephraim as the "unwise child" who holds back when the time for birth is at hand.

Conclusion

This investigation of Gal 4:19 began with a suggestion that Paul's maternal metaphor has two poles — a "near" point and a "far-off" point. The near point is Paul's physical suffering for the sake of the gospel, through which he displays Christ crucified. In light of the echoes of Jeremiah's and Isaiah's maternal imagery for God, I suggest that the far-off point is God's apocalyptic labor in which the apostle shares, just as Jeremiah enacts God's anguish at the destruction of Jerusalem. This dual focus illuminates the shift in subjects of the two clauses of Gal 4:19, in which Paul is the subject of the first clause, and God is the implied subject of the passive verb in the second clause. The prophetic echoes of ὠδίνω, however, imply that God is also the dual subject of the first clause. In other words, Paul's embodied proclamation represents and enacts God's "labor," both as divine anguish in the midst of apocalyptic warfare, and as divine power creating and nurturing the new people of God.[113] It is a theophany of the God of Jeremiah and Isaiah, who also portray God's intense involvement with humanity in anthropomorphic, relational metaphors. The maternal imagery employed by the apostle in 4:19, like the paternal imagery of 4:6, draws on this biblical tradition of language about God, and cannot be understood apart from it.

Yet although the echoes of Jeremiah and Isaiah amplify Paul's metaphor, they do not tell the whole story. Paul interprets his scars as the branding marks of Jesus. From his perspective, his suffering is precisely a christophany, because what the prophets foretold is now coming to pass in the advent of Christ. Therefore the "far-off" and "invisible" referent of ὠδίνω as divine suffering has come near and become visible in the concrete, historical crucifixion of Jesus of Nazareth. This necessitates a revision of the earlier description of Paul's imagery, because in a sense both "poles" of his metaphor have material referents — Paul's physical suffering and Christ's physical crucifixion.

Nonetheless, in another sense the second pole remains far off, precisely because Christ's crucifixion was a unique event in human history. As far as we know, neither Paul nor his converts were physically present at Golgotha; therefore, in this sense Christ's death remains unfamiliar and in-

---

113. See also Phil 3:10; Rom 8:17. Colossians 1:24 attests to an early Christian tradition that ascribes to Paul's physical suffering a completion of what is lacking in Christ's sufferings.

accessible to them.[114] Rather, this punctiliar event has invaded Paul's experience through the apocalypse of God's Son in him, and it continues to "come home" to his converts through the apostle's preaching. As "Christ is formed in" them, the Galatians too will display over time the unique crucifixion of God's Son through their own interaction and suffering for the sake of the gospel.[115]

Insofar as 4:19 concludes the pericope, which begins, "Become like me, because I have become like you," it draws on the shared history of the apostle and his converts. This "history," as noted in chapter two above, displays two kinds of "continuity": a "temporal" continuity of promise, connecting both Paul and the Galatians with their origin in God's gracious call, and a "relational" continuity, creating unity between Paul and his converts "in Christ." Both kinds of "continuity" are maintained by God's gracious action, but both also require concrete expression in the lives and relationships of the apostle and the Galatians over time. Paul's apocalyptic "labor pains" build on this shared history, with its "temporal" and "relational" continuity, by contributing a vivid image to his preaching of the apocalyptic gospel's lasting capacity to intersect with and realign the linear narratives of his converts.

The vivid image of protracted labor pains proclaims this "staying power" in two ways: it conveys the notion of "temporal" continuity by bringing together punctiliar and linear motifs, and it conveys the cosmic and personal dimensions of life "in Christ" by bringing together divine and human action. The punctiliar event that Paul preaches is God's new creative invasion of the cosmos through the crucifixion of Jesus. But God as revealed in the crucifixion is entirely consonant with God as revealed in the suffering and proclamation of the prophets, just as the God who "apocalypsed his son" to Paul is the God who first set aside and called the apostle from birth.[116]

---

114. The same observation obtains, of course, for all of Paul's subsequent readers. Paul's reference to his preaching as a "placard" of Christ crucified before his converts' eyes (3:1) remains a metaphor, as does his interpretation of his own scars as the "stigmata" of Jesus (6:17).

115. The question of whether such "formation" is ever complete remains open. Nonetheless, one still can say that Paul has in mind the practice of sacrificial love, as displayed in the fruit of the Spirit (Gal 5:13-25). See Gaventa, *Our Mother*, 37.

116. In Fretheim's words (*Suffering of God*, 166), "we should note that the prophet's life as embodied Word of God is partial and broken. . . . Yet, in the prophet we see decisive conti-

Therefore, by referring to God's apocalyptic "labor pains," ὠδίνω evokes both the physical suffering of Christ on the cross and the continuity of divine faithfulness as portrayed by the promise to Abraham and by the prophets. By referring to Paul's intensely personal, indeed physical, demonstration of the gospel in 4:13-14, 20, it evokes the apostle's relationship with his converts, through which the crucifixion of Christ is displayed over time. As the climax of his appeal to "become like me," it tells them that, just as his participation in Christ involves suffering for the sake of the gospel, so the formation of Christ in them will take a cruciform shape. Just as the transforming and sustaining power of God is paradoxically displayed through Paul's "weakness," so it will be with the Galatian congregations. In this way Paul's maternal imagery evokes the relational matrix through which the apocalyptic gospel intersects with and realigns the narrative of God's children — a set of relationships characterized by the sacrificial, proactive and boundary-crossing love of the "Son of God, who loved me, and gave himself for me" (2:20).

---

nuities with what occurs in the Christ-event. God's act in Jesus Christ is the culmination of a long-standing relationship of God with the world that is much more widespread in the OT than is commonly recognized." Similarly Mauser (*Gottesbild*, 17) claims: "The Old Testament God in human form (ἐν μορφῇ ἀνθρώπου) is the proclamation of the incarnate God. And the Old Testament person *(Mensch)*, who in a certain sense receives his or her life in the form of God (ἐν μορφῇ θεοῦ), is the messenger of the human Jesus, whom the Christian confession identifies as true God *(vere deus)*."

Chapter Five

"Children of the Free Woman"

I f in Gal 4:19 Paul confronts his readers with a "metaphor squared," in the "allegory" of 4:21–5:1 he confronts them with a network of extended metaphors multiplied exponentially.[1] Coming together in this passage are the

---

1. The expression "metaphor squared" was coined by Gaventa, *Our Mother,* 4-5. Paul's "allegory" is closer to "typology" in that it proceeds under the banner of Gal 3:8: "Scripture prepreached the gospel to Abraham." See Hays's discussion in *Echoes of Scripture,* 105-11. Hays's definition of typology as a "species of the genus *allegorical interpretation*" is particularly helpful: "the allegorical sense latent in the text's figures is discovered not by a reading that ascends from the material to the spiritual but by a reading that grasps the preliminary in relation to the ultimate" (215 n. 87).

By way of contrast, both Daniel Boyarin and Elizabeth Castelli see "allegory" as the key to interpreting this passage. Drawing on contemporary literary theory, both argue that Paul's "allegory" does indeed "ascend from the material to the spiritual," and furthermore, that in so doing it closes off and reduces the meanings of its "characters," rendering them as mere "ciphers." For discussion see Boyarin, *A Radical Jew: Paul and the Politics of Identity* (Berkeley and Los Angeles: University of California Press, 1994), 32-36; and Castelli, "Allegories of Hagar: Reading Galatians 4:21-31 with Postmodern Feminist Eyes," in *The New Literary Criticism and the New Testament,* ed. Elizabeth S. Malbon and Edgar V. McKnight, JSNTSup 109 (Sheffield: Sheffield Academic Press, 1994), 232. In my view the embodied character of Paul's discourse, as well as the expectation of future apocalyptic judgment to be found even in Galatians (e.g., 5:5, 21; 6:6-9), argue against such an antimaterialistic reading of Paul. One may compare Castelli's reductionistic reading of Paul's "allegory" with Soskice's open-ended understanding of metaphor.

It is interesting to note that Deutero-Isaiah also appropriates the patriarchal traditions "typologically," although it is not possible to determine in what form those traditions were available to the prophet. In *Prophet Reads Scripture,* 60, Sommer defines typological allu-

Genesis stories of Abraham's two sons and their respective mothers, Isaiah's story of the "barren woman" (Isa 54:1) with its implicit references to both Sarah and Jerusalem, and the metaphors of "Jerusalem now" and "Jerusalem above." The complexity of the allegory increases with the probability that the apostle is retelling and reinterpreting Scriptures that his converts have heard from the other missionaries in Galatia.[2] Add to this the fact that he sets the context for this interpretation of the Genesis narrative with his own retrospective "story," and the allegory invites a multistoried reading of its function within the larger framework of the letter.[3]

Thus Paul's auditors find themselves in an endlessly reverberating echo chamber, or to change the metaphor, a hall of mirrors. Although the Teachers probably first claimed the slogan "Jerusalem is our mother," Paul distinguishes between "present Jerusalem in slavery with her children," and free "Jerusalem above" — "*she* is *our* mother."[4] By the time both the Teachers and Paul speak of "Jerusalem our mother," this feminine image of the holy city has been developed in a variety of ways within Second Temple Judaism.[5] Furthermore, the apostle refracts the birth narratives of Isaac and Ishmael through the lens of Isa 54:1. This lens in itself is multifaceted, insofar as Isaiah appropriates the motif of the barren woman who has chil-

---

sions as positing "correspondences between diverse people, events, and places, thus asserting that one may be understood in light of the other or that one provides a pattern that the other follows." Furthermore, he argues (134) that such a pattern of correspondence characterizes Deutero-Isaiah's use of the widespread traditions concerning the patriarchs: "The typological relationship between Abraham and the exiles is straightforward: just as Abraham and Sarah were vouchsafed an unlikely — indeed unbelievable — promise of abundant progeny, so are the exiles; just as the ancestors went in small numbers from Mesopotamia to Canaan, so will the Judean community; just as the ancestors trusted in YHWH and acted accordingly, so must the exiles."

2. Barrett, "The Allegory of Abraham, Sarah, and Hagar in the Argument of Galatians," in *Essays on Paul*, 154-70.

3. See B. Longenecker, *Triumph*, 168 n. 41: "Paul seems to assume that, if his audience will ever be in a position to hear new tones of meaning in the Hagar-Sarah narrative, it is at this point in the letter. This is significant, since presumably such would not have been the case at the outset of the letter. In this regard, Paul's plea that they become like him (4.12) continues to resound even throughout the interpretative exercise in 4.21-31."

4. So Mussner, *Galaterbrief*, 26; Martyn, *Galatians*, 441, 462-63.

5. See Norman Porteous, "Jerusalem-Zion: The Growth of a Symbol," *Living the Mystery: Collected Essays* (Oxford: Blackwell, 1967), 93-111; Callaway, *Sing, O Barren One*; Humphrey, *Ladies and the Cities*; Kamila Blessing, "The Background of the Barren Woman Motif in Galatians 4:27" (Ph.D. diss., Duke University, 1996).

dren miraculously and transforms it into a promise to the exiles.[6] The prophet also develops themes and images from earlier prophets, so that the paradoxical motif of the barren mother is richly intertextual as well as tradition laden.[7]

Clearly the labyrinthine character of Gal 4:21–5:1 invites exploration on many levels. In this chapter I will explore only one level: the contribution of Isa 54:1 to Paul's interpretation of Sarah's story in Gal 4:21–5:1. Linked to this is the role of the prophetic text in Paul's contrast between the impotence and futility of the Teachers' message and the generative and nurturing power of the nonnomistic gospel. I will argue that Isa 54:1 encapsulates the combined stories of "the barren woman" and the city of Jerusalem, and that this "story" functions in Galatians both as a picture of God's transforming power and as a promise of a lasting community and habitation for God's people in "Jerusalem above." The movement in this story of reversal — in which the barren and desolate woman becomes a joyful mother and the ravaged city becomes a nurturing metropolis overflowing with inhabitants — undergirds the movement in Paul's letter from his anxious labor pains to his confidence that his converts will remain steadfast in the freedom of the gospel (Gal 4:11, 19; 5:10). As a picture of God's power and a promise of an enduring dwelling place, the saga of "mother" Jerusalem in 4:26-27 prepares the way for Paul's description of the Spirit-led community (5:13–6:16).

As will become clear, the allegory as a whole plays a pivotal role in the letter, drawing together themes from the preceding section, in particular the question of the Galatians' origin in the faith, and anticipating the ultimate *telos* of new life in the Spirit — eternal life (6:8). Earlier in the letter, Paul's testimony delineated two "pasts" for both himself and his converts — one under the dominion of the enslaving powers that belong to the "present evil age," and the other originating in God's gracious call. Galatians 4:21–5:1 recapitulates this retrospective narrative through its contrast between the slavery of the son born κατὰ σάρκα and the freedom of the son born through the promise, κατὰ πνεῦμα. At the same time, however, the citation of Isa 54:1 in Gal 4:27 turns the Galatians' attention to the

6. In addition to the stories of Sarah (Gen 11:30), Rebekah (Gen 25:21), Rachel (Gen 29:31; 30:22-23), Samson's mother (Judg 13), and Hannah (1 Sam 1), one may note also Ps 113:9: "He gives the barren woman a home, and makes her the joyful mother of children."

7. See Sommer, *Prophet Reads Scripture*, passim, for Deutero-Isaiah's appropriation of earlier prophetic texts and patriarchal traditions.

future, preparing the way for a contrast between two destinies. One destiny belongs to those who continue to live in slavery to the powers of this age; in Paul's eyes they have no real future, but are destined to be "cast out" (4:30) and disinherited (5:21). The future belongs to the children of "Jerusalem above"; this future, named as the "hope of righteousness" (5:5) and guaranteed by the inheritance of the Spirit, is to shape the present life of the Christian communities in Galatia.

Due to the multilayered quality of the passage itself, the following investigation is unavoidably complex. It will proceed along five lines of inquiry: (1) What is the place and function of 4:21–5:1 in the letter as a whole? (2) What is the place of Isa 54:1 in the structure of Gal 4:21–5:1? (3) How does Isa 54:1 relate to Sarah's story in the Genesis narrative? (4) What is the relationship between the barren woman and the maternity of Paul? And, to be examined in chapter six, (5) What is the connection between Paul's allegory, with its two "family trees," and the opposition between the flesh and the Spirit in Gal 5–6?

Galatians 4:21–5:1 in the Structure of the Letter

In Relation to 3:6–4:20

Paul's interpretation of Gen 16–21 and Isa 54:1 is the second of two roughly parallel exegetical sections (the first being Gal 3:6–4:7) that deal "with the genetic identity of the Galatian churches."[8] The first exegetical section tells the Galatians that through their baptism into Christ they are "children of God" and therefore also children of Abraham (3:26-29).[9] The second section tells them that they are children of the free, not the slave, woman. Through the thematic connection between these two interpretations of Abraham's "children," 4:21–5:1 forms an *inclusio* with the argument that

---

8. Martyn, *Galatians*, 432. See p. 296 also for parallels between the passages, with 3:1-5 corresponding to 4:8-20, and 3:6–4:7 corresponding to 4:21–5:1. In this way the Sarah-Hagar allegory forms an *inclusio* with the previous exegetical section. R. Longenecker (*Galatians*, 199) notes a "rough parallel" between the two exegetical sections.

9. The conclusion of the first exegetical section emphasizes the converts' identity as God's children and heirs, not as Abraham's children. The Spirit does not impel them to cry, "Abba, Abraham!" but "Abba, Father!" (4:6-7). On Paul's modulation of "descent from faithful Abraham" into "descent from God," see Martyn, *Galatians*, 302-6.

begins at 3:1.[10] It picks up the association of "law" with "flesh," in opposition to the Spirit (3:2-4); the motif of "inheritance" (3:18, 29; 4:7); the contrast between slavery and freedom (4:1-10); and the use of birth imagery in reference to the founding of churches (4:19).[11]

These observations suggest a strong connection between 4:21–5:1 and 3:1–4:20. There are differing opinions in the secondary literature as to whether the allegory functions primarily as a supplementary illustration or adds something substantively new to the preceding theological argument. Luther thought that the addition of an allegorical picture added persuasive power to Paul's proclamation of freedom from the law.[12] Burton treats it as "a supplementary argument . . . apparently as an after-thought."[13] Betz, on the other hand, sees it as a forceful use of the Abraham story to form the climax of the *probatio* beginning in 3:1.[14] Since C. K. Barrett proposed that the Galatians first heard the Genesis passages from Paul's opponents, many have seen Paul's exegesis as a strategic defensive move by the apostle.[15] For example, James D. G. Dunn argues that Paul has been forced by his opponents' use of the Genesis passages into giving his converts an alternative interpretation of the birth narratives of Isaac and Ishmael.[16]

But Paul's argument is not purely defensive, for even as the apostle takes up a story first taught to the Galatians by the Teachers, he turns it against them and to his own purpose by equating the law-inscribing mission and its adherents with Hagar and Ishmael.[17] In 4:21–5:1, by designating Hagar and Sarah as two covenants, and by using the "missioning" verb γεννάω to describe their respective pregnancies and deliveries, Paul speaks of two distinct Jewish Christian missions to the Gentiles.[18] The "Hagar

10. Martyn, *Galatians*, 296, 409.

11. On the motif of birth imagery, see Martyn, *Galatians*, 451-54; idem, "Covenants of Hagar and Sarah," *Theological Issues*, 198; Engberg-Pedersen, *Paul and the Stoics*, 328 n. 7.

12. Luther, *Galatians*, 414.

13. Burton, *Galatians*, 251. So also Oepke, *Galater*, 147.

14. Betz, *Galatians*, 238-40.

15. Barrett, "Allegory of Abraham, Sarah, and Hagar," 158; followed by Dunn, *Galatians*, 243; R. Longenecker, *Galatians*, 200; Martyn, *Galatians*, 433; Hays, *Galatians*, 300.

16. Dunn, *Galatians*, 243.

17. Hays (*Galatians*, 300) says that in 4:21 "Paul goes on the offensive, taking the battle to the Missionaries' home turf."

18. As Martyn has noted (*Galatians*, 451-54), in Paul's retelling of the stories of Sarah and Hagar, he substitutes the verb γεννάω, in both its masculine (vv. 23, 29) and feminine (v. 24) forms, for the verb τίκτω, which occurs in the LXX. On the basis of Paul's other uses

covenant" represents the law-observant mission of the Teachers, carried out in the name of the church in Jerusalem ("Jerusalem now") and bearing children into slavery to the law. The "Sarah covenant" represents the circumcision-free mission, led by Paul, carried out under the sponsorship of "the heavenly Jerusalem" who "guides the true church below," and bearing children into freedom.[19] As indicated by the present tense verbs throughout the pericope, the allegory primarily concerns a division between different Jewish Christian missions rather than the relationship between Christianity and Judaism, or the destiny of the literal city of Jerusalem.[20] According to many interpreters, the climax of the passage comes in v. 30, and the imperative "cast out the slave woman and her son" is Paul's command to the Galatian congregations to expel the circumcising Teachers and their followers.[21] If so, then the primary emphasis of the pericope falls on the negative command of v. 30. There are weighty reasons, however, for arguing that v. 30 is not the climax of the pericope, and indeed that the imperative ἔκβαλε in that verse is not spoken as an exclusionary command to Paul's auditors.

First, the negative command to "cast out" in v. 30 is enveloped by three positive triple imperatives in 4:27/Isa 54:1 ("rejoice, break forth, and

---

of γεννάω in Phlm 10 and 1 Cor 4:14-15, Martyn (451) has argued convincingly that the apostle uses this verb to speak of the "genesis of Christians and of Christian churches through the power of the gospel entrusted to him by God."

19. Ibid., 466.

20. Following Mussner, *Galaterbrief,* 332; *pace* Lightfoot, *Galatians,* 184; Schlier, *Galater,* 160; Burton, *Galatians,* 267; Betz, *Galatians,* 251. Martyn is followed by Dunn, *Galatians,* 250; and Hays, *Galatians,* 303, although both see "Jerusalem now" as also symbolizing Israel. Commenting on Mussner, Barclay agrees that Paul is attacking Jewish Christians, not Jews, but perceptively adds, "Paul is attacking Jewish-Christians for their Jewish presuppositions, and for wanting to make Gentile believers live like Jews"; this amounts to "an implicit attack on law-observant Judaism for its cultural imperialism" (*Obeying the Truth,* 250 n. 50).

21. This has been argued most forcefully by Martyn, *Galatians,* 445-46. See also Hays, *Galatians,* 306. On the basis of a parallel with Rom 12:1, Charles Cosgrove, "The Law Has Given Sarah No Children," *NovT* 29, 3 (1987): 232, argues that διό, ἀδελφοί begins the next section, leaving 4:30 as the sole climax of 4:21-30. Cosgrove's argument falters in that he fails to attend to the immediate parallel address to the Galatians as ἀδελφοί in 4:28, which drives home the issue of identity as central to the passage. Cosgrove (234) contends, rather, "Here, as in 3:1–4:11, not the question of status ('justification,' 'sonship') but whether 'life in the Spirit' depends on law-keeping is in view." Yet the questions of identity and "life in the Spirit" are inseparable, as Cosgrove himself maintains; "sonship" is intimately related to "life in the Spirit," because the status of "sonship" brings with it the inheritance of the Spirit.

shout!") and two imperatives in Gal 5:1 ("stand fast, do not submit"). When these abundant imperatives receive equal weight, they suggest that the primary purpose of the allegory is to reaffirm to the Galatian Christians their identity as children of the free woman.[22] Second, it is interesting to note further that ἔκβαλε is a second person *singular* imperative. The only other occurrences of this verb form are the imperatives in 4:27, which, like 4:30, are embedded in a scriptural citation. These earlier singular imperatives are addressed to the barren woman, not to the Galatians themselves; as such, they witness to Paul's auditors concerning the partial fulfillment of Isaiah's prophecy. When Paul does want to tell his Galatian congregations what to do, he consistently uses second person *plural* imperatives (4:12, 21; 5:1, 13, 15, 16; 6:1, 2) or third person singular (6:4, 6, 17).[23] On occasion he also uses the hortatory subjunctive in the first person plural (6:9-10). In no other instance does he use the second person *singular* to issue a direct command to his congregations.[24] These observations must call into question the assumption that the imperative in 4:30 directs the Galatians to cast out the Teachers and their followers. I suggest, rather, that the singular imperatives embedded in the scriptural citations of 4:27 and 4:30 depict for the Galatians the contrasting destinies of the children of the free woman and the children of the slave.[25] If so, the weight of Paul's exhortation falls on the plural imperatives in 5:1, with their affirmation of the Galatians' new identity and freedom.[26] Thus the restatement of Christ's

---

22. See, e.g., Barclay, *Obeying the Truth*, 92: "Sarah and Hagar represent two covenants, the basis of two very different family identities." Charles Cousar argues helpfully that the repeated vocative addresses to the "brothers and sisters" in vv. 28 and 31 supply the application of the allegory, with 5:1 as a transitional conclusion (*Galatians*, Interpretation [Atlanta: John Knox, 1982], 103).

23. The use of the singular here may highlight Paul's warning that each individual will bear his or her own judgment before God. See David Kuck, "'Each Will Bear His Own Burden': Paul's Creative Use of an Apocalyptic Motif," *NTS* 40, 2 (1994): 289-97. See also Schlier, *Galater*, 202.

24. In 1 Cor 5:13, the one place in his letters where an imperative embedded within a scriptural citation clearly *does* command action (exclusionary at that!), Paul changes the verb to a plural from its singular form in the LXX (Deut 13:5; 17:6; 19:19; 21:21-24; 22:21, 24; 24:7).

25. For more extended discussion of this proposal, see Susan Eastman, "'Cast Out the Slave Woman and Her Son': The Dynamics of Inclusion and Exclusion in Gal 4:30," *JSNT* 28 (2006): 309-36.

26. Thus Betz, *Galatians*, 251. Hays (*Galatians*, 306) argues that v. 31 is a restatement of vv. 26, 28.

liberating activity and the two imperatives of 5:1 make it the climax of both the pericope and indeed of the letter, by summing up what precedes and introducing what follows.[27] This proposal finds support from the extensive connections between 4:21–5:1 and 5:2–6:18.

In Relation to 5:1–6:18

In addition to the connections between Paul's scriptural argument in 4:21–5:1 and his earlier reworking of the Abraham story, there are also strong connections between the passage and the latter part of the letter. These connections are carried forward by the thematic links of "law" with "flesh," and "promise" with "Spirit," and by the related themes of "freedom" and "inheritance." First, the association of "law" with "flesh," and "promise" with "Spirit," sets the stage for the conflict between the "flesh" and the "Spirit" in 5:16-25. The link between "flesh" and "law" is circumcision; the allegory is addressed to those who want to be "under law" (4:21), while in 4:22–5:1, to be "under law" is equated with being born into slavery by the power of the flesh.[28] In 4:29 those born according to the flesh persecute those born according to the Spirit; in 5:10-12 the circumcision mission is "troubling" the Galatians, while Paul is "persecuted" because he does not preach circumcision; and in 6:12 those concerned with fleshly appearance "compel" the Galatians to be circumcised.

In 5:18, however, the apostle insists that those who are led by the Spirit are not "under law." Just as, having begun by the Spirit rather than the law, they cannot be completed (ἐπιτελεῖσθε) by the flesh (3:3), so now being led

---

27. See Martyn, *Galatians*, 407. On 5:1 as the theme of the letter, see Hays, *Galatians*, 306; Engberg-Pedersen, *Paul and the Stoics*, 329 n. 10.

28. The association of "flesh" with "circumcision" was well established in Jewish tradition: "Thus shall my covenant be in your flesh for an everlasting covenant. But an uncircumcised male who is not circumcised in the flesh of his foreskin, that person shall be cut off from his people" (Gen 17:13-14). Ezekiel thunders against the presence of "foreigners uncircumcised in heart and uncircumcised in flesh" as a profanation of the temple. One readily can imagine the Teachers using such texts to persuade the Galatians to be circumcised. In Philo the circumcision of the flesh is seen as an aid against the desires of the flesh (*Spec.* 1.9). See also Gen 17:23-25; Lev 12:3; Gen 34:24 LXX; Jer 9:25 LXX; Sir 44:20; Jdt 14:10; *Jub.* 15:13-33; 4 *Ezra* 1:31; 1QH X, 23. See also *b. Shebu'ot* 13a and *b. Sanhedrin* 99a for later references to the "covenant of flesh." For helpful discussion see Barclay, *Obeying the Truth*, 203-4.

by the Spirit they will be set free from "completing" the desires of the flesh (πνεύματι περιπατεῖτε καὶ ἐπιθυμίαν σαρκὸς οὐ μὴ τελέσητε, 5:16). The setting for this liberation is precisely in the Galatians' communal life as the arena of conflict between "the flesh" and "the Spirit" (5:17), echoing the conflict between the one "born according to the flesh" and the one "born according to the Spirit" in 4:23 and 29. Thus the argument about "genetic identity" in 4:21–5:1 anticipates the ethical outworking of that identity in 5:1–6:10.[29] Because the Galatians are "children of promise" (4:28), they have received the promised Holy Spirit (4:6-7) so that they will bear the fruit of the Spirit (5:22-23).

Second, the theme of "freedom," which comes to the fore in the identification of the Galatians as children of the free woman in 4:26 and 31, dominates the description of life in the Spirit beginning at 5:13.[30] In 3:23–4:10 the apostle outlines freedom in negative terms, as freedom from slavery to the law and the *stoicheia;* in 5:13–6:10 he outlines the positive consequences of being "children of the free woman." It is the children of the free woman who receive the inheritance — the promised Spirit — and thus through the community-building fruit of the Spirit proleptically display the new creation. The children of the slave woman, however, have a different destiny. In 4:30 the slave woman and her son, born by the power of the flesh, are cast out from the inheritance promised to those born by the power of the Spirit.[31] Similarly, in 5:4-5 those seeking to be justified by law are cut off from Christ and the "hope of righteousness."

As a "Pauline Bridge"

The foregoing analysis indicates that 4:21–5:1 has strong connections with both the "theological" section beginning at 3:1 and the "paraenetic" sec-

---

29. Regarding the relationship between 4:29 and 5:13-24, Robert Jewett notes, "the character of 'flesh' is formally the same in both passages. In both, it stands in opposition to Christ and his realm. In both passages it is the flesh which takes the offensive against the spirit and in both it reduces man to slavery" (*Paul's Anthropological Terms: A Study of Their Use in Conflict Settings,* AGJU 10 [Leiden: Brill, 1971], 102-3).

30. Hansen (*Abraham in Galatians,* 151) highlights the antitheses of ἐλευθερία-δουλεία and πνεῦμα-σάρξ in 4:21-31 as providing the basis for the "ethical appeal" of 5:13–6:10.

31. The translation of κατὰ σάρκα and κατὰ πνεῦμα as "by the power of the flesh" and "by the power of the Spirit" is that of Martyn, *Galatians,* 435.

tion that follows.[32] The pericope moves the Galatians forward from identifying themselves as Abraham's offspring to the present social implications of their identity and destiny as "children of the free woman." This transitional function has been proposed most explicitly by Troels Engberg-Pedersen: "We have two opposed views here: either to take 4:21-31 to go with the whole section that begins in 3:1 or to take it rather with what comes after the section (and as being introduced by 4:12-20). Solution? 4:21-31 is *a Pauline bridge*."[33] This connection is clearest in the "transitional conclusion" supplied by 5:1: "For freedom Christ has set us free. Stand fast, therefore, and do not be subject again to a yoke of slavery." This climactic appeal suggests that 4:21–5:1 has a transitional function in two ways. First, it connects the themes of identity in 3:6–4:7 with the concerns for behavior in the Galatian congregations in 5:13–6:10.[34] Second, it turns the attention of Paul's converts from a focus on the past to a focus on the future. In what way does Isa 54:1 contribute to such a transition? The first step is to ask what part it plays within the structure of the scriptural argument in 4:21–5:1.

---

32. Given these links between Gal 4:21-31 and the rest of the letter, there is a persuasive edge to R. Longenecker's argument that the pericope forms part of an "appeals and exhortations" section, which in turn is part of 4:12–6:10 as a major "request" section. The difficulty with Longenecker's position is that it does not give due weight to the parallels between the two exegetical sections, 3:6–4:7 and 4:21-31 (*Galatians*, 184-86, 199). Longenecker is followed by Matera, *Galatians*, 173, although Matera argues that the "Rebuke and Appeal" section begins at 4:1. Hansen (*Abraham in Galatians*, 141-46) also follows Longenecker in arguing that the "request" section begins at 4:12.

As noted earlier, the distinction between "theology" and "paraenesis" in Paul's thought is itself problematic. See Richard Hays, *The Moral Vision of the New Testament* (San Francisco: HarperSanFrancisco, 1996), 18-19; Engberg-Pedersen, *Paul and the Stoics*, 136-38, 326-27 n. 6.

33. Engberg-Pederson, *Paul and the Stoics*, 328 n. 7. See also Engberg-Pedersen's discussion on 133-34. Cosgrove makes a similar point: "the motif of sonship in freedom provides a most appropriate conceptual means of transition from the ideas developed in the letter up to this point and the concrete exhortations to follow (see 5:1; 5:13), facilitating in the widest sense the movement from indicative to imperative" ("Law Has Given," 235).

34. The notions of identity and behavior derive from Barclay's analysis of the situation in Galatia (*Obeying the Truth*, 75).

Isaiah 54:1 in the Structure of Galatians 4:21–5:1

The apostle organizes his treatment of the birth narratives of Ishmael and Isaac in two opposing columns, signaled by his use of the military verb συστοιχέω in 4:25.[35] These two columns of opposing "characters" can be set forth as follows:

v. 22 "For it is written, 'Abraham had two sons'":[36]

v. 22 son of the slave girl	son of the free woman	A
v. 23 born "according to the flesh"	born "through promise"	B

v. 24 "These are two covenants"

v. 24 from Sinai
      bearing children for slavery
v. 25 Hagar (Mount Sinai in Arabia)[37]
      present Jerusalem
      in slavery with her children
v. 26

                        Jerusalem above
                        free
                        "She is our mother"

---

35. For the interpretation of συστοιχέω in light of Pythagorean columns of opposing principles laid out in Paul's allegory in opposing columns, see Lightfoot, *Galatians*, 181; Lagrange, *Galates*, 127-28; Betz, *Galatians*, 245; Dunn, *Galatians*, 244; Martyn, *Galatians*, 438-40, 457-66; Hays, *Galatians*, 303.

36. I have identified scriptural markers by underlining, vocative addresses by bold type, and imperatives by italics.

37. The textual evidence is fairly evenly divided between manuscripts that include Hagar in 4:25 ("Hagar is Mount Sinai in Arabia") and those that omit Hagar ("Sinai is a mountain in Arabia"). The inclusion of Hagar is more difficult and therefore, in my view, more likely. According to this reading, the neuter τὸ goes with "Hagar" rather than Sinai, thereby utilizing the name "Hagar" as a cipher representing Sinai. The association of Hagar and Sinai with Arabia might further Paul's attack on the other missionaries' teaching by associating Ishmael with non-Jews. For extensive discussion of this possibility, see especially R. Longenecker, *Galatians*, 205-6; Peder Borgen, "Some Hebrew and Pagan Features in Philo's and Paul's Interpretation of Hagar and Ishmael," in *The New Testament and Hellenistic Judaism*, ed. Peder Borgen and Søren Giversen (Aarhus: Aarhus University Press, 1995), 151-64; Martyn, *Galatians*, 437-38. Both Mussner, *Galaterbrief*, 322-25; and Borse, *Galater*, 169-71, argue for the shorter reading.

v. 27 "For it is written":

v. 27		*Rejoice, break forth and shout*
		barren one who does not bear
		not in labor
	has a husband	desolate one
	fewer children	many more children
v. 28		**You, brothers and sisters**, are
		children of promise, like Isaac
v. 29	born according to flesh	born according to the Spirit A′
	persecutes	persecuted

v. 30 "But what does the Scripture say?"

v. 30	*cast out* (implied object of verb)	*cast out* (implied subject of verb)
	not inherit	
v. 31		**We, brothers and sisters**, are
		children of the free woman B′

5:1 Transitional conclusion

| v. 1 | | For freedom Christ has set us free |
| | yoke of slavery | *Stand fast, do not submit again* |

Paul's "table of opposites" is usually laid out in a condensed fashion so that the antinomies are directly opposite each other, including antitypes that are implied but not named. The advantage of such a condensed version is that it allows one to see at a glance the pattern of polar opposites. The disadvantage is that it tempts the interpreter to fill in the blanks without first asking if Paul had a reason for leaving them blank.[38] Thus, for example, Lightfoot sets the pattern by supplying "Sarah, the freewoman" opposite "Hagar, the bondwoman," and "Ishmael, the child after the flesh" opposite "Isaac, the child of promise."[39] The usual explanation given for

---

38. This disadvantage is noted correctly by Karen Jobes, "Jerusalem Our Mother," *WTJ* 55 (1993): 301: "The significance of the unfinished character of the parallel is often overlooked as interpreters have not hesitated to fill in the Sarah-side of the construction using the force of logical parity."

39. Lightfoot, *Galatians*, 181. Lightfoot also further qualifies the two covenants as "old" and "new," and "present Jerusalem" as "earthly Jerusalem" in contrast with "heavenly Jerusa-

Paul's omission of these important names is that argued by Barrett: apparently the Galatians already know the story from the Teachers, since Paul simply assumes their familiarity with the main characters and hurries on to make his points.[40] When the allegory is laid out verse by verse, however, the lacunae in the parallel columns become more obvious, and perhaps also the logic and flow of the apostle's argument may become apparent in new ways.

A glance at the passage as outlined above demonstrates that it is structured by three appeals to Scripture (vv. 22, 27, 30), two vocative addresses (vv. 28, 31), and six imperatives (three in 4:27; one in 4:30; two in 5:1). The first and third scriptural references to the stories of Abraham's two sons in Genesis form a rough chiasm surrounding the central citation of Isa 54:1. Perhaps because they are so problematic, these Genesis references have received considerable attention in the secondary literature; concomitantly, the imperative of 4:30 — "cast out the slave woman and her son" — is given more weight than the triple imperative of 4:27.

As Barrett argues, the story of Abraham, Hagar, and Sarah "is a part of the Old Testament that Paul would have been unlikely to introduce of his own accord," because "its plain, surface meaning supports not Paul but the Judaizers."[41] The characters and concepts associated with these references fall primarily in the left-hand column. They include "Hagar," "Sinai," "Arabia," "present Jerusalem," "born according to the flesh," "slavery," "cast out," and "shall not inherit." In other words, they refer to all that which, identified with "present Jerusalem," is in slavery to the powers that govern "this present evil age" (1:4), and is thus fated to be "cast out" and "cut off" (4:30; 5:4).

The citation of Isa 54:1, however, has received relatively little notice, despite the likelihood that it is introduced by Paul himself, not the Teachers.[42] Accordingly, little attention is paid to its triple imperatives: "Rejoice, break

---

lem," thus perhaps illustrating the dangers of supplying words that are not actually in the text. As Hays argues (*Galatians*, 302), the contrast is not between an "old" and a "new" covenant, but between the old covenant of Sinai and the older covenant God made with Abraham. See also Dunn, *Galatians*, 249. Nonetheless, both Hays (303) and Martyn (*Galatians*, 456) supply "Sarah" and "Ishmael" in their depiction of Paul's oppositional columns.

40. Barrett, "Allegory," 161-65.

41. Ibid., 162.

42. See Jobes, "Jerusalem Our Mother," 301. On Paul's introduction of Isa 54:1, see Barrett, "Allegory," 164-66; R. Longenecker, *Galatians*, 215; Martyn, *Galatians*, 441.

forth, and shout!" The characters and concepts associated with Isa 54:1 fall primarily in the right-hand column as belonging to the eschatological "Jerusalem above," whose children wait for the "hope of righteousness" (5:5).[43] "Freedom," "promise," "inheritance," miraculous birth, and heavenly city — these are the themes that carry Paul's auditors forward by highlighting their characteristics as "children of promise."

"Isaac" (v. 28) is the one proper name from Genesis appearing on this side of the table; even here, however, the Galatians are not identified directly with Isaac, but they are "like Isaac" (κατὰ Ἰσαάκ), because their "birth" is also "through the promise" and therefore κατὰ πνεῦμα. By qualifying the identity of the new community in Christ as "like Isaac," Paul tells his converts that their continuity with the family tree of Abraham comes solely through the continuity of promise.[44] Nonetheless, for the remainder of the letter the stories about Abraham's offspring cease to play a direct role in Paul's preaching; they have rather an indirect role in the ensuing description of life in the Spirit, through the two elements highlighted by the rough chiasm noted above — the conflict between flesh and Spirit (vv. 23, 29), and the Galatians' continuing identity as "children of the free woman" (vv. 22, 31).

On the other hand, Isa 54:1 provides the characteristics of the city that belongs to the future. This city is overflowing with inhabitants, a living demonstration of divine plenitude in the face of human impossibility.

43. Frequently, Paul introduces Scripture quotations with the formula, "as it is written" (καθὼς γέγραπται). See, e.g., Rom 1:17; 3:4, 10; 4:17; 8:36; 9:13, 33; 11:8. In his other uses of γάρ to introduce a quote, the quote substantiates his immediately preceding claim. See, e.g., Gal 3:10; Rom 9:15, 17; 10:10-13. In my view the γάρ introducing the citation from Isaiah links it with the preceding verse: "Jerusalem above" is "our mother" because she corresponds to the "barren" and "desolate" woman who miraculously bears many children. Isaiah 54:10-12 presents a picture of exalted Jerusalem that recurs in later Jewish and Christian descriptions of "heavenly Jerusalem" (e.g., Tob 13:16-17; Rev 21:10-21) as well as of the elect community (4Q164= 4QpIsa d). The depiction of Jerusalem as a desolate woman, eschatologically transformed into a joyful mother, is frequent in later Jewish texts, both prior and subsequent to the destruction of Jerusalem. See, e.g., 2 *Bar.* 4:1-7; 4 *Bar.* 5:35; 4 *Ezra* 9:26–10:59. See the discussion in Andrew Lincoln, *Paradise Now and Not Yet: Studies in the Role of the Heavenly Dimension in Paul's Thought with Special Reference to His Eschatology*, SNTSMS 43 (Cambridge: Cambridge University Press, 1981), 18-27.

44. The expression "continuity of promise" was coined by Käsemann, "Justification and Salvation History," *Perspectives on Paul*, 68-69, in regard to Rom 4: "Rom. 4:17ff. depicts Abraham's faith as a relation to that God who reveals himself in history, gives offspring and hence sets faith in the continuity of promise and fulfilment, present and future."

Thus if the Galatians want to know the antitype to Hagar, they will need to see the birth narratives refracted through this prophetic lens. When they do, they will see God's transforming power magnified through the story of the barren woman. They also will find their own place in the story affirmed, as Paul emphasizes in the parallel direct addresses, "You, brothers and sisters," and "we, brothers and sisters" (vv. 28, 31). At the heart of the chiasm formed by references to the "son of the free woman" born through the promise/Spirit (4:23, 26-29), Isa 54:1 grounds the apostle's central affirmation of the Galatians' new identity as miraculous children of the free woman, in direct antithesis to the exclusion of the "slave woman and her son." Thus, in contrast to the exclusionary imperative of Gal 4:30, the climactic imperatives of 5:1 accent the stability and freedom of those whose identity derives from the promise and the Spirit.[45]

Isaiah 54:1 in Relationship to Sarah's Story

The centrality of Isa 54:1 in the structure of Gal 4:21–5:1 prompts a closer look at the relationship between the prophetic passage and the stories of Abraham's family. That relationship has elements of both continuity and transformation, as the story of the "barren woman" in Isa 54 both fulfills and transcends Sarah's story. I will look at each of these elements in turn, asking how they relate to Paul's preaching of the staying power of the gospel.

Continuity: The Barren Woman and Sarah

Paul's warrant for introducing Isa 54:1 into the story of Abraham's two wives and two sons is not immediately apparent. Unlike the anonymous woman of the Isaiah passage, Sarah has a husband and she (presumably) also has labor pains.[46] Hagar is the one who is, properly speaking, without a husband, and who in the story is made desolate in the wilderness (ἐπλανᾶτο τὴν ἔρημον, Gen 21:14). But Hagar is nowhere in view in Isa 54:1,

---

45. See Cousar, *Galatians*, 103: "This branch of the family is connected to the new age." The warning that the son of the slave woman, begotten by the power of the flesh, shall "not inherit," is echoed by the warning that those who do the works of the flesh "shall not inherit the kingdom of God" (5:21).

46. Indeed, Sarah's labor pains are explicitly mentioned in Isa 51:2.

nor is Sarah mentioned by name; the poem is in praise of Jerusalem restored, not Sarah.[47] How, therefore, does the apostle connect the Isaiah
passage to Sarah, and to what end?

The textual link between Isa 54:1 and Sarah's story is the word "barren"
(στεῖρα).[48] The connection becomes explicit when Isa 54:1 is placed next to
Gen 11:30:

Εὐφράνθητι στεῖρα ἡ οὐ τίκτουσα (Isa 54:1)

Καὶ ἦν Σάρα στεῖρα καὶ οὐκ ἐτεκνοποίει (Gen 11:30)

By alluding to Jerusalem as a "barren woman," Isaiah implicitly refers to
the ancient motif of the barren matriarch, of which Sarah is the quintessential example. The prophet appropriates this motif as a promise to Jerusalem that God will transform her into a vibrant city. But the "barren
woman" in Isa 54:1 is anonymous; does Isaiah have Sarah in mind here? An
internal intertextual echo suggests a positive answer. In 51:1-3 (LXX) Sarah's story explicitly prefigures God's astonishing way of fulfilling the divine promise in a new time:

> Hearken to me, you who pursue deliverance
>   [οἱ διώκοντες τὸ δίκαιον],
> You who seek the Lord.
> Look to the rock from which you were hewn,
> And to the quarry from which you were dug.
> Look to Abraham your father,
> And to Sarah who bore you [τὴν ὠδίνουσαν ὑμᾶς],
> For he was but one when I called him,
> But I blessed him, and made him many.
> For the Lord will comfort Zion,
> He will comfort all her waste places,
> And will make her wilderness like Eden,
> Her desert like the garden of the Lord.

47. See Hays, *Echoes of Scripture*, 118.

48. On Paul's use here of *gezerah shawah*, see Barrett, "Allegory," 164; Barclay, *Obeying
the Truth*, 92 n. 45; R. Longenecker, *Galatians*, 215. Jobes ("Jerusalem Our Mother," 309) says,
"barrenness is the note that resounds in the intertextual space between Galatians and Isaiah."
It would be more precise to say that "barrenness" resounds in the intertextual space between
Genesis and Isaiah, since στεῖρα does not occur in Galatians outside the citation of Isa 54:1.

Reminding the exiles of their family history, here Isaiah finds in the story of Sarah and Abraham a witness to the power of God to deliver and multiply, to transform desolation into abundance. Hays has argued persuasively for an "internal echo" connecting Isa 51:1-3 with 54:1, "hinting at the correspondence between the city in its exilic desolation and the condition of Sarah before Isaac's birth, a correspondence that also implies the promise of subsequent blessing."[49] Given this correspondence between the city and the barren matriarch, Isaiah paves the way for Paul to connect Sarah with Jerusalem. In Hays's argument:

> Consequently, Paul's link between Sarah and a redeemed Jerusalem surely presupposes Isa. 51:2, even though the text is not quoted in Galatians 4. It is Isaiah's metaphorical linkage of Abraham and Sarah with an eschatologically restored Jerusalem that warrants Paul's use of Isa. 54:1. The effect of Paul's allusive use of the quotation, however, can be better described the other way around: the citation of Isa. 54:1 metaleptically evokes the whole rippling pool of promise found in the latter chapters of that prophetic book.[50]

Central to that "pool of promise" is the assurance that the Gentiles will come to worship the God of Israel (Isa 49:6; 51:4-5; 52:10; 54:2-3; 55:5).[51] On this basis Hays concludes, "The 'many children' of Isa 54:1 are to be found precisely in the Gentile churches."[52] To be precise, the many children in the Galatian congregations demonstrate that the time of fulfillment has begun for the eschatological city, and thus anticipate the ultimate fulfillment of the promise to Sarah that she will indeed become the "mother of a multitude" (Gen 17:16). It is in this sense that the Gentile Christians may be called Sarah's "spiritual children" just as, through Christ, they are "Abra-

49. Hays, *Echoes of Scripture*, 119-20. See also Lagrange, *Galates*, 129; Lincoln, *Paradise Now*, 23.

50. Hays, *Echoes of Scripture*, 120.

51. See Hays, *Galatians*, 304.

52. Hays, *Echoes of Scripture*, 120. Hays clarifies that Paul's use of Isa 54:1 as a reference to Gentiles is an "extraordinary hermeneutical inversion" in which "Paul extends the logic of reversal at work in the text well beyond the referential sense envisioned in the original." In Isa 54:3 LXX, the barren woman's children ("seed") will "inherit the Gentiles" — the Gentiles are possessed by Jerusalem, not included in the redeemed people of God. Again, the extent of Paul's "hermeneutical inversion" is apparent in light of Isa 49:2-23, where the Gentiles come to "mother Jerusalem" and bow down with their faces to the earth.

ham's seed, heirs according to promise" (3:29). In Paul's proclamation, the many "children" of the Gentile Galatian churches adumbrate the eschatological fulfillment of this promise of offspring, apart from the law.

But the other missionaries also may have referred to Jerusalem as "mother" in their preaching to the Gentiles in Galatia.[53] Indeed, Isaiah's promise that the Gentiles will seek Israel's God includes the promise to Jerusalem that "the uncircumcised and the unclean shall enter you no more" (Isa 52:1). Thus one still must ask what *Paul's preaching* gains by setting the Genesis narratives specifically in the context of Isa 54:1.

Transformation: From Children of Sarah to Children of the Free Woman

In wrestling with this question, we may use two earlier observations as exegetical guides: the woman in Isa 54:1 is anonymous, and the place opposite "Hagar" in Paul's oppositional columns is taken by the "barren woman." First, Sarah is not mentioned by name in either Isa 54:1 or Galatians. To put it another way, while indeed "Paul causes Abraham to drop from sight" in the allegory, as Martyn notes, Sarah never even appears on stage.[54] This is not to deny that as the quintessential "barren matriarch" she is implied by Isa 54:1, particularly as it appears in Paul's allegory. But if the apostle simply wanted to call on Sarah by name as witness to the power of God to multiply Abraham's children, he had 51:1-3 ready to hand as a persuasive scriptural "proof." Why does he not use it rather than 54:1? Why does he instead choose a text in which the matriarch is merely implied, rather than the only direct reference to Sarah in Isaiah?

---

53. The idea of Jerusalem as a mother city of refuge for Gentile converts is already present in Isa 54:15 LXX: "Proselytes will come to you through me and will take refuge in you." In *Joseph and Aseneth*, the proselyte Aseneth plays a role analogous to that of Jerusalem, as she is given the name "City of Refuge, because in you many nations will take refuge with the Lord God" (*Jos. Asen.* 15:7, trans. Charles Burchard, *OTP* 2:246). See also Zech 2:15 LXX. Rabbinic traditions connect Sarah with Jerusalem as the mother who nourishes proselytes. See, e.g., *Pesiq. Rab Kah.* 22:1. See discussion in Martyn, *Galatians*, 463 n. 189. In addition, *Tg. Isa.* 54:1 and *Pesiq. Rab.* 32:2 refer to Isa 54:1 to link Sarah with Jerusalem. See R. Longenecker, *Galatians*, 215; Florian Wilk, *Die Bedeutung das Jesajabuches für Paulus*, FRLANT 179 (Göttingen: Vandenhoeck & Ruprecht, 1998), 193 n. 22.

54. Martyn, *Galatians*, 434.

One possibility is that Sarah's "absence" repeats the point the apostle makes earlier in reference to the paternity of Abraham: a linear "fleshly" descent has no place in the description of the new community that exists "in Christ." Just as in Gal 3:6–4:7 the apostle modulates the formula "children of Abraham" into "children of God," so here in 4:21-31 he replaces the implicit "children of Sarah" with "children of the free woman."[55] Given this replacement, it is not precisely correct to name "the free woman" as Sarah. Rather, the role of Sarah in the birth narratives provides the category of "free woman," which Paul takes up and expands through the story of the barren woman in Isa 54:1.

This proposal finds support in the second observation: in the two oppositional columns of Gal 4:21–5:1, the lacuna opposite "Hagar" is filled in by "the barren one who does not bear." By replacing "Sarah" with this description of the barren woman's desperate situation, Paul emphasizes the limitation of natural human abilities, represented by Hagar, in contrast with the plenitude of God's fulfillment of the promise.[56] Within the Genesis narrative itself, Abraham's alliance with Hagar is an interruption in the pattern of "promise-fulfillment," analogous to the way in which Gal 3:15-18 depicts the Sinaitic law as interrupting God's promise to Abraham. The patriarch's "fleshly" liaison with Hagar brings forth only one son, who faces an uncertain future in the wilderness (Gen 21:10-14), whereas Sarah bears, through God's promise, a son who will have "offspring as numerous as the stars of heaven" (Gen 22:17).[57] As noted above, Isa 54:1 is not exactly parallel, but it metaphorically makes the same point: the "woman who has a husband" has the human "means" to bear children, and she does — but relatively few. The woman who is both desolate and barren is doubly hopeless, from a purely human perspective, yet God

---

55. In Martyn's formulation, "Descent from God is the picture with which Paul ends his exegetical exercise (4:7)" (*Galatians*, 306; see 302-6 for Martyn's argument).

56. This contrast plays on the multivalent uses of "flesh" in Galatians: it is associated with the "works of the law" in 3:1-5; it is a power opposed to the power of the Spirit in 5:13-24; here in 4:23, 29 it refers to a method of procreation that is merely human. Burton (*Galatians*, 252) translates κατὰ σάρκα in v. 23 as "by natural generation"; Hays (*Galatians*, 301) refers to the "'fleshly' stratagem of having Abraham impregnate Hagar." For analysis of Paul's use of the term "flesh" in Galatians, and the argument that it refers to "what is merely human," see Barclay, *Obeying the Truth*, 208. At least in the allegory of 4:21–5:1, κατὰ σάρκα appears to refer to a "merely human" capacity to bear children.

57. Paul ignores both the promise in Gen 21:13 that God also will make a nation of Ishmael, and God's care for Hagar and Ishmael in the wilderness (Gen 21:17-21).

abundantly blesses her with many children. Similarly, warns Paul, the Galatians' alliance with the law-inscribing Teachers will bear few children for an uncertain future (Gen 21:10/Gal 4:30), in contrast with the numerous children of the "barren woman" in Isa 54:1/Gal 4:27. One might paraphrase Paul's citation of Isa 54:1 to read: "More are the children of the woman who must rely solely on God's promise than of the woman who can rely on her own fertility."

Thus, through the lens of Isaiah, the role of the barren matriarch in the Genesis narrative becomes paramount insofar as her natural ability to bear children is inversely related to the display of God's power through her. Paul's citation spotlights this inverse relationship, because it is so striking in the Isaiah passage. The extreme shame and hopelessness associated with barrenness in ancient Israel is well attested by the biblical texts.[58] The poet amplifies the woman's desperate situation by piling on the negative descriptors ("not bearing children," "desolate") in order to magnify her utter transformation from despair to joy, as the familiar lament of the individual barren woman is radically changed through the paradoxical imperative "Sing, O barren one." Lest the reader miss the point, Isa 54:4 spells out the reversal of status in negative terms:

Do not fear, for you will *not* be ashamed;
Do not be discouraged, for you will *not* suffer disgrace;
For you will *forget* the shame of your youth,
And the disgrace of your widowhood you will remember *no more.*

The barren woman rejoices, of course, because she miraculously now has more children than she can manage. She is the city overtaken by a veritable population explosion.[59]

---

58. See, e.g., 1 Sam 1:1-11; 2 Sam 6:23; Gen 16:2; 20:18; 30:1-2. See discussion in Darr, *Isaiah's Vision*, 98. Callaway, *Sing, O Barren One*, 109, also notes the way Paul links sterility and barrenness with "death" — specifically the "deadness of Sarah's womb" — in Rom 4:16-17.

59. Darr, *Isaiah's Vision*, 179. Such a dramatic movement from barrenness to abundant offspring is adumbrated in Isa 49:14-21. Isaiah 54:1, however, intensifies the scope of the change in Jerusalem's situation. In 49:21 the mother is "childless" (ἄτεκνος), but in 54:1 she is "barren" (στεῖρα). In 49:22-25 Jerusalem's promised multiplication of offspring will be due to their return from exile; 54:1, however, implies that the abundant progeny come through a miraculous birth. The actual terminology of childbirth is absent in the earlier passage; it is introduced into Isa 54 through the poet's appropriation of the barren matriarch motif as an image of Jerusalem.

The story of the barren woman in Isa 54:1 encapsulates a story of "mother Jerusalem," which threads through the remainder of the prophetic book and is taken up in a variety of ways in later Jewish apocalyptic texts. Therefore it is possible that Paul's citation of Isa 54:1 evokes not simply the "rippling pool of promise" in the latter half of Isaiah, but the storied shape of that promise. It is not necessary to argue that Paul has specific texts other than Isa 54:1 in mind, but simply that he cites a verse that summarizes a widespread and well-known "plot" concerning the destruction and redemption of Israel.[60] In the first part of the story, Jerusalem is represented by a woman who becomes desolate and childless, both cast off by her divine "husband" and bereaved of her children. In the second part of the story, her fortunes are reversed by divine favor, and she is again beloved and the joyful mother of children. By linking Isa 54:1 with his reference to "Jerusalem above," Paul claims for the heavenly city this story of the barren woman's movement from dereliction to fulfillment.[61]

60. In later rabbinic tradition, Sarah, Rachel, Rebekah, Leah, the mother of Samson, and Hannah are listed with Zion, on the basis of Ps 113:9 and Isa 54:1, as the "seven barren ones" (*Pesiq. Rab Kah.* 141). As Callaway concludes: "Any one of the barren mothers can be understood as a sign of what God has done for Israel and of what he will do for Israel. As a group they present the entire salvation history 'telescoped' around seven figures. As individuals, *each bears in her own story the theme of promise and fulfillment which is the theme of Israel's story*" (*Sing, O Barren One*, 123; emphasis added). For further discussion, see particularly Callaway, 13-57, 120-23. Wilk (*Bedeutung*, 193) notes that the story tradition of the barren woman begins with Sarah and culminates with Jerusalem, similarly to the way Paul "begins" with Sarah and ends with Jerusalem our mother: "The special significance of the Sarah-Zion analogy is shown in the fact that Sarah stands at the beginning, and Zion at the end, of the trajectory tracing God's merciful acts (*Gnadenerweise*)."

61. The most striking references to "heavenly Jerusalem" as a bereaved and restored mother of her inhabitants are in the post–70 C.E. book *4 Ezra*. See *4 Ezra* 7:26; 8:52; 9:38–10:54; 13:36. See also *2 Bar.* 4:2-4; 32:2-7. The motif of a heavenly Jerusalem may originate with the idea of a heavenly pattern to which the earthly temple corresponds (Exod 25:40; 1 Chr 28:19; Wis 9:8). See also *1 En.* 90; 91:16; *2 En.* 55:2 (longer recension); Rev 3:12; 21:2; 21:9–22:5; Heb 11:10, 16; 12:22. Hebrews 11:10 attests to an early Christian tradition associating Abraham with eschatological Jerusalem: "He looked forward to the city which has foundations, whose builder and maker is God." The closest verbal parallel to Gal 4:26 is *4 Bar.* 5:35 (*Paraleipomena Jeremiou* 27, ed. and trans. Robert A. Kraft and Ann-Elizabeth Purintun, SBLTT Pseudepigrapha Series 1 [Missoula, MT: Society of Biblical Literature, 1972]), which contrasts "the city above, Jerusalem" (τὴν ἄνω πόλιν Ἰερουσαλήμ), with the destruction of present Jerusalem. For further discussion see Porteous, "Jerusalem-Zion," 235-52; Frederick F. Bruce, *The Epistle to the Galatians*, NIGTC (Grand Rapids: Eerdmans, 1982), 220-21; Lincoln, *Paradise Now*, 18-22; R. Longenecker, *Galatians*, 213-16.

Two observations support this suggestion that Paul evokes the story of Jerusalem's redemption through his citation of Isa 54:1 in conjunction with "heavenly Jerusalem." First, Paul was not alone in connecting Isa 54 with descriptions of eschatological Jerusalem; such a connection occurs elsewhere in a variety of ways. Prior to Jerusalem's destruction, the picture of the city built of precious stones (Isa 54:11-12) recurs in the vision of glorified Jerusalem in Tob 13:16-17. The same imagery also informs the later description of the heavenly Jerusalem in Rev 21:10-21, further testimony that the proclamation of a lasting city in Isa 54 outlasted the second destruction of Jerusalem and developed into imagery for a heavenly Jerusalem. In both of these instances, the imagery from Isa 54 is taken up in reference to eschatological Jerusalem. But it is also used to refer to existing communities of faith. At Qumran Isa 54:11-12 is interpreted as referring to the "congregation of his elect," which is a present reality even as it will be the foundation of eschatologically restored Jerusalem (4Q164).[62] In the New Testament as well, two passages apply Isa 54:13 to the community of faith, where the new age is already partially present. In the Fourth Gospel, Jesus apparently alludes to Isa 54:13 in order to claim that everyone who has learned from God will come to him (John 6:45). Paul himself appears to echo the promise of Isa 54:13a in 1 Thess 4:9: "Concerning brotherly love, you do not need anyone to write to you, because you yourselves have been taught by God to love one another." It is not possible to determine whether Paul alludes specifically to Isa 54:13a, given the promise elsewhere of God's role as Teacher, as in Isa 30:20-21 and Jer 31:34. But it is clear that the apostle expects his converts in Thessalonica to experience direct instruction from God, just as he expects the Galatians to be

---

62. McKenzie's comment on Isa 54:11-17 speaks in a sense for later apocalyptic interpretations of that passage: "The point of the imagery is that Yahweh is founding a lasting city, one that will not again suffer the fate of the Jerusalem of the monarchy. What would the prophet have said if he were told that the restored Jerusalem would be laid in ruins in 70 A.D. by the legions of Titus? But the vision of the prophet here approaches the eschatological; the lasting city of Yahweh's good pleasure is not a material reality of walls and buildings located at a definite point of longitude and latitude; it is the community of the redeemed, of all those who are 'instructed of Yahweh' and are 'established in righteousness'" (*Second Isaiah*, 140). It is questionable, however, whether either Isaiah or later apocalypticists see "eschatological" and "material" as mutually exclusive categories. Isaiah 54:14-17 describes the city's security in quite concrete terms. Note also the material reality of the heavenly city in *4 Ezra* 10:55. See Michael Stone, *Fourth Ezra: A Commentary on the Book of Fourth Ezra*, Hermeneia (Minneapolis: Fortress, 1990), 335.

led by the Spirit, and that this expectation accords with the description of redeemed Jerusalem in Isa 54.[63]

The variety and abundance of these references to Isa 54 suggest its currency in the realm of Jewish apocalyptic expectation during the time of the Second Temple, supporting the likelihood that Paul also would be familiar with such an apocalyptic interpretation of the passage. This leads to the second observation supporting his evocation of the story of Jerusalem as a desolate and restored mother — its occurrence in other first-century texts. To take one example, *4 Ezra*, although later than Paul's letters and considerably different in its theology, provides a striking parallel to Paul's appropriation of the barren woman's story in relationship to a heavenly Jerusalem.[64] After the destruction of Jerusalem in 70 c.e., the author of this apocalyptic book struggles to come to terms with God's apparent injustice. The seer questions God's justice and mercy, and receives a series of visions that lead him to an acceptance of God's inscrutable ways.[65] In the fourth vision (9:26–10:59) he sees a woman who grieves bitterly. When he questions her, she tells him that she was barren for thirty years, but that finally God answered her prayers and gave her a son (9:43-46). But on the night of the son's marriage, he died, and now his bereaved mother is inconsolable (10:1-4). When he hears this story, Ezra responds with a remarkably unsympathetic form of "consolation": "What is your individual grief com-

---

63. One may also note other Second Temple Jewish texts in which the motif of the barren woman is appropriated to speak about spiritual "fruit" in an ethical sense. For example, in Wis 3:13 the righteous "barren woman . . . will have fruit when God examines souls," whereas the offspring of the unrighteous are "accursed." See also Philo's interpretation of Isa 54:1 as an allegory of the history of the soul, in which the "barren" soul receives the divine seed and "brings forth new life in forms of precious quality and marvellous loveliness, wisdom, courage, temperance, justice, holiness, piety and the other virtues and good emotions" (*Praem.* 27.159).

64. For dating *4 Ezra* in the last decade of the first century, see Stone, *Fourth Ezra*, 9-10; Bruce Metzger, "The Fourth Book of Ezra," *OTP*, 1:520. In contrast with Galatians, one may note that in *4 Ezra* it is precisely through the "sowing of the law" that God's righteous ones are to bring forth eschatological "fruit" (9:31; see also 3:20). *Fourth Ezra* anticipates the future salvation of righteous individuals, and the future advent of the Messiah; Paul proceeds from the conviction that the Messiah has come, the eschatological age has begun, and God is creating a new corporate people who are not defined in relationship to the law but solely in relationship to the Christ.

65. On "the transition of Ezra from skeptic to believer" as the central theme of the book, see John J. Collins, *The Apocalyptic Imagination: An Introduction to Jewish Apocalyptic Literature*, 2nd ed. (Grand Rapids: Eerdmans, 1998), 199-200; Stone, *Fourth Ezra*, 24-38.

pared to what the whole earth suffers? Look, we're all mourning, because 'Zion, the mother of us all, is in deep grief and great affliction' [10:7]. So 'shake off your great sadness and lay aside your many sorrows' [10:24]!"[66]

As Ezra speaks to the woman, she is transformed before his eyes and becomes "an established city, and a place of huge foundations" (10:42). An angel tells the astonished seer that the woman is really Zion; her son represents the temple that Solomon built, and the son's death represents the destruction of Jerusalem (10:43-48). Yet in the very midst of her grief and lamentation, the woman now is revealed to the seer as Zion in its glory: "the weeping Zion is the glorious Zion incognito."[67] Here the desolate city has a heavenly counterpart that exists in glory, has a material reality (10:55), and comforts Ezra in his grief.[68] Michael Stone comments, "Mourning for the city or Zion has been, of course, the central motive of the book so far; that mourning finds its consolation in the present chapter. The use of 'city' in the context of consolation is significantly dominant."[69] The city is built on huge foundations, it is established, it guarantees a sure future for its inhabitants.

There are, to be sure, significant differences between the stories of the barren women in *4 Ezra* and in Isa 54:1. In the first, the miraculous gift of a son is but a prelude to subsequent bereavement and restoration, as if *4 Ezra* begins where Isaiah's story of the barren woman ends. Nonetheless, the triumphant climax of Isaiah, with its promise of a new creation (Isa 65:17; 66:22), developed into the apocalyptic hope of a new creation, which reverberates in *4 Ezra* (7:75), as indeed it reverberates in Gal 6:15.[70] Whatever the

---

66. Stone (*Fourth Ezra*, 318-20) perceptively remarks that the woman represents the seers' earlier questions, and the seer takes on the role of the angel who spoke to him earlier in the book (4:1; 5:33). In comforting the woman, Ezra comforts himself and displays his progress in understanding. See also Collins, *Apocalyptic Imagination*, 206.

67. Humphrey, *Ladies and Cities*, 74. For the existence of preexistent, heavenly Jerusalem as a city that is now hidden and will be revealed, see also 7:26; 8:52; 13:36.

68. It is not clear whether the vision reveals the hidden, glorified identity of earthly Jerusalem or promises the transformation of the city from an earthly to a heavenly state. For extensive discussion of the relationship between suffering Jerusalem and heavenly Zion in *4 Ezra*, see Humphrey, ibid., 74-76.

69. Stone, *Fourth Ezra*, 336.

70. For the motif of new creation, see *Jub.* 1:29; 4:24-26; 11QT XXIX, 7-10; 1QH XI, 13; 1QS IV, 25; *1 En.* 72:1; 91:15-16; *4 Ezra* 7:75; *2 Bar.* 32:6; 44:5-15; *L.A.B.* 3:10; 16:3; 32:17. For the derivation of this apocalyptic motif from Isa 65-66, see Stone, *Fourth Ezra*, 239; Wolfgang Kraus, *Das Volk Gottes: Zur Grundlegung der Ekklesiologie bei Paulus* (Tübingen: Mohr/Siebeck, 1996), 247-52; Martyn, *Galatians*, 565 n. 64; Hays, *Galatians*, 345.

source of the story for the writer of *4 Ezra*, its adaptation in that apocalyptic book indicates its currency and vitality as a symbol of both transformation and hope for a lasting salvation.[71] So also in Gal 4:26-27, the combined images of Jerusalem above and the barren woman are richly allusive, redolent with this promise of transformation and ultimate stability.

In Isaiah as in *4 Ezra*, one is struck by both the "hermeneutic of reversal" and the promise of continuity that shape the depiction of Jerusalem as a barren and desolate woman who miraculously becomes the mother of countless children.[72] By citing Isa 54:1 Paul has chosen a verse that tells this story in a nutshell.[73] It can be traced throughout Isa 49–66, as the text resignifies tropes that previously conveyed Jerusalem's despair and desolation, but now are reversed and employed to describe her expectation and abundance.[74] As a city she will be rebuilt in glory (54:11-12); as a wife she will be restored to her husband and rescued from the shame of her abandonment (54:4-8); as a mother she will rejoice in her abundant off-

71. For the argument that *4 Ezra* appropriates an existing tale, perhaps 1 Sam 1–2, see Stone, *Fourth Ezra*, 311. In Humphrey's view (*Ladies and Cities*, 166), "for the reader of the apocalypse, the Woman-City symbolism will have already evoked ideas of Israel as the Bride of Yahweh, with promises of fruition (Isa. 54.1-14)." For the metaphorical linkage between women and cities, and the function of the metaphor to depict transformation and inspire hope, see Humphrey, 23: "Whether the hope of an ideal Zion is earthly or heavenly, preexistent, present or future, the general Old Testament idea is retained that God has as his spouse and habitation those who are faithful, and is preserving them, despite outward appearances. In *Aseneth*, *4 Ezra*, the Apocalypse and *Hermas*, this hope is made concrete within the apocalyptic form through the event of transformation or transfiguration experienced by the female figure."

72. For the "hermeneutic of reversal" in Deutero-Isaiah's allusions, see Sommer, *Prophet Reads Scripture*, 36-46.

73. Many commentators note the climactic and central role of Isa 54 within Isa 40–66. Westermann (*Isaiah 40–66*, 271) speaks of "the exceptional nature of ch. 54 as compared with all that precedes it." Abma (*Bonds of Love*, 84) maintains: "Chapters 54 and 55 together can be considered as the grand finale of Deutero-Isaiah. . . . Decisive moments in the dynamics of the book have taken place, such as Yhwh's arrival in Zion (52:8-10) and the people's recognition that the pioneering work of the servant was for their good (53:4-6). These crucial moments form the necessary background for the two final chapters, for the glorious song about Zion's future (chap. 54) and for the colourful invitation to come to Zion and enjoy there the good things of life (chap. 55)." For a similar evaluation of the climactic role of Isa 54, see McKenzie, *Second Isaiah*, 140.

74. Extensive discussion of the "story" in Deutero-Isaiah "of a woman's life from bereavement and barrenness in ch. 49 to the birth of a son in ch. 66" is provided by John Sawyer, "Daughter of Zion and Servant of the Lord in Isaiah: A Comparison," *JSOT* 44 (1989): 91.

spring (49:19-21; 54:1-3; 66:7-9) and nourish them as God nourishes them (66:11-13).

This story of transformation from barrenness to fecundity comes to a climax in 66:7-14, which pictures Jerusalem as a mother painlessly birthing a nation and nursing her children. John Sawyer notes concerning the relationship between 54:1 and 66:1-14:

> Coming as it does at the very end of the book of Isaiah, [66:1-14] picks up themes familiar to us from earlier passages. Of these the most significant is 54.1-10. . . . There the woman was promised a husband and lots of children: here the birth of her first child is described. Chapter 54 is written in the future tense, full of promises and assurances; this passage is in the past tense with an account of how she gave birth to a son. . . . But here, as in ch. 54, the emphasis is on the birth itself, as an act of new creation, on the mother rather than on the child. In fact who is born here is not clear: one child as in v. 7, or more than one as in the second half of verse 8, or a whole nation as in the first half of v. 8. . . . [T]his is not about the birth of a son as in [chs.] 9 and 11, but about birth as opposed to death, fecundity as opposed to barrenness.[75]

By highlighting the fecundity of God's promise, and the movement from promise to fulfillment in Jerusalem's story, Sawyer's comments train a spotlight on God's redemptive power, as that power brings to pass that which is humanly impossible.[76] This celebration of powerful redemption resounds in the joyful imperatives of 54:1, in which the barren matriarch's reversal of fortune is taken up and transcended by the promise to Jerusalem and, ultimately, to the whole creation.

The promise of Israel's redemption encapsulated in 54:1 suggests that such a celebration of God's new creative power also reverberates through Gal 4:21–5:1, and carries Paul's argument forward into his description of life in the Spirit in Gal 5–6. The issue is one of power.[77] After asking his converts, "You who want to be under law, do you not hear the law?" the apostle sets before them Isaiah's vivid picture of God's redemptive activity in contrast with human futility. This picture fills out the distinction stated earlier by Paul in

75. Ibid., 97.

76. Abraham's old age and Sarah's barrenness are also no barrier to God's life-giving power in Rom 4:17-19.

77. See Martyn, *Galatians*, 435.

3:21b-22, between the restraining power of the law and the life-giving power of Christ's faithfulness: "If a law had been given which could make alive [ὁ δυνάμενος ζῳοποιῆσαι] then righteousness would indeed be by the law [ἐκ νόμου]. But the scripture imprisoned all things under sin [ὑπὸ ἁμαρτίαν], that what was promised might be given through the faithfulness of Jesus Christ [ἐκ πίστεως Ἰησοῦ Χριστοῦ] to those who believe."[78] Here the law's power is limited to a specific purpose; it intensifies human limitations and is powerless to give life.[79] In 4:21–5:1 the law fulfills the same limiting function in the left-hand column of Paul's "Table of Opposites" as the circumcising mission bears children into slavery. In the right-hand column, however, the transformation of the barren and desolate woman in Isa 54:1 sidelines the command of circumcision, and instead highlights the theme of God's new creative power in the birth narratives as well (see pp. 137-38). This picture of transformation sets the stage for Paul's ensuing exhortation concerning life in the Spirit, in which divine power rather than law-observance will transform the shared life of the Galatian congregations.

Four insights into the contribution of Isa 54:1 to Paul's message can be gleaned from the foregoing observations about the relationship between Isa 54:1 and the Genesis narratives. First, by citing a verse that implicitly refers to Sarah, Paul interprets the conversion of the Gentile Galatians as a sign of God's fulfillment of the promise to Abraham and Sarah. Through the Gentiles' reception of the Spirit, apart from observance of the Sinaitic law, they are living proof that God brings that promise to fruition apart from the law. As such they are "children of promise, like Isaac," not through the fleshly act of circumcision, but because they also are begotten by the power of the promise.

Second, by citing a verse that echoes Sarah's story but does not mention her by name, and indeed subsumes her story into that of Jerusalem, Paul further modifies his converts' self-understanding as "children of promise." That is, just as he modulates "children of Abraham" into "children of God," so now he modulates the implicit "children of Sarah" into "children of the barren woman." This modulation supports the apostle's

---

78. On the translation of ἐκ πίστεως Ἰησοῦ Χριστοῦ, see Hays, *Faith of Jesus Christ*, 132-56; Martyn, *Galatians*, 263-77.

79. In Rom 8:3 Paul paints a similar contrast between the weakness of the law and the powerful action of God in Christ.

earlier claim that the Galatians are God's children solely through the promise, not through lineal descent.

Third, the story of the barren woman in Isa 54:1 displays God's transformative power in the midst of human weakness. Through this picture of transformation, Paul claims that the point of Abraham's complicated family life is the contrast between divine plenitude and human limitation. Like the children of the woman who has a husband, "Hagar's children" have been born through merely human initiative and capabilities — and they are limited by the extent of those same capabilities. The barren woman's children, however, are born and live only by the power of God's promised Spirit, and they increase in number through that same limitless power. One might say that the two sets of "children" metaphorically represent two "family trees," one κατὰ σάρκα and the other κατὰ πνεῦμα. The difference between the two family trees is analogous to the difference between a "gospel κατὰ ἄνθρωπον" and Paul's apocalyptic gospel. In the latter, God accomplishes what is humanly impossible.

Finally, by linking the story in Isa 54:1 with the eschatological image of heavenly Jerusalem, a lasting habitation, secure and free from oppression, the apostle sets before his converts a triumphant picture of the future that belongs to the "children of promise." This picture supports Paul's proclamation of the staying power of the gospel by turning his converts' attention from the past to the future, from their origin in God's call to their *telos* as children of the heavenly city. In chapter six I will suggest some of the ways Gal 5–6 develops the social implications of that eschatological future for his converts' communal life here and now.

Taken together, these observations demonstrate that Isa 54:1 plays a central role in the function of Gal 4:21–5:1 as a "Pauline bridge," to recall Engberg-Pedersen's term: in line with the programmatic question of 3:3, it moves Paul's auditors from the question of their origin to that of their corresponding "end." That is, it acknowledges the concern for Abrahamic descent and "genetic identity" that occupies 3:6-28, but it also emphasizes the Galatians' ultimate identity as miraculous children of the free eschatological city, thereby preparing the way for the implications of that new identity in 5:1–6:16. As a sign of God's transforming power, Isa 54:1 displays to the Galatians the power that will bring them from their first calling "in grace" to their completion by the Spirit. As a picture of the heavenly city that guarantees a future for God's people, no matter how hopeless things look on earth, it is a ringing affirmation of the ultimate destiny of the children of promise: "Jerusalem above is free, and she is our mother." The story of this city portrays a sweeping reversal on a cosmic level, as it moves from human barrenness to divine abundance, and from suffering to joyous birth without suffering.

What a triumphant picture of the "relational matrix" to which Paul and the Galatians belong! One might add, what an apparent contrast to the apostle's appeal to join with him in suffering for the sake of the gospel, taking on the identity markers of "co-crucifixion" with Christ. Recalling Paul's "labor" in Gal 4:19, one senses here a certain tension between these two pictures of life "in Christ," and of the power that sustains that life. Thus before turning to the apostle's exhortation concerning the communal life of the Galatians (Gal 5–6), it will be helpful to explore the relationship of Isa 54:1 to Paul's own preaching.

The Barren Woman and the Maternity of Paul

No Labor Pains?

If στεῖρα is the *Stichwort* that links Isa 54:1 to Sarah's story in Gen 11:30, ὠδίνω is the *Stichwort* that links the prophetic text to Paul's apostolic "labor" in Gal 4:19. The textual link is shaped by an ironic, paradoxical pattern of reversal: in 4:19 Paul suffers labor pains with his Galatian converts; in Isa 54:1 the barren woman has children *without* enduring labor pains. This contrast raises questions about the relationship between Paul's "maternity" and the barren woman's fecundity. That is, if the many children of Isa 54:1 include Paul's Gentile converts, one must ask what the connection is between his apostolic suffering and the barren woman's painless delivery.

One may begin by noting that in Isa 54:1 the metaphor of "labor pains" signifies terror and anguish, in an echo of the experience of devastation that is seared into Jerusalem's memory (see Jer 6:24; 4:31; 13:21; 22:23). The difference now is that Jerusalem does not have to go through that devastation again — such "labor pains" are a thing of the past. But paradoxically "childbirth" itself has not come to an end; rather, the promised multitude of children signifies the plenitude of God's restoration of Jerusalem. Thus Isa 54:1 highlights the story of mother Jerusalem as one of movement from futile "labor pains" to divinely given fecundity that bypasses the pain of labor. As noted above, this story culminates in 66:7-9, where the birth of

Zion's children is so speedy that she does not suffer in childbirth.[80] Thus, by naming the barren woman as οὐκ ὠδίνουσα, 54:1 both consigns her suffering and futility to the past and anticipates the miraculous state of salvation that is depicted in 66:7-14. This transformation of the imagery of childbirth reflects the scope of Isaiah's vision, insofar as childbirth without labor pains is unprecedented not only in Jerusalem's "story" but also in women's experience ever since the first mother was told she would bring forth children "in pain" (Gen 3:16).[81] In Katheryn Darr's words, "Mother Zion escapes the birth pangs that, according to Gen 3:16, have been everywoman's lot since Eve, the first progenitrix."[82]

---

80. Isaiah 66:7-9 echoes and amplifies the reversal limned by 54:1:

> Before she was in labor
> she gave birth;
> Before her pain came upon her
> she delivered a son.
> Who has heard of such a thing?
> Who has seen such things?
> Shall a land be born in one day?
> Shall a nation be delivered in one moment?
> Yet as soon as Zion was in labor
> she delivered her children.
> Shall I open the womb and not deliver?
> says the Lord;
> Shall I, the one who delivers, shut the womb?
> says your God.

The emphasis in the MT of 67:9 is on God's faithfulness and power to complete the birth process. The LXX differs somewhat, emphasizing rather a judgment on Israel's failure to trust in God's sovereignty over both birth and barrenness: "Behold, I gave this expectation [of the miraculous birth of the nation], yet you do not remember me, says the Lord. Behold, do not I make the childbearing [γεννῶσαν] and the barren woman [στεῖρα]? says the Lord" (66:9). In both versions, however, the transformation of the childbirth metaphors in v. 7 remains; the birth miraculously bypasses the pain of labor. For extensive discussion of the reversal of labor pains in 66:9 in relationship to both 37:3 and 54:1, see Darr, *Isaiah's Vision*, 221-24; Sawyer, "Daughter of Zion," 98.

81. The reference to "the days of Noah" in 54:9 also communicates the cosmic scope of Deutero-Isaiah's proclamation and hope. Westermann (*Isaiah 40–66*, 275) maintains, "There is no place in Deutero-Isaiah which indicates more clearly — though this is not said in so many words — that the turning-point which he had to proclaim had a significance which far transcended Israel herself, and affected the whole world."

82. Darr, *Isaiah's Vision*, 222.

The picture in Gal 4:19 could not differ more: the apostle suffers *pro-tracted* labor pains with the Galatian congregations — pains that he fears will end in an aborted birth rather than a healthy delivery. He fears that his work among them has been in vain (4:11), that their own suffering has been in vain (3:4), that having begun by the Spirit they will not be completed by the Spirit (3:3). There is a stark contrast between the situations of the apostle and the barren woman. That contrast points to either a total dislocation between Paul's mission and the promise of Isa 54:1 or a developmental relationship between the mission and the promise. As we have seen, the first possibility is precluded by the many strong connections between Paul's mission and the promise; indeed, the Gentile congregations themselves adumbrate the fulfillment of the promise of abundant progeny.

The second possibility, however, promises to be more fruitful. According to this reading, the movement in the barren woman's story, from anguish and futility to joy and fecundity, implies a similar movement in the birth and ongoing life of the Galatian churches. That is, through the textual link of οὐκ ὠδίνουσα, Isaiah's image of labor-free childbirth functions in Galatians as an eschatological fulfillment of Paul's apostolic "labor" in Gal 4:19. As a counterpoint to Paul's missionary "labor," Isa 54:1 provides a sneak preview of the end of the story, even as it tells the Galatians that they themselves prove the truth of the story. If so, then the story of the barren woman encapsulated in Isa 54:1 promises that the God who labors is also the God who delivers.[83] For this reason, the "barren woman" is summoned to "rejoice, break forth, and cry out" in Gal 4:27/Isa 54:1. Perhaps this triple imperative is an answer to Paul's own "perplexity" and desire to "change his voice" in Gal 4:20.

The Heavenly Jerusalem and Paul's Mission

If Isa 54:1 thus provides an eschatological promise in counterpoint to the apostle's missionary "labor" in Gal 4:19, it also may clarify the relationship between Paul's mission and the barren woman, whose miraculous delivery describes the maternity of "Jerusalem above." Such a clarification is wel-

---

83. One recalls the LXX of Isa 66:9, with its emphasis on the sovereign power of God: "Behold, do not I make the childbearing [γεννῶσαν] and the barren woman [στεῖρα], says the Lord?"

come, in that the tension between Paul's "labor" in 4:19 and the absence of labor pains in 4:27/Isa 54:1 necessitates careful qualification of the proposal that identifies "Jerusalem above" with the circumcision-free mission to the Gentiles. Martyn's precise formulation, in which "Jerusalem above" *sponsors* such a mission, minimizes the difficulty: "The Galatians' birth identity is analogous to Paul's apostolic identity, for their mother is God's promissory church in heaven — *she* is *our* mother — in the sense that they were born by the power of God's promise in the circumcision-free mission to the Gentiles."[84] To be precise, however, the Galatians' birth identity is analogous to that of Paul only in their birth as Christians by the power of God's promise, but not in their birth through the circumcision-free mission to the Gentiles. Rather, in recounting his own genesis in the faith, the apostle repeatedly ascribes it to a direct apocalypse from God apart from human mediation (1:12, 15-16). The distinction is important: that which has power to bring to birth and to liberate both Paul and the Galatians is not the mission itself but God's fulfillment of the promise, of which the mission is a servant.

Indeed, the childbearing role of "Jerusalem above" correlates with the role of the promise throughout the passage. This generative role can be seen through the interchangeable references to the promise and the maternity of the free woman. In 4:23 the son of the free woman is begotten "through the promise"; in 4:26 "Jerusalem above is free and she is our mother"; in 4:28 the Galatians are "children of promise"; in 4:31 "we are children of the free woman." As the climax of the passage, 5:1 spells out just what it means to be "children of the promise": "For freedom Christ has set us free." Christ is the "seed" who inherits the promise to Abraham, bringing liberation from the law and the *stoicheia;* fundamentally it is Christ's act of liberation that powerfully begets both the apostle and the churches he founds through the circumcision-free mission (3:16; 3:21–4:7).[85]

---

84. Martyn, *Galatians,* 441. Note also Martyn's comparison, *Theological Issues,* 207 n. 25, of the two covenants in Gal 4:24 with the similar language of covenants in 2 Cor 3: "Whereas in Galatians 4 Paul speaks of his circumcision-free mission as the (Sarah) covenant itself, in 2 Corinthians 3 his mission is in the *service* of the (new) covenant, a locution that may help us to understand how in Galatians Paul can include himself among the children of the Sarah/circumcision-free mission (note *'our* mother')."

85. Hays (*Echoes of Scripture,* 121) rightly notes 3:29 as the key to the relation between Paul's "ecclesiocentric" hermeneutic and christology: "Because the Gentile believers have 'put on Christ' in baptism (Gal 3:27), they have become united with him in a way that allows

Thus while there is a correspondence between the maternity of "Jerusalem above" and the generative preaching of the apostle's circumcision-free mission to the Gentiles, there is also an important distinction between them. In a sense, this distinction correlates with that between the promised culmination of salvation and the suffering and conflict that characterize life in "the present evil age." Perhaps nowhere else in Galatians is the tension between "already" and "not yet" in Paul's eschatology so pronounced as in the counterpoint between Paul's apocalyptic "labor" in 4:19 and the absence of "labor" in 4:27/Isa 54:1.[86] On the one hand, Paul suffers in solidarity with Christ, and he appeals to his converts to share with him in this suffering. The eschatological reservation of Gal 5:5 must be given its due: "Through the Spirit, by faith, we expectantly await the hope of righteousness."

On the other hand, even now "Jerusalem above" bears children without pain; the new creation that Isaiah announced is already proleptically present through the numerous Gentile Christians who comprise those children. Thus, by telling the Galatians that they belong to "Jerusalem above," Paul emphasizes the incursion of future apocalyptic events into the present time. In Andrew Lincoln's words:

> the emphasis in Paul's statement is on *realized* eschatology. . . . [I]t is when his emphasis is on realized eschatology that the apostle exchanges temporal categories for spatial. This realized aspect of Paul's eschatology is underlined by the double use of the present tense (ἐστιν) — the heavenly Jerusalem *is* free, she *is* our mother. The heavenly city represents an order which is now being realized and the benefits of which can now be experienced by the believer.[87]

---

them to participate — vicariously — in his inheritance and his destiny." See also Lincoln, *Paradise Now*, 26.

86. This tension is also present in the mixture of spatial and temporal references that contrast "Jerusalem now" and "Jerusalem above," implying for the latter Jerusalem a status that is both heavenly and eschatological. Stone's comments (*Fourth Ezra*, 335) on Ezra's vision of the heavenly Jerusalem are apropos for Gal 4:26 as well: "The revelation of the city is not tied by the author to an eschatological or heavenly context. The city is seen as real . . . ; Ezra is commanded to enter it and experience it (10:55-57). Questions as to whether the city is the heavenly Jerusalem or an eschatological one should probably be answered with an ambiguous 'Yes!'"

87. Lincoln, *Paradise Now*, 21-22.

This use of the present tense does not mean that in Galatians as a whole Paul proclaims *only* a realized eschatology. The letter ends with a ringing statement of Paul's suffering as a mark of solidarity with the crucified Christ (6:17); and as the previous chapters have shown, throughout the letter he calls on his converts to join with him in suffering for the sake of the gospel. One recalls Schütz's comments on Paul's call for universal subordination to the gospel: "All of this makes sense only where power and the gospel are thought of within the milieu of a history moving to fulfillment, where there is still a frontier to cross, a *telos* yet to arrive. The final judgment is the final and unmistakable manifestation of power. . . . This is only to say that in the very nature of the case apostolic authority cannot be final."[88] The future "frontier to cross" is why the distinction between "Jerusalem above" and the present circumcision-free mission to the Gentiles is so important; it sets a limit on the identification of the apostle's action with that of God. Without such a distinction, that mission would be in danger of becoming a *telos* in itself, rather than a servant of God's mission.[89]

Nonetheless, here in Gal 4:27 Paul anticipates the certain fulfillment of God's eschatological promise, just as Isa 54:1 anticipates the climax of Jerusalem's story in Isa 66. The saga of the barren mother contributes to the apostle's contrast between "childbirth" by the power of the flesh and "childbirth" by the power of the promise. And the image of "Jerusalem above" contributes to his contrast between the destinies of those "begotten" by the flesh and those "begotten" by the Spirit, as it evokes a vivid eschatological picture of the lasting city where God's salvation reigns. Together, these images carry forward the communal life of the "children of promise," in contrast with that of the children born "according to the flesh." Thus Gal 4:26-27 underwrites Paul's proclamation of the durative force of the nonnomistic gospel by depicting the sovereign power of God as the one who both "births" the Galatian congregations and will bring them to completion (3:1-3). In the remainder of the apostle's letter, he displays to his converts what "completion by the Spirit" looks like, in contrast with the false hope of "completion by the flesh."

---

88. Schütz, *Paul and Anatomy*, 285.

89. On the tension between "already" and "not yet," see Dunn, *Galatians*, 254, who cautions against identifying "heavenly Jerusalem" with the church.

Chapter Six

Two "Family Trees": The Opposition between the Flesh and the Spirit

I n the previous chapter we saw that the conflict between the children of the "flesh" and those of the Spirit sets the stage for the opposition between the flesh and the Spirit in Gal 5:13–6:18. This conflict plays out in the daily life of the Galatian congregations, insofar as Paul's familial metaphors in Gal 4 provide a heuristic way to conceptualize the respective qualities of communal life in the realm of the flesh and the Spirit.[1] That is, Paul's goal is that Christ "be formed" among his converts (4:19), and he knows that such formation does not happen in a vacuum: either it will be stunted in an environment shaped by the destructive interplay between the law and the flesh as oppressive powers, or it will flourish in communities led by the Spirit. Therefore, in the oppositional columns of his allegory (see chapter five above), the apostle lists the characteristics of two "family trees" deriving from the slave and the free woman. In 5:13–6:10 he sets forth

---

1. Implicit in this suggestion is a conviction that the understanding of Paul's metaphorical language is not well served by "translating" it into nonrelational terms such as "realm" or "sphere." Rather, my heuristic proposal is an attempt to take seriously Amos Wilder's comments about metaphorical and symbolic language in the New Testament, and to apply them to Paul's metaphors: "We should reckon with what we can learn about metaphorical and symbolic language from students of poetry: that it cannot really be translated, least of all into prose; that its meaning is to be thought in terms of its own distinctive mode of communication; that this kind of report of reality — as in a work of art — is more subtle and complex and concrete than in the case of a discursive statement, and therefore more adequate to the matter in hand and to things of importance" (*Early Christian Rhetoric: The Language of the Gospel* [Cambridge: Harvard University Press, 1964], 125).

these family traits under the headings of "the flesh" and "the Spirit"; they describe two relational matrices within which either deformation or formation takes place.[2] That 5:13–6:10 is bracketed by arguments against those who enjoin and receive circumcision suggests a close correspondence between the relational matrix constituted by the flesh and the nature of communal life under the tutelage of the other missionaries.[3]

Because a detailed investigation of Paul's argument in Gal 5–6 would require another book, in this chapter I will merely sketch out some connections between the oppositional columns in 4:21–5:1 and the characteristics associated with the flesh and the Spirit in 5:13–6:10 (see pp. 137-38). In the left-hand column of Paul's allegory, one finds the family traits of the

---

2. This way of conceptualizing the roles of the flesh and the Spirit in Gal 5 is similar to Martyn's interpretation (*Galatians*, 525) of the "works of the flesh" as "marks of a community under the influence of the Flesh," and the "fruit of the Spirit" as "marks of a community in which the Spirit is fruitfully active," but with a subtle difference. Martyn (532-33) speaks exclusively in corporate terms: "They have become marks of community character, so that if one speaks of 'character formation,' one adds that it is the community's character that is being formed by the Spirit (cf. 4:19)." In my view Paul has both the community and its individual members in view. That the categories of "individual" and "corporate" are not mutually exclusive is indicated by the apostle's references to "Christ in me" (2:20), the Spirit sent into "our hearts" (4:6), and the responsibilities of individual believers (6:1-9). These references imply that perhaps 4:19b also should be translated to refer to both individuals and the corporate community, so that Christ is formed "in and among" the Galatians. There is a circular interplay between the formation of the community and the formation of the individuals in it; it is through participation in a community led by the Spirit that individuals are shaped by Christ, but they in turn contribute to the community's character, so that it corporately bears the fruit of the Spirit. For Paul's concern with individual as well as corporate character-formation, see Barclay, *Obeying the Truth*, 231: "Paul lays a significant emphasis on the *character* of the moral actor — rather than, for instance, the enumeration of his *duties*. . . . His concern is for the fundamental direction of a person's life."

3. The structure of Gal 5–6, in which references to circumcision and its practitioners bracket the discussion of life in the spirit, is explicated by Frank Matera, "The Culmination of Paul's Argument to the Galatians: 5:1–6:17," *JSNT* 32 (1988): 79-91 (83); B. Longenecker, *Triumph*, 81; Martyn, *Galatians*, 544 n. 6. This structure is problematic for those who see in Gal 5:13 an abrupt shift to a "second front," in which Paul addresses a "libertine" faction in Galatia; e.g., Wilhelm Lütgert, *Gesetz und Geist: Eine Untersuchung zur Vorgeschichte des Galaterbriefes*, BFCT 22.6 (Gütersloh: Bertelsmann, 1919); James H. Ropes, *The Singular Problem of the Epistle to the Galatians* (Cambridge: Harvard University Press, 1929); Lightfoot, *Galatians*, 208; Burton, *Galatians*, 291; Jewett, "Agitators," 209-12; R. Longenecker, *Galatians*, 235-38. For arguments against the "two-front" theory, see especially Mussner, *Galaterbrief*, 367; Barclay, *Obeying the Truth*, 14-16.

relational matrix instigated by the Teachers' preaching: those who belong to this family tree are enslaved (4:22, 24, 25; 5:1), identified with the law of Moses (Sinai, 4:24; note also the "yoke of slavery," 5:1), persecutors (4:29), and excluded from the inheritance of Abraham (4:30). They derive their existence and family lineage from "the flesh" (4:23, 29), they are few in number (4:27), and they stand under the threat of disinheritance (4:30).

The "barren woman" and her children, on the other hand, are free (4:22, 26, 31; 5:1); they owe their existence as a family to God's miraculous activity (4:27); they are children of promise (4:28) and of the Spirit (4:29); and they are numerous (4:27). Paul treats them as acting subjects, addressing them directly as "brothers and sisters" (4:28, 31), and exhorting them directly to "stand fast" and resist the enslaving yoke of the law (5:1). As those born by the power of the Spirit, "through the Spirit" they wait for the "hope of righteousness" (5:5).

The Flesh

These two family trees appear as strictly antithetical in Paul's allegory, just as the opposition between the flesh and the Spirit is nonnegotiable in Gal 5–6. Yet it is by no means certain that Paul's auditors saw things in such a clear-cut way — quite the opposite is more likely. He introduces his allegory by addressing them as "you who want to be under the law" (οἱ ὑπὸ νόμον θέλοντες εἶναι, 4:21).[4] Such a wish would be entirely positive from the standpoint of the other missionaries and their followers, in that the law promised protection and guidance, including protection from the desires of the flesh.[5] But Paul's "allegory" responds to his converts' wish to be "under the law" by connecting the law typologically with the flesh and with slavery as characteristics of Hagar's family tree — the family system that derives its existence from "the flesh."

---

4. For the possibility that the Galatians learned the phrase ὑπὸ νόμον from the Teachers, see Joel Marcus, "'Under the Law': The Background of a Pauline Expression," *CBQ* 63, 1 (2001): 72-83. Marcus notes connections between "under the law" (an expression without parallel in the LXX or other Jewish texts), "the yoke of the law" (*m. Abot* 3:5), and "the yoke of slavery" (Gal 5:1). He also notes (74) the rabbinic expression "to bring near under the wings of the Shekinah" as a "common image for conversion."

5. For the argument that the Teachers taught the Galatians that the law would help them resist the "evil inclination," see Martyn, *Galatians*, 290-94. See also Joel Marcus, "The Evil Inclination in the Letters of Paul," *Irish Biblical Quarterly* 8 (1986): 8-21.

This interplay between law, flesh, and slavery resurfaces in the puzzling verses of 5:16-18:

v. 16: But I say, walk by the Spirit and you will in no way complete
the desire of the flesh [καὶ ἐπιθυμίαν σαρκὸς οὐ μὴ τελέσητε].

v. 17: For the flesh desires against the Spirit and the Spirit against
the flesh,
For these are opposed to each other,
So that you may not do what you wish [ἵνα μὴ ἃ ἐὰν θέλητε
ταῦτα ποιῆτε].

v. 18: And if you are being led by the Spirit, you are not under the
law [ὑπὸ νόμον].

Few verses in Galatians receive such sharply divergent interpretations as these.[6] Verses 16 and 18 correspond in their parallel references to walking by the Spirit and being led by the Spirit, suggesting also some kind of connection between the results of the Spirit's leadership: freedom from "completing" the desires of the flesh, and freedom from being "under the law." But recalling that at least some of Paul's converts *want* to be "under the law," one must ask whether they hear such freedom as self-contradictory rather than as "good news." The question may aid in understanding the puzzle of v. 17: who are Paul's addressees here, what do they want to do, and why are they unable to do it?[7] I suggest that 4:21 provides a clue through its similar combination of θέλω and ὑπὸ νόμον. The logic would proceed as follows: in the allegory of 4:21–5:1 Paul addresses his converts' desire to be under the law by warning them that the law will lead them into slavery, precisely because it is aligned with the flesh. In 5:16-18 he again addresses the same people, telling them that they cannot be led by the Spirit and under the law at the same time. His argument proceeds in three steps: having aligned the law with the flesh (4:21–5:1), in 5:16 he proclaims the power of the Spirit over the desires of the flesh; in v. 17 he names the conflict between the flesh and the Spirit, such that the Galatians, having re-

6. For a summary and evaluation of the commentaries, see Barclay, *Obeying the Truth*, 112-16.

7. The question of whether to translate ἵνα as ecbatic or telic is probably insoluble, but also not materially significant for the sense of the passage: either the conflict between the flesh and the Spirit serves the purpose of frustrating the Galatians' desired actions, or results in such frustration.

ceived the Spirit into their hearts (4:6), may not do what they wish — that is, go "under the law" by "going under the knife." Finally, 5:18 drives home the same point: they cannot simultaneously be led by the Spirit and under the law.[8]

If this analysis is correct, then one characteristic of the family matrix generated by "the flesh" is an attempt to be both under the law and led by the Spirit. According to Paul's apocalyptic vision, such an attempt is futile because both the flesh and the law as mediated through fleshly observance belong to the "present evil age," which is passing away, whereas the coming of the Spirit marks the advent of the new creation. Furthermore, this attempt to live a "dual existence" is not only futile, it is deadly, in that it severs its adherents from Christ (5:2-4) and consequently also from the relational matrix in which their divisions have come to an end (3:28). Outside that relational matrix, outside the shared identity that exists only "in Christ" and not in the law, the community becomes vulnerable to the "works of the flesh" that will rip it apart (5:19-21).

Thus a second family trait of the "flesh" is interpersonal and intercommunal strife, as described in the "works of the flesh": "enmity, strife, jealousy, anger, selfishness, dissension, party spirit, envy" (5:20-21). The works of the flesh also include sexual sins, drunkenness, and carousing. Paul emphasizes, however, the divisive elements in the characteristics of the flesh by warning against them in 5:15, 26.[9] These unsavory attitudes and actions are prefigured in Paul's depiction of Gen 21:9 as a situation of family strife instigated by Ishmael against Isaac: "As at that time the son born according to the flesh persecuted the son born according to the Spirit, so also now" (4:29).[10] Such a typological correspondence suggests that those who practice the "works of the flesh" express their identity as children of the slave woman, born according to the flesh through the fleshly practice of "works of the law" — that is, circumcision. Therefore

---

8. See also Martyn, *Galatians*, 531: "the note of tragic failure in 5:17 is one that Paul directs only to the Galatians who are attempting the impossible, that is to follow both Christ and the Sinaitic Law."

9. For the argument that 5:15 metaphorically describes the communal effects of the curse of the law in Deut 28:53-57, see Eastman, "Evil Eye," 74-75.

10. The manifest injustice of Paul's accusation against Ishmael has been abundantly discussed in the commentaries: it has no basis in Genesis, although there are some parallels in rabbinic texts (e.g., *Pesiq. Rab.* 48.2). For discussion and review of the literature, see Mussner, *Galaterbrief*, 329-31; R. Longenecker, *Galatians*, 200-206.

the "works of the law" that threaten to divide the Galatian communities are intertwined with the divisive "works of the flesh." Ironically, the law-inscribing mission of the Teachers increases the Galatians' vulnerability to the "flesh, with its passions and desires" (5:24); indeed, it is precisely the Teachers and their followers who are most in danger of succumbing to those passions. Paul himself practiced such works of the flesh in his former "zeal" (1:14); now he finds himself treated as an "enemy" (ἐχθρός) by the Galatians who have fallen under the Teachers' "troubling" influence (4:16).

Yet a third characteristic, disinheritance, connects the slave woman's children with the family matrix represented by the flesh. Quoting Gen 21:10, but changing "my son Isaac" to "the son of the free woman," Paul proclaims, "The son of the slave will not inherit with the son of the free woman" (4:30). This distinction between the status of the slave and the status of the free son as the heir picks up on the same distinction in 4:7. Paul's earlier numerous references to "inheritance" suggest that it is the "blessing of Abraham . . . the promise of the Spirit" (3:14, 18, 29; 4:7).[11] But his subsequent reference to disinheritance (5:21b) adds a further meaning: those who continually practice the works of the flesh "will not inherit the kingdom of God." Numerous commentators identify 5:21b as a pre-Pauline formula, perhaps used by Paul in prebaptismal catechesis, and they claim that the "inheritance" language here has nothing to do with κληρονομέω and κληρονόμος elsewhere in the letter.[12] Yet surely the references to inheritance in 3:14, 18; 4:30; and 5:21b invite further investigation, suggesting a link between the kingdom of God and the promise of the Spirit. Such a link is strengthened by connections between the Spirit and the "kingdom of God" elsewhere in Paul's letters. For example, in phraseology reminiscent of the fruit of the Spirit, the apostle proclaims that "the kingdom of God is not eating and drinking, but righteousness and peace and joy in the Holy Spirit" (Rom 14:17). The context is Paul's concern that the health of the Christian fellowship not be weakened by abuses of Christian freedom — a context similar to that of Gal 5:21. In another passage similar to 5:21, Paul precedes a long vice list with the warning, "the unrighteous will not inherit the kingdom of God" (1 Cor 6:9-10). But he immediately assures the Corinthians that they have been "washed, sanctified, justified in the name of the Lord Jesus Christ, and in the Spirit of our God," and adds a

---

11. Hays, *Galatians,* 276-77.
12. See, e.g., Betz, *Galatians,* 281, 284-86; R. Longenecker, *Galatians,* 258.

radical statement of freedom from the law: "All things are lawful for me" (1 Cor 6:11-12). In these passages, as in Gal 5:21, the apostle refers to the inheritance of the kingdom of God in the context of communal concerns, in relationship to the Spirit, and in distinction from the law. The implication is that the inheritance of the Spirit and the inheritance of the kingdom are intimately related, so that within the community led by the Spirit, the kingdom is partially present through the fruit of "righteousness, peace, and joy in the Holy Spirit."

Returning then to the question of the *dis*inheritance of the family tree represented by the flesh, the link between the Spirit and the kingdom suggests that disinheritance from the kingdom of God includes exclusion from the "family" led by the Spirit. Such exclusion is the outworking of the incompatibility between life under the law and life led by the Spirit: insofar as a communal matrix that practices the "works of the flesh" reveals its genesis κατὰ σάρκα, like the slave woman's children it also is "cast out" from the communal life of the Spirit that *proleptically* displays the kingdom of God. Hence Paul's insistent concern for the quality of his converts' communal life (5:15, 26). It is this concern that grounds his series of individual imperatives in 6:1-8.[13]

At the same time, Paul's repeated warning in 5:21b of a *future* disinheritance serves as a reminder that the kingdom of God is adumbrated, not fully realized, in the community led by the Spirit. There are yet a future judgment and an eschatological hope. Paul's attention turns emphatically to this future in 6:2-9, as he employs two eschatological motifs referring to divine judgment — "each person will bear the burden [of God's judgment]" (6:5), and "one reaps what one sows" (6:7-9).[14] Paul uses these mo-

---

13. On the relationship between individual responsibility and community life in Gal 6, see especially Kuck, "Each Will Bear," 289-97; Barclay, *Obeying the Truth*, 158-70. Both Barclay and Kuck emphasize the future orientation of Paul's appeal here.

14. The interpretation of 6:5 as a reference to judgment is supported by 5:10: "The one who is troubling you will bear the judgment [βαστάσει τὸ κρίμα]," as well as by the frequent use of "burden-bearing" language in reference to divine judgment in other Jewish and Christian texts. For the argument that 6:5 refers to the final judgment, see Schlier, *Galater*, 202; Mussner, *Galaterbrief*, 401; Bonnard, *Galates*, 125: "Mutual help in the church, but solitude of the person before the judgment of God." See also Barclay, *Obeying the Truth*, 162 n. 5; Kuck, "Each Will Bear." One also finds in *4 Ezra* 7:104-105 a striking parallel. The motif of "sowing and reaping" recalls the earlier motif of "fruit" and anticipates the final harvest at the last day. See Schlier, *Galater*, 204-5; Bonnard, *Galates*, 127. On "fruit" as an eschatological motif, see Barclay, *Obeying the Truth*, 119-21. *Fourth Ezra* speaks of the Torah sown in the hu-

tifs to encourage the Spirit-led community, but also to warn those who persist in practicing the "works of the flesh," including, in light of Paul's link between the law and the flesh, the law-inscribing practices enjoined by the Teachers.[15] In a relational matrix shaped by the nexus of the flesh and the law, individuals end up "sowing to their own flesh" (6:8) rather than investing in the shared good of the community. The result, warns Paul, is that the law, which promised to bring the Galatians to completion (3:3), ends up, in tandem with the flesh, delivering them over to corruption: "The one who sows to his own flesh will from the flesh reap corruption" (6:8). *This* is what "completion by the flesh" looks like; *this* is the bleak outcome of the family tree engendered and formed by the interaction of the flesh, which belongs to the transitory present age, and the law, which is unable to give life (3:21).[16]

I have suggested three connections between Hagar's typological family tree and the community shaped by the flesh: the fatal attempt to be simultaneously "under the law" and led by the Spirit, interpersonal conflict, and disinheritance. These connections are not exhaustive, but rather suggest a metaphorical family system represented by the flesh in opposition to the Spirit. It is important to note that these negative evaluations of "flesh" in Galatians all occur where it is opposed to the Spirit. Thus "flesh and blood" in 1:16, and Paul's reference to his life "in the flesh" in 2:20, refer simply to human, corporeal existence.[17] The birth of Ishmael κατὰ σάρκα also refers to an event instigated and limited by human capabilities; by as-

---

man heart, with the purpose of bringing forth fruit that is an eternal reward. See especially *4 Ezra* 9:31; also 3:20, 33; 4:30; 6:28; 8:6. Stone (*Fourth Ezra*, 73) suggests a possible connection to the fruit of the tree of life, which gives eternal life.

15. Barclay, *Obeying the Truth*, 164, 212. Martyn (*Galatians*, 553) argues that "sowing to one's own flesh" specifically refers to circumcision. In my view it certainly *includes* circumcision, but the context set by the list of "works of the flesh" implies a larger range of meanings. See also Betz, *Galatians*, 308.

16. Cf. 1 Cor 15:50: "Flesh and blood cannot inherit the kingdom of God."

17. See Barclay, *Obeying the Truth*, 205: "As [the Spirit's] opposite, σάρξ is caught up into the dualism inherent in all apocalyptic thought and is thus associated with 'the world' and 'the present age' which stand in contrast to the new creation. *It is this apocalyptic dualism which gives to σάρξ its negative 'colouring':* just as the present age is an evil age (1:4), so the flesh is at best inadequate and at worst thoroughly tainted with sin" (emphasis original). In association with the flesh, as in "the covenant in the flesh," the law also takes on this negative coloring. Compare *4 Ezra* 9:31-37, where the Torah continues forever, despite the judgment on those who are unable to keep Torah because of the evil inclination sown in their hearts.

sociation, the works of the law fall into the same sphere of human capabilities and their corresponding limitations. In this respect, Barclay's definition of flesh as "merely human" is helpful, because it captures the curiously "flat" quality of the existence that Paul depicts under the heading of "the flesh."[18] This family tree is a closed system, determined only in relationship to the past, because ultimately it has no future; turned in upon itself, with each individual egocentrically focused, because it does not share in the transcendent cosmic dimension brought by the sending of the Spirit into human hearts; unable to produce anything truly new because it belongs only to the "present evil age" — rather like a Hollywood B movie that is re-run endlessly.[19]

The picture changes dramatically when Paul sets forth the family traits of the community that draws its life from the promise and the Spirit. Indeed, Barclay says, in comparison with the flesh, "As regards the Spirit, here in Galatians (as elsewhere) a much fuller picture of personified power is evident: the Spirit cries 'Abba' (4.6), leads Christians (5.18) and is displayed in miraculous power in their midst (3.5). The Spirit is no less than the divine power unleashed in the dawning of the new age, the source of new life (εἰ ζῶμεν πνεύματι . . . 5.25)."[20] A closer look at the Spirit's activities will reveal both its role as the glue that holds together the cosmic and personal dimensions of the new relational matrix, which Paul and his converts share "in Christ," and its related role in bringing the Galatians from their genesis to their future completion in the faith. In both of these roles, the Spirit carries forward the family identity of the community born miraculously by the barren woman, belonging to the eschatological heavenly city, and therefore partaking of the new creation.

---

18. Barclay, *Obeying the Truth*, 206.

19. It is through association with the present evil age that the flesh may be said to have a *limited* cosmic dimension and enslaving power. Käsemann's comments are helpful (*Perspectives on Paul*, 26): "existence is always fundamentally conceived from the angle of the world to which one belongs. Existence is 'flesh' in so far as it has given itself over to the world of the flesh, serves that world and allows itself to be determined by it. But since confrontation with the creator is characteristic of this world, and since this confrontation has in fact always meant the isolation and rebellion of the creature, 'flesh' is also the sphere of the demonic."

20. Barclay, *Obeying the Truth*, 213. Barclay adds in a footnote (n. 90): "The texts in which σάρξ is personified are, in fact, remarkably few in comparison with the range of personal statements made about the Spirit."

The Spirit

In comparison with the family system defined by the flesh, the relational matrix led by the Spirit has both transcendent and personal dimensions, because the Spirit is closely aligned with Christ. The Spirit is given, received, and continually supplied where the message of Christ's faithfulness is preached and heard with faith (3:2-5). The Spirit is the Spirit of God's Son, and the sending of the Son is the occasion for the sending of the Spirit into human hearts (4:4-6). Thus the Spirit is in "our hearts," just as Paul claims, "Christ lives in me" (2:20). One would expect, therefore, that the Spirit carries on the work of forming Christ in and among the Galatians (4:19); it is this work of formation that the Spirit continues in 5:16-23, warring against the flesh (5:17), leading the Galatians (5:18), and bringing forth community-sustaining fruit (5:22-23).[21] In all of these ways, Paul depicts the divine activity of the Spirit as filling out the cosmic dimensions of the relational matrix in which Paul and the Galatians live.

At the same time, however, the Spirit's activities are also human activities, personally and corporately embodied in the Galatians' life together. The Spirit cries "Abba, Father," in the Galatians' hearts, but they also cry "Abba."[22] Just as Paul treats the "children of promise" as acting subjects in 4:28–5:1, so here he directly exhorts those who are led by the Spirit. The Galatians are commanded to "walk by the Spirit," who makes them alive

---

21. Barclay (ibid., 119-20) summarizes the various interpretations of "fruit" in 5:22: as a reference to the "spontaneous" quality of Christian behavior (Burton, *Galatians,* 313; Oepke, *Galater,* 140: "Fruit (καρπός) designates life's (outward) expressions as an organic outcome of the inner nature"; a reference to growth of character (George Duncan, *The Epistle of Paul to the Galatians* [London: Moffat, 1934], 173); a focus on virtues as a gift (Schlier, *Galater,* 187; Mussner, *Galaterbrief,* 385). Barclay (*Obeying the Truth,* 119-20) helpfully points instead to the numerous references to "fruit" in the Old Testament and intertestamental literature: Israel is a fruit-bearing tree (Ps 80:8-18; Isa 5:1-7; 27:2-6; Jer 2:21; Ezek 15:1-8; 17:1-10; 19:10-14), 121 n. 41; it fails to bear fruit (Isa 5:1-7; Jer 2:21; 8:13; 24:8-10; Mic 7:1ff.), 121 n. 42; it will again bear fruit in the eschatological future (Isa 27:2-6; 37:30-32 [MT פֶּרִי; LXX σπέρμα]; Jer 31:27-28; 32:41; Ezek 7:22-4; Hos 14:5-8; Joel 2:18ff.; Amos 9:13-15; *Jub.* 16:26; 1QS VIII, 20; *1 En.* 93:2-10), 121 nn. 43-44. In at least two of these passages, Isa 32 and Joel 2, the fruit comes from the Spirit. In Wis 3:13 the righteous barren woman "will have fruit when God examines souls."

22. In the parallel passage in Rom 8:15-17, Paul says, "When *we* cry, 'Abba! Father!' it is the Spirit himself bearing witness with our spirit that we are children of God, and if children, then heirs."

(5:16, 25); *they* have crucified the flesh (5:24); they individually may "sow to the Spirit" for the corporate good (6:8). The imperatives of 5:25–6:10 exhort the Galatians to act out what the Spirit works in and among them, because *they all*, having received the Spirit (3:2, 5), are πνευματικοί (6:1).[23] Thus, since the Spirit creates the fruit of gentleness (5:23), they are to treat the trespasser with gentleness (6:1); since the Spirit creates the fruit of goodness (5:22), they are to "share all good things" with their teachers (6:6), and to "work the good [ἐργαζώμεθα τὸ ἀγαθόν] to all" (6:10). By acting out the fruit bestowed by the Spirit, they themselves "sow to the Spirit" — "the one agricultural metaphor recalls the other."[24]

The picture created by Paul's description of the Spirit's action, combined with his exhortations concerning the Galatians' behavior, is thus of a community in which human action and interaction is guided and sustained by God's action. This dialectical relationship has been described in terms of the relationship between the indicative and the imperative moods, as believers' "repetition" of what Christ has done, and as an "overlay of Subjects."[25] As Barclay puts it, "The power and leading of the Spirit and even the gift of the fruit of the Spirit do not diminish but rather enhance the demand to work and to sow to the Spirit. . . . Paul saw the divine indicative in peculiarly dynamic terms — it was not simply a matter of what God *had* done (in election etc.) but what he *continued to do* in and for the believer."[26] One sees here the peculiar combination of cosmic and personal dimensions in the relational matrix to which Paul recalled the Galatians in 4:12-20. In Gal 5–6 it is the Spirit who holds together that

23. Barclay, *Obeying the Truth*, 157; Martyn, *Galatians*, 543.

24. Barclay, *Obeying the Truth*, 165. Note also the conjunction of the metaphors of "sowing" and "fruit" in Jas 3:18: καρπὸς δὲ δικαιοσύνης ἐν εἰρήνῃ σπείρεται. See also *4 Ezra* 3:20-22; 9:31-32, where "fruit" is meant to come from the Torah sown like seed in the human heart, but the continuing presence of the evil inclination stunts the growth of the seed. See commentary by Stone, *Fourth Ezra*, 73, 308-9.

25. For discussion in terms of indicative and imperative, see Barclay, *Obeying the Truth*, 225-27; for the notion of "repetition," see Martyn, *Galatians*, 547-48; for an "overlay of Subjects," see Hays, *Faith of Jesus Christ*, 224: "The Spirit given as our Helper effects a mysterious personal union with Christ. Thus the story does not simply shift from Christ as Subject in one sequence to humanity as Subject in the next. Instead, there is a complex overlay of two Subjects, so that Paul can attribute his own life and activity to 'Christ in me' (Gal 2:20)."

26. Barclay, *Obeying the Truth*, 226-27. In contrast with Fowl's assessment of Paul's personal narrative ("Learning to Narrate," 347), one sees here no competition between divine and human action, but rather divine action strengthening human action.

"matrix" and energizes the human participants to bring forth the fruit of loving service so that "Christ is formed" among them.

I argued above that Paul's description of life in the Spirit names the characteristics of the family tree that has its genesis in the promise rather than the flesh. Insofar as the Spirit is the source of the Galatians' own mutual service, the transformed community limned by Gal 5–6 is adumbrated by the "barren woman" who is figuratively their "mother." Just as she cannot bear children κατὰ σάρκα, so they cannot bear the fruit of the Spirit by the power of the flesh.[27] Both kinds of "fruitfulness" are impossible at the "merely human" level; nonetheless God brings them to pass — at the human level. Thus there is a correspondence between the fruit of the Spirit (5:22-23) and the "fruitfulness" of the barren woman who bears children according to the promise and the Spirit (4:23, 27-29).[28] Indeed, those who miraculously bear the "fruit of the Spirit" are expressing their identity as children of the free woman (4:31); it may be that the sacrificial mutual service produced by that "fruit" is the greatest miracle "worked among" them through the Spirit (3:5), so that they themselves may "work the good to all people, and especially to the household of faith" (6:10). This fruit shows itself in two related, paradoxical family traits — the fulfillment of the law and mutual sacrificial service.

First, it is the convergence of divine and human action that leads to the fulfillment of the law as a paradoxical mark of the family matrix that derives its identity *not* from the law but from the Spirit. In contrast to the futility of "fleshly" attempts to live under the law, here the law is fulfilled (5:14; 6:2).[29] The clue to this fulfillment is in the perfect passive

27. Nor could a "gospel" κατὰ ἄνθρωπον generate new life and bring the gift of the Spirit (1:11).

28. In Gen 30:2; Ps 131:11 (ET 132:11); Mic 6:7; Lam 2:20, καρπός refers metaphorically to offspring, as in "the fruit of the womb." Barclay suggests, "Since Paul refers to the 'blessing of Abraham' (3:14), it may be relevant to note that that blessing reads 'El Shaddai bless you and make you fruitful and multiply you' (Gen 28:3-4). If this is coming true literally through the inclusion of Gentiles (Gal 4:27), it is also being fulfilled in a metaphorical sense, through the 'fruit of the Spirit'" (*Obeying the Truth,* 122 n. 46).

29. The contrast is analogous to, but not identical with, that between Hagar's attempt to fulfill the promise, and Sarah's (reluctant!) reliance on the promise of God: "Regarding the *birth* of churches among the Gentiles, it is the Law of Hab 2:4, Genesis 16–21, and Isa 54:1 that is being brought to completion in the circumcision-free mission (Gal 3:11; 4:21–5:1; cf. Rom 10:15, 18). As regards *daily life* in those churches, what has been brought to completion is the Law of Lev 19:18" (Martyn, *Galatians,* 491). Contrary to Martyn (503-14), however, I do

πεπλήρωται in 5:14: "Through love be slaves of one another, for the whole law has been fulfilled in one word, 'You shall love your neighbor as yourself.'" Earlier in Galatians, Paul refers to the "fullness of time" (πλήρωμα τοῦ χρόνου), the time when the Son became a member of enslaved humanity (4:4). The perfect tense of πληρόω in 5:14 suggests that Paul there refers to a past event with continuing consequences in the present; the passive voice raises the question of the implied subject of the verb. One might therefore infer that here in 5:14 he refers to God's past act in sending his Son, and the Son's faithful self-giving on behalf of enslaved humanity. This inference finds further support from the content of the "one word" — "You shall love your neighbor as yourself." Paul's own narrative makes clear that the one who has enacted such love in the past is indeed the Christ "who loved me and gave himself for me" (2:20).[30] Therefore it is Christ who has fulfilled perfectly the intent of the law of Moses. The preceding sentence and the connecting γάρ indicate, however, that this fulfillment is not a substitute for the Galatians' mutual love and sacrificial service, but the foundation of such love. Thus Christ's fulfillment of the law also becomes the basis for Paul's command in 6:2: "Bear one another's burdens, and so fulfill the law of Christ."[31] Here again one sees the "overlay of Subjects" that characterizes the community led by the Spirit.

Second, the community led by the Spirit is to manifest the family trait of mutual service — literally, slavery (5:13). Paul extends the relational

---

not think that Paul cites Lev 19:18 in Gal 5:14 in order to refer to the original promise to Abraham rather than the Sinaitic law. The familiarity of Lev 19:18 as a summary of the Mosaic law, plus the fact that in Rom 13:8-10 Paul cites it as a summary of the commandments, imply that here in Gal 5:14 also the apostle quotes Lev 19:18 as a summary of the Mosaic law. See Sanders, *Paul, the Law*, 96. Christ's singular fulfillment of the summary of the law provides the guidance and empowerment for the human fulfillment of that law (Gal 6:2).

30. In Hays's words ("Christology and Ethics," 274), "*Agapē* finds its definitive expression for Paul in the figure of the preexistent Son of God who gave himself up for us (cf. Gal 1:4; 2:20) on the cross." See also Martyn, *Galatians*, 547-49.

31. Some scholars take "the law of Christ" as a reference to the Mosaic law; so, e.g., Sanders, *Paul, the Law*, 98. Others, such as Hays ("Christology and Ethics," 276, 286-90), take it as a reference to the pattern of Christ's life. I wonder if the distinction between these two interpretive options is hard and fast, given the close connection between Gal 5:14 and 6:2. That is, if, as Hays puts it, the "law of Christ" refers to "the structure of existence . . . embodied paradigmatically in Jesus Christ," that structure of existence fulfills the intent of the Torah of Moses encapsulated in Lev 19:18. In this sense, Christ can be said to be the τέλος νομοῦ in Rom 10:4, both as fulfilling the law's intent and as bringing to an end the law as the way to righteousness.

metaphors that permeate his letter in a surprising and shocking direction. As the earlier analysis of Gal 4 showed, those relational metaphors are fluid: by the inspiration of the Spirit, the Galatians cry out, "Abba! Father!" (4:6); Paul addresses the Galatians as both "brothers and sisters" (4:12) and "my children" (4:19); he is a mother in labor with them (4:19); and together both he and his converts are children of Jerusalem above, children of the free woman (4:26, 31). The ethical outworking of their new identity as children of the free woman is to be mutual service to "all, but especially those of the household of faith" (6:10). The exhortations of Gal 5–6 are bracketed by familial imagery.

Given this fact, it is striking that neither the paternal nor the maternal metaphors continue into those exhortations, even when Paul throws the weight of his personal authority behind his warning against circumcision (Ἴδε ἐγὼ Παῦλος λέγω ὑμῖν — 5:2). Rather, Paul addresses the Galatians with only two household metaphors; he calls them "brothers and sisters" (5:13; 6:1), and he tells them to be slaves of one another (5:13): "Do not use your freedom as a staging area for the flesh, but through love be slaves of one another." It is hard to imagine a more radical expression of Christian freedom than this abrupt and startling convergence of "family roles," particularly given Paul's contrast between the children of "Hagar" and those of the free woman. The liberty with which Paul employs and rearranges familial metaphors indicates, at least potentially, a corresponding fluidity in the structure of the new family system led by the Spirit.[32] Having repeatedly warned his converts against slavery to the law, now the apostle audaciously exhorts them to become slaves. As in the fulfillment of the law, here the connection between the Galatians' identity as children of the free woman and their call to be slaves is "in Christ." Christ is the one who was "born under the law" (4:4); therefore the new family system, which takes its bearings from Christ, has as its hallmark the same willingness to serve one's brothers and sisters sacrificially.[33]

Through such mutual service, the Galatians live out their inheritance

---

32. For similar observations about Paul's family imagery in 1 Thessalonians, see Malherbe, "God's New Family," 121: "The letter teems with the language of family, but the picture that emerges is neither consistent nor hierarchical."

33. Taken to its logical conclusion, the "overlay of Subjects" in the Christian community would include a willingness to subject oneself to the law for the sake of one's compatriots in the faith. Practically speaking, this is what Paul enjoins in Rom 14:13-21. Given the polemics of his Letter to the Galatians, however, he does not draw this conclusion here.

as children of the free woman. That is, they live out the gift of the Spirit that they have received as free sons and daughters (4:4-7). In contrast with the children of the slave woman, those who practice the works of the flesh, as children of the free woman they live in light of their eschatological hope.[34] Those who live by the power of the Spirit "eagerly await the hope of righteousness" (5:5). Being freed from the divisive "works of the law" and "works of the flesh," they bear the community-building fruit of the Spirit (5:16-18, 22-23). They "sow to the Spirit" and "reap eternal life" (6:8). They belong to the "new creation," "the Israel of God" (6:15-16). The picture of the redeemed community in chs. 5–6 fills out the reverse implication of 3:3: *this* is what "completion" by the Spirit looks like. Thus the apostle exhorts his converts, "Let us not grow weary in well-doing [τὸ καλὸν ποιοῦντες], for in due season we shall reap, if we do not lose heart. So then [ἄρα οὖν], let us work the good [ἐργαζώμεθα τὸ ἀγαθόν] for all people, especially those of the household of faith [τοὺς οἰκείους τῆς πίστεως]" (6:9-10).[35]

Conclusion

The analysis in this and the previous chapter suggests several ways in which Paul's citation of Isa 54:1 contributes to the transitional function of Gal 4:2–5:1, and supports his thematic exhortation in 5:1: "Stand fast, therefore, and do not again be subject to a yoke of slavery." The story of the barren woman affirms to the Galatians their own identity as free children of promise, and therefore as a sign of God's fulfillment of the promise to Abraham and Sarah. It also spotlights the theme of God's power and pleni-

---

34. Again, the comments of Malherbe ("God's New Family," 123) on 1 Thessalonians are relevant to Galatians as well: "It is by virtue of being an eschatological community, children of the day and of the light (5:4-5), that they are likewise to continue their own edification and nurture (5:11). It is this eschatological dimension that makes the psychagogical description that follows different. Unlike pagans, who also engaged in admonition and comfort, and helped their fellows, the Thessalonian brothers were to do so because . . . they believed in God's eschatological purpose for them."

35. B. Longenecker's comments on 6:9-10 are helpful: "If the Galatians imagined salvation to involve 'works' of the law (2.16; 3.2, 5) and 'doing' the things of the law (3.10, 12; cf. 5.3), even Paul's message of freedom from the law includes an aspect of 'working' and 'doing' (cf. 6.4). Paul is insisting that his gospel, rather than being ethically deficient, includes the social dimension within its remit" (*Triumph*, 81). See also Barclay, *Obeying the Truth*, 94.

tude in the Genesis narrative, proclaiming that it is God's power, not human endeavor, that also will bring the Galatians to the fruitfulness given by the Spirit. By subsuming the story of the individual barren woman into the story of Jerusalem's transformation from barrenness to fecundity, Isa 54:1 encapsulates the story of God's transformation of the corporate people of God. In the reversal of both Sarah's and Jerusalem's desperate straits, God does what is humanly impossible. For this reason, the movement in the story of the barren woman, from desolation to abundance, undergirds the movement in Paul's preaching to the Galatians, from the "perplexity" of 4:19-20 to the rejoicing of 4:27. By providing a sneak preview of the end of the story, the miraculous birth described in Isa 54:1/Gal 4:27 supplies a counterpart to Paul's apostolic "labor" in Gal 4:19, promising that his "labor" is not in vain. The present tense verbs describing "Jerusalem above" emphasize the incursion of eschatological reality into the present experience of the churches birthed by Paul's mission; at the same time, the tension between Paul's "labor" and the barren woman's painless delivery suggests that his churches also live in the tension between human suffering and divine power.

Through such an assurance of God's abundance over against human impotence, Isa 54:1 thus contributes to the apostle's contrast between the communities signified by the two mothers and the births of their respective sons. This contrast between futility and fruition sets up the ensuing conflict between the powers of "the flesh" and "the Spirit" in 5:1–6:8, but it also drives home the certainty of divine plenitude that forms the basis for "life in the Spirit" and guarantees its ultimate fruition and completion (3:3). Like Paul's own "testimony," the barren woman's "story" thus functions as a promise to the Galatians: "The God who labors is the God who delivers; stand fast, therefore, in the liberating power of the gospel. Don't be like Hagar, resorting to 'fleshly stratagems' to ensure your identity as God's children. Be like the barren woman, trusting that the God who works miracles among you will bring you to completion (3:3-5)."[36]

These observations indicate that the maternal imagery of Gal 4:19 and 27 does indeed provide clues to the nature of the relational matrix that Paul limns for his congregations. First, the spotlight on God's transforming power is consistent with the "line of movement" disclosed both by Paul's retrospective narrative, in which God in Christ moves into the cos-

---

36. The term "fleshly stratagem" comes from Hays, *Galatians*, 301.

mos and Paul moves into the sphere of the Galatians' existence, and by his identification with the prophetic call to embody God's involvement with humanity. That is, in each instance the transforming power comes from God in spite of human limitations; it is the divine initiative that moves the story forward from promise to fulfillment. If one speaks of a "history" thus created by the gospel, it is a history in which the movement from beginning to *telos* cannot be made without reference to God's action.

But, second, the history created by the gospel cannot be described without reference to human action as well — specifically, the human community in which the boundary-crossing love of God is to be enacted over time. The nature of the community thus becomes crucial in mediating the transforming power of God. In this regard, the maternal images of Gal 4:19 and 27 seem to present rather different pictures of the relational matrix that Paul and his converts share in Christ. In the apostolic suffering of 4:19, God's movement into the human sphere becomes visible through the weakness and persecution of the apostle, and Paul implicitly calls on his converts to share with him in enduring persecution for the sake of the gospel. In the victorious image of "Jerusalem above" rejoicing with her many children, such suffering is nowhere in sight. We may discern in these contrasting images the two functions of maternal metaphors that we noted in the gendered language of Guerric, abbot of Igny: such metaphors convey a radical reversal of values, and a promise of nurture and sustenance. Taken together, the contrasting images depict the tension in which the Galatians will discover the power of God sustaining their life together in Christ. This is the tension between human weakness and divine power, and it is adumbrated in Paul's paradoxical description of his converts' initial experience of the Spirit: "Did you suffer [ἐπάθετε] so many things in vain? If indeed in vain. Does the one who supplies the Spirit to you and works miracles [ἐνεργῶν δυνάμεις] among you do so by works of the law, or by the message of faith [ἐξ ἀκοῆς πίστεως]?"

The suffering and the eschatological power of the Spirit are contemporaneous, and the Galatian community is to join with Paul in living at the nexus of the two.[37] Both will shape their life together. On the one hand,

---

37. One sees the same reasoning at work throughout 2 Corinthians, as evident in Paul's description of his experience in Asia: "We were so utterly, unbearably crushed that we despaired of life itself. Why, we felt that we had received the sentence of death; but that was to make us rely not on ourselves but on God who raises the dead" (2 Cor 1:8b-9 RSV).

losing sight of the reality of present suffering and persecution would risk living in a delusional state, as if, in this "present evil age," it were possible to give birth to and sustain new life in Christ without experiencing conflict and pain. For Paul such a delusion would be an abdication of his apostolic calling to preach the cross of Christ (5:11) and a surrender to insipid "people pleasing" (1:10). One recalls Käsemann's acid comments on the subject of salvation history:

> Abraham does not know the country to which his exodus is to take him. He hears the promise of heirs without understanding how that promise can be fulfilled. What he sees speaks against it. From a human and earthly point of view, Sarah's laughter is completely justified and the expression of a realism which the church ignores at its peril. Sarah's laughter is faith's constant companion. . . . For Paul, salvation history is therefore exodus under the sign of the Word and in the face of Sarah's justifiable laughter. Its continuity is paradoxical because it can only endure when God's Word, contrary to the earthly realities, creates for itself children and communities of the pure in spirit.[38]

The reality of suffering and weakness manifests the power that sustains Paul and his converts — the "staying power of the gospel" — as quite simply the power that comes from God alone, the one who continually "supplies the Spirit" to the community of faith (3:5).[39]

On the other hand, by losing sight of the eschatological future — the "heavenly Jerusalem" — the Galatians risk falling prey to an overtly or subtly despairing acceptance of the status quo. Without hope, suffering makes no sense — "we are of all people most to be pitied" (1 Cor 15:19). Over against such a danger, Paul sets a vivid picture of the Galatians' destiny as children of the free woman, giving them a hope that produces endurance and sustains their present life together.

Therefore, finally, Paul's metaphors provide the family imagery that prepares the way for the contrast between the family system generated by the flesh and that generated by the promise and led by the Spirit. The characteristics of the first family tree are listed in the divisive "works of the

---

38. Käsemann, *Perspectives on Paul*, 69-70.

39. One notes in Käsemann's "paradoxical continuity" a similarity to Martyn's formulation of "theological continuity" and "anthropological discontinuity." But note also that such continuity endures on an *anthropological* level by creating "children" and "communities."

flesh." This branch of the family is generated and sustained by "merely human" capabilities, and therefore stuck in the "present evil age," cut off from Christ and destined for corruption. The family generated by the "barren woman," on the other hand, relies solely on God's promise, bears the "fruit of the Spirit," and belongs to the new creation. Paradoxically, the members of this relational matrix, sustained only by the God who continually supplies the Spirit to them and works miracles among them (3:5), find themselves called to responsibility as acting contributors to the fruitful character of their community. Insofar as that community transcends the "old age" division between circumcision and uncircumcision, by "faith working through love" (5:6), it will be in conflict with the present evil age and therefore experience suffering. Simultaneously, it will display the crucified Christ and mediate the transforming power of God over time, thereby adumbrating the new creation (6:15). This is the "completion" to which Paul calls his converts in Galatia, as he recalls them to the transcendent and personal relationship that they share with him and with each other "in Christ."

Chapter Seven

Paul's Mother Tongue and the Staying Power of the Gospel

Anyone familiar with Pauline studies will recognize an underlying polemic in the foregoing studies of Paul's "mother tongue." Like the literature professors whom Le Guin criticizes for teaching literature as if it were only "father tongue," we also may run the danger of reading and teaching Paul's Letters as if they were *only* "father tongue," that is, unidirectional, objective, and authoritarian.[1] As scholars we may seek objectivity and distance, or alternatively we may name our inability to do so, but surely it is a mistake to think that Paul himself seeks such objectivity and distance when he writes to his converts. Precisely the opposite is the case. Because he bases his appeal to the Galatians on his own "story" and his relationship with his auditors, Paul's preaching is intensely personal and emotional, with not even a pretense of disinterestedness or objectivity. Rather, the "overlay of subjects" so evident in his relationship with both Christ and his converts calls into question any rigid distinction between objectivity and subjectivity. Paul's whole way of speaking, from his claim that Christ lives in him to his designation of his scars as the stigmata of Jesus, renders such a distinction nonsensical. It is this "overlay of subjects" that animates the apostle's "native tongue," so that we fail to hear and understand him insofar as we attempt to translate that "native tongue" into purely objective discourse. Rather, in order to hear Paul's voice fully, it is necessary to listen again to his "mother tongue," to the intensely relational inflections of his voice, the language of his maternal "labor" with his con-

---

1. Le Guin, "Bryn Mawr," 153.

verts. Paul uses the intimate imagery of family life to draw his converts back into the thread of conversation that mediates their life together.

This investigation of Paul's language has focused on three aspects of the apostle's discourse in 4:12–5:1, all under the banner of "mother tongue": the relational network evoked in 4:12-20, the representational embodiment of his message, and the use of maternal metaphors in 4:19 and 4:21–5:1. My working hypothesis has been that close attention to Paul's mode of proclamation will illuminate the contribution of this section of Galatians to the letter as a whole. In particular, I have proposed that Paul's enactment of the gospel and his maternal metaphors give motivational force to his message by communicating the staying power of the gospel. According to this interpretation, 5:1 is a climactic summary of the apostle's overriding concern for his converts: "For freedom Christ has set us free. Stand fast, *therefore,* and do not again become subject to a yoke of slavery." Galatians 4:12-31 provides the basis and motive force for this exhortation, precisely because its two pericopes display the transforming and sustaining power that grounds the apostle's appeal. In 4:12-20 Paul gathers together the preceding theological and autobiographical strands of the letter, reminding the Galatians of the relational matrix that they share "in Christ" and recalling them to that shared relationship. In 4:21-31 he interprets the birth narratives of Ishmael and Isaac through the lens of Isa 54:1, thereby highlighting the plenitude of God's gracious fulfillment of the promise, over against the limitation of merely human effort. The contrast between the children "born according to the flesh" and those "born according to the Spirit" sets up the ensuing contrast in Gal 5:13–6:10 between life in the Spirit and life at the nexus of the flesh and the law.

Thus, by summing up the first half of Paul's argument and setting the stage for the second, 4:12–5:1 plays a pivotal role in the letter as a whole, turning the Galatians' attention from questions about their origin in the faith to assurances about their ultimate destiny as "children of the free woman" (4:26). At the same time, the passage also turns from a reaffirmation of their identity as God's children to exhortations about the outworking of that identity in their behavior (5:13–6:10). At stake in this pivotal passage is the source and nature of the power necessary to effect and sustain such a change in the Galatian churches. The apostle's discourse in Galatians provides clues to the nature of this power by limning narrative patterns of correspondence between Paul's preaching to the Gentiles, their conversion to Christ, and Christ's apocalyptic entry into the realm of human affairs. These patterns disclose a dynamic mimetic reversal at the heart of the gospel: because God in Christ participates in the human story, God initiates and sustains human participation in Christ's story through the gift of the Spirit.

The apostle's use of both personal and cosmological language further discloses the nature of the gospel's staying power. The personal character of Paul's appeal bases it in experience; it is indeed a kind of emotional, relational "mother tongue" that offers "experience as truth."[2] But because the dramatic change in his life demonstrates both the transforming power of God and the ongoing life of Christ "in" him, the apostle's preaching is also cosmological in scope. Paul even interprets his own physical scars as a placard of Christ crucified. In all of these ways, his means of communication exceeds a rhetoric of pathos; it is rather an "embodied" proclamation in which the message is communicated through the medium of the apostle's story, his previous encounters with his auditors, and even his own body. His relationship with the Galatians, in which he "became like" them, enacts the boundary-crossing love of God, who "sent forth his son, born of a woman, born under the law, to redeem those who were under the law, so that we might receive adoption as sons" (4:4-5).

This mutually participatory interaction between God and humanity is adumbrated in prophetic texts, fulfilled in Christ, and recapitulated in Paul's preaching to the Galatians. In Jeremiah, Isaiah, Ezekiel, and Hosea, the prophet's communication is at times multivocal, employing both spoken word and prophetic sign-acts, and mingling the voices of God, the prophet himself, and the people. In this sense, the prophet acts as a representative figure. Analogously, the shape of Paul's life is a sign of God's transforming grace; his relationship with his converts displays Christ's relationship with humanity; Paul's body is a sign of Christ crucified.

Thus in the preaching of both the classical prophets and Paul, the content of the message is indissolubly joined with a representational, embodied mode of proclamation. Far from being an authoritarian pronouncement from on high, such preaching comes from people who themselves are subject to the message they proclaim. For this reason it is not *authoritarian,* because it does not concentrate power in the messenger. Rather, the messenger becomes poignantly vulnerable. At the same time, this mode of

---

2. The offering of experience as "truth" is part of Le Guin's description of "mother tongue," ibid., 150.

communication is peculiarly *authoritative,* because the messenger's shared experience with his auditors renders him credible and therefore powerful.[3]

Keeping these summary observations in mind, I want to offer some concluding reflections on the gospel's power to "create a history," and its relationship to Paul's mode of proclamation as "mother tongue."

The Power of the Gospel to Create a History: Four Reflections

Reclaiming the Past

Paul's testimony reclaims the past for the new history being created by the gospel. In one sense, the gospel history begins with the advent of Christ in human history, and begins in the apostle's own life with the apocalypse of Christ in him. Yet the God who sent his Son and revealed him in and to Paul is also the God who set aside the apostle in his mother's womb. Paul's reclamation of the past becomes clear when one notes that Paul's own story displays continuity and discontinuity in both desirable and undesirable ways. On the one hand, the apocalypse of Jesus Christ in him occasioned a radical break with his "former life in Judaism"; on the other hand, that former life was itself an interruption of the movement from Paul's call "from my mother's womb" to the fulfillment of that call.

The apostle describes a similar double discontinuity in the Galatians' story: the good news is that although formerly they were enslaved under the *stoicheia,* now they have been set free in Christ; the bad news is that now regression under the law is severing them from their first calling in grace. These observations suggest that the history created by the gospel does not simply negate either Paul's or his converts' pasts, but rather affirms their original and originating call by God; seen from the vantage point of that gracious call, there is no past outside the embrace of God's purposes.

Paul's "mother tongue" furthers this reclamation of the past in several ways. It is a language that carries with it the memory of God's revelation to

---

3. In *Merriam-Webster's Collegiate Dictionary,* 11th ed. (Springfield, MA: Merriam-Webster, 2003), 83, "authoritarian" is defined as "1: of, relating to, or favoring blind submission to authority . . . ; 2: of, relating to, or favoring a concentration of power in a leader or an elite not constitutionally responsible to the people." "Authoritative" is defined as "having or proceeding from authority."

Israel, through the calling of Abraham, and also through the preaching of the prophets. Paul's mingling of βίος and message displays in his person an enactment of God's prior calling, and communicates through his own person a promise of continuity as well as transformation.

Time and Relationships

That Paul appeals to his converts in relational terminology suggests that their continuous movement from call to completion is mediated by their interaction in Christ. Conversely, the law delivers discontinuity in the temporal progression of their life in Christ, because it disrupts the relational unity within the Galatian congregations as well as between the Galatians and Paul. Thus one begins to see that the gospel "creates a history" in that it creates a *community*.

If this is the case, then the shared history of Paul and his converts, as those histories converge through and in Christ, does not display "theological continuity" and "anthropological discontinuity," to recall Martyn's terms. Perhaps the language of *time* and *relationships* would be more helpful for describing the gospel's power to create a history, because it replicates Paul's own terminology; he uses temporal markers to depict the radical break in his own life, and he uses the language of human interaction to depict the threat posed to his congregations by the other missionaries' insistence on law observance. At the same time, he exhibits in his own person a kind of temporal continuity sustained by the God who first set him aside and then revealed his Son in him, and he appeals for continuity in the fellowship that he shares with the Galatians. Paul's intensely personal, reciprocal appeal, couched in fluid familial metaphors, communicates to the Galatians that their "story" in Christ will be carried forward by the relational network to which they belong. As noted earlier, the gospel thus "creates a history" by creating a community that finds its unity in Christ alone, apart from the divisive effects of the law. The continuity thus created is both "theological" and "anthropological" in that it is sustained by God but also displayed through flesh-and-blood individuals and communities. In other words, it is a temporal continuity mediated by a network of transcendent and personal relationships.

Divine Movement

It is not adequate, however, to say that the gospel creates a history by creating a community, by involving Paul and his converts in a relational network through which the power of God sustains their new life in Christ. The other missionaries also have such a communal vision, and could say the same. Therefore a further qualification of the power of the nonnomistic gospel is needed, and it is at this point that Martyn's emphasis on the "line of movement" becomes crucial.[4] In Gal 4:12-20 the apostle's polemical contrast between the circumcising missionaries and himself distinguishes them precisely on the basis of the direction of the "line of movement." As noted in chapter two, when Paul says, "Become like me, *because* I have become like you," he implicitly contrasts their reciprocal relationship with the other missionaries' demand for unidirectional mimesis. When, in short order, he warns the Galatians that "they want to shut you out, so that you will seek them," he contrasts the conditionality and exclusivity of the circumcision mission with the graciousness and vulnerability of his own preaching to the Galatians.

Despite the apostle's polemical rhetoric, more is at stake here than different styles of preaching, or different personalities, or even apostolic authority. Rather, only by crossing the boundaries to become like the Gentile "others," without first requiring that they become like him, can Paul fully communicate the grace of God who took the initiative to liberate enslaved humanity. The powerful good news of the gospel is this divine movement into the sphere of human bondage, thereby setting humanity free to become like God.[5] Martyn is at his most eloquent in describing this liberating divine initiative: "See that in the literal crucifixion of Jesus of Nazareth God invades without a single if. Not *if* you repent. Not *if* you learn. Not even *if* you believe. The absence of the little word if, the uncontingent, prevenient, invading nature of God's grace shows God to be the powerful and victorious Advocate who is intent on the liberation of the entire race of human beings."[6]

The nature of this grace as transforming power is found in its dy-

---

4. Martyn, "Events in Galatia," 167. See discussion in chapter one.

5. The most succinct expression of this reversal is in 2 Cor 5:21: "For our sake he made him who knew no sin to be sin, so that in him we might become the righteousness of God."

6. Martyn, *Theological Issues*, 289.

namic, presuppositionless movement into the domain of human bondage under the powers of the present evil age, quite apart from any entry requirements. Because this gracious movement is not contingent on human observance of the law, its power to transform persists despite human disobedience and failure. At the same time, Paul is convinced that this grace comes home to the Galatians insofar as they experience it in human interaction. His enactment of the gospel, by "becoming like" the Galatians and by suffering persecution, is essential to the communication of God's grace in Christ. Such a form of discourse conveys a "history" that is far from docetic. Enmeshed in human experience and interaction, like the apostle himself, it also displays weakness and vulnerability.

Weakness and Incompletion

Reclaiming the past, mediated in the present by the community of faith, and disclosing God's gracious participation in human affairs, the "history" created by the gospel thus far looks visible and glorious. But such is not the case, as becomes evident in Galatians in the tension between Paul's suffering and "labor pains," and the victorious, pain-free childbirth of "Jerusalem above." Thus, finally, Paul's temporal and relational language does not depict an uninterrupted, victorious progression of gospel history, but rather an often painful story marked by the tension between beginning and completion. Rowan Williams's epigrammatic and poignant description of human "wholeness" could well be applied to the communal identity of the churches in Galatia: "My 'health' is in the thinking or sensing of how I am *not* at one with myself, existing as I do in time (change) and language (exchange)."[7] That is, the foregoing investigation of Paul's proclamation of the power of the gospel to "create a history" has disclosed an intimate link between the operation of God's transforming power through time ("change"), and the mediation of that power through human relationships ("exchange"). Short of the eschaton, the gospel history is incomplete; in conformity with the crucified Christ, it is a history of suffering, conflict, and apparent powerlessness.

Thus, as Williams's comments intimate, the history and community created by this gospel remain essentially open and incomplete in them-

---

7. R. Williams, *Lost Icons*, 151; emphasis added.

selves. They are informed at all times by Paul's eschatological reservation, and that "in-formation" limits the degree to which either the apostle or his converts "embody" the power of God. The only bodily markers available to the apostle this side of the eschaton are the stigmata of Jesus that accompany his communication of Christ crucified. Similarly, the community that originates from the "barren woman" lives always at the intersection of its own limitation and weakness, and God's limitless provision. This means that the communal history and the historical community created by the gospel will always look weak and fragmentary, pointing beyond themselves to a *telos* yet to arrive, and bearing within themselves a space, an emptiness where the transcendent "Other" can be revealed.

The open-ended, evocative nature of metaphors makes them especially suited to communicate such a history. Denoting without fully defining, referring without fully describing, metaphors effectively point beyond themselves to a God who never can be fully articulated. As we have seen in the tension between Paul's apostolic labor and the labor-free childbirth of the barren woman in Isa 54:1, it is the nature of the gospel community and history to do the same. The Gentile congregations in Galatia adumbrate the fulfillment of the promise of abundant progeny, but they also point beyond themselves to a future hope of righteousness. A community is not a metaphor because it is not a figure of speech; it may, however, function as a model that, like metaphors, functions as a signifier, a pointer, to invisible realities.

Paul's *maternal* metaphors in particular display the distinctive character of the gospel's transforming and sustaining power in three ways. First, they communicate a reversal of expectations about the nature of power and authority. The paradoxical power of God is veiled in suffering and upsets the cosmic hierarchy by exalting the lowly; it is the barren woman who rejoices, because her barrenness becomes the opportunity for God's abundant provision to become manifest. Similarly, it is the persecuted apostle whose mission engenders a multitude of Gentile believers in Christ, even as he worries that his labor may be in vain. The fecundity of the barren woman and the apostle's maternal labor both point beyond themselves to hint at the paradoxical nature of God's power mediated through suffering. God's labor on Israel's behalf, and God's labor in Christ, bring forth that which is humanly impossible.

Second, Paul's maternal metaphors set forth a vivid picture of God's enduring care for the community of faith. By evoking the storied promise of Isa 54:1, "Jerusalem above" denotes the mother-city who tenderly cares for her inhabitants, and who becomes a lasting refuge for God's children. Paul, no less than his converts, is the child of this city. The maternal image gives durative force to Paul's proclamation of the gospel's staying power. At the same time, it continues to limn an eschatological hope that remains in the future.

Finally, the familial imagery of mothers and children in the allegory of 4:21–5:1 provides a heuristic metaphorical construct for describing the contrasting aspects of communities led only by the Spirit, and communities that attempt to live simultaneously under the direction of the Spirit and the law. That is, as children of promise the Galatians have been born into "the household of faith," a family system with certain characteristics — mutual sacrificial service, the fruit of the Spirit, bearing one another's burdens. To describe such behavior as belonging to a family system generated by the promise of God, rather than by blood relations, is rather different than describing it simply as belonging to the sphere of existence under the power of the Spirit. Far from being sentimental, such family imagery creates a conflict between identification with one's biological family of origin and identification with the new family in Christ. The implication is that the relational matrix involving Christ, Paul, and the Galatians is to be formative at the most fundamental level, and that the community and history created by the gospel are intensely intimate and experiential.

Mother Tongue and Metaphor

Faced with Paul's metaphorical language, readers generally take one of three interpretive options. They may, like Castelli, focus on the dangerous and potentially coercive power of the metaphor — in particular the paternal metaphor — reading it in effect as a totalizing and ontological claim about the nature of God. In his study of metaphor in the Psalms, William Brown describes this collapse of the metaphor's distinction between the subject and the image: "When metaphors, for example, become literalized to the point that they exclude other metaphors for the same subject or target domain, particularly in the case of God, they function as idols. Such has been said of the exclusive use of masculine imagery for God."[8] When

8. William Brown, *Seeing the Psalms: A Theology of Metaphor* (Louisville: Westminster John Knox, 2002), 10.

Paul's family metaphors are read in this way, the only option appears to be rejection of his family imagery as oppressive and destructive. One purpose of the present study's focus on Paul's *maternal* metaphors is precisely to counter such a totalizing reading and rejection of Paul's parental imagery.

In order to counter the dangers of idolatrous misperceptions of God, a second option is to "translate" the metaphors into a different linguistic medium. One also may attempt such "translations" in order to make Paul's language more accessible to modern ears. For example, Engberg-Pedersen writes of Paul's Galatian passages describing the "effect of the Christ event on human beings": "The metaphorical terminology in many of these passages is quite striking and it is obvious that they are attempts on Paul's part to express a key experiential side of his thought. In view of the metaphorical character of the writing, there is an urgent need to try to advance to at least some clarity about what is Paul actually talking about. Thus we need some kind of translation."[9] Indeed, Engberg-Pedersen's whole project is to provide a "translation" of Paul's Letters that may provide a "real option" for at least understanding Paul in the twenty-first century. But Soskice's careful analysis of metaphor in both scientific and religious language argues strongly that such a "translation" is neither possible nor desirable. Indeed, it undercuts Engberg-Pedersen's assumption that modern scientific thinking can and indeed must dispense with metaphor. Perhaps more to the point, Engberg-Pedersen's translation project requires him to reduce Paul's "cosmology" to his "ethics," because he assumes that the apostle's cosmology is incoherent for contemporary readers and therefore not a "real option." At stake here is the close connection between the "interchange in Christ" at the heart of Paul's gospel and the mode of his proclamation of that gospel through relational metaphors. To "translate" his personal, passionate, vivid, and specific imagery about both God and human beings into abstract anthropological statements is to strip the apostle's language of its power and to distort his message. It is to collapse the "far-off point" of the metaphor into its "near point" in human experience, and thereby to deny the metaphor completely. Barclay makes just such a criticism of Engberg-Pedersen's comments on Paul's metaphorical language: "it leaves me with an uneasy feeling that to bracket out the Pauline 'metaphors' . . . of substantive change, of death and new life in Christ, made possible by an 'invasion' of divine grace, is to lose the heart of his religious

9. Engberg-Pedersen, *Paul and the Stoics*, 146. See also 334-35 n. 33.

convictions, and to fail to resonate with contemporary religious experience, whose expression is, after all, *necessarily* metaphorical."[10]

These comments highlight the relationship between religious language and daily life; if the metaphor expresses the real, flesh-and-blood experience of Paul and his auditors, it also speaks to the real experience of contemporary readers of Paul. In the present study I demonstrate this link between Paul's gospel and the concrete interaction and experience of his communities. Thus, whether the interpreter attempts to "translate" Paul's metaphors in order to avoid idolatry or simply to render them more accessible to modern ears, I suggest here that such attempts cannot help but distort our understanding of the apostle's letters. Brown states the problem in terms that speak eloquently to the interpretation of Paul's Letters as well:

> to eschew the power of metaphor in theological discourse for fear that idolatry is the unavoidable result would, in effect, sever any connection between God and the world of human perception. The outcome would be an impoverishment of theological discourse. . . . Interpreting Scripture into a more conceptually precise language will not retrieve its original meaning. Such a program, akin to demythologization, dispenses with the image that is so integral to its message, an aberrant form of allegorizing that serves only to tame the text.[11]

Clearly what I propose in this reflection about Paul's mode of proclamation is that attempts to translate Paul's "mother tongue" into "conceptually precise language" do indeed impoverish both theological interpretation of his letters and the power of those letters to speak to the apostle's readers today.

---

10. John Barclay, review of T. Engberg-Pedersen, *Paul and the Stoics, Biblical Interpretation* 9, 2 (2001): 236.

11. Brown, *Seeing the Psalms,* 10-11. Engberg-Pedersen's project of "translation" is indeed a project of "demythologization," insofar as he takes it as axiomatic that Paul's cosmology is not a "real option" for contemporary readers. The echo of Bultmann is not accidental; Engberg-Pedersen's approach is quite similar in aim to Bultmann's, as he himself acknowledges (*Paul and the Stoics,* 28-29), although he thinks that by comparing Paul to the Stoics he has found an ancient interpretive context that avoids the anachronism of Bultmann's existentialist anthropology. The further question arises whether Engberg-Pedersen has not interpreted Stoicism anachronistically by separating Stoic ethics from Stoic cosmology. See the criticisms of J. Louis Martyn, "De-apocalypticizing Paul: An Essay Focused on *Paul and the Stoics* by Troels Engberg-Pedersen," *JSNT* 86 (2002): 72-77.

The comments of Brown and Barclay point toward a third option in interpreting Paul's metaphorical language, and that is to allow the metaphors to speak in and to the context of human social constructs today. This option is fraught with dangers: the danger of idolatry, as mentioned above; the danger of anachronistic applications of familial imagery; the danger of abusive and coercive appropriations of such imagery; the evocation of destructive family experiences and painful memories. To some degree, as noted earlier, Paul's own eschatological reservation provides a check on such dangers. But it is also the case that family metaphors are dangerous because they are powerful, and they are powerful because they draw on foundational experiences. As Brown suggests, "it is on the anvil of experience that metaphor is forged. The poetic metaphor draws on a stock of common, immediate, and sometimes controversial images and events and transforms them into icons, into intimations of divine activity and reflections of human character."[12]

Paul's maternal metaphors evoke the most formative of human relationships, that between parent and child. Their evocative power suggests rich possibilities for reading Paul's maternal metaphors today, such that they function not as an obstacle to understanding but rather as a vehicle that connects the text with the contemporary reader on a multitude of levels — emotion, memory, and thought. Again, Brown's perceptive comments about imagery in the Psalms may speak of Paul's "mother tongue" as well, in a passage that deserves to be quoted at length:

> If genres function to create expectations in the reader that help determine the meaning of the text, then so does the text's deployment of imagery. The inviting and invasive nature of the metaphorical image effectively serves as the bridge that spans the yawning chasm between ancient and (post)modern worldviews and sensibilities. Such is in keeping with the essential role of metaphor, namely, that of "transferring" meaning, and in transference there is reception and, invariably, transformation. In the reader's appropriation of metaphor, the poetic text itself comes to be read in a different way, as *both* understood and appreciated — the two cannot be separated. Archetypal in scope, the most powerful metaphors share a "strangely common" ground between text and interpretation, even between the poet and the reader.[13]

12. Brown, *Seeing the Psalms*, 213.
13. Ibid., 11.

In other words, metaphorical imagery stimulates an interactive engagement with the text. The resulting "transference" of meaning reaches beyond the text's original recipients to contemporary readers, involving them also in a process of reception and transformation. Here the "inviting and invasive nature of the metaphorical image" means that there can be no distinction between "understanding" and "appropriation" — the metaphor cannot be held at a distance, but (metaphorically speaking) gets under the reader's skin.[14] Herein lie its power and danger. In terms of Le Guin's linguistic image, it is a kind of "mother tongue" that renders one vulnerable, and that "goes two ways, many ways, an exchange, a network."[15]

Conclusion

Finally, when these insights about the power of Paul's relational, embodied, and metaphorical mother tongue interface with the criticisms of Castelli and the caution of Williams regarding the corruptibility of religious language, the resulting conversation turns necessarily to the character of the reading community. Williams underlines the importance of that community in the following reflection on the nature of the incarnation as "the embodiment of God's act to create a moving and expanding network of saving relationship":

> If the Church exists, as it does, at an angle to the forms of human association we treat as natural, the temptation is to seek to ignore or abolish these forms: to treat people as if they were not deeply and permanently moulded by their natural and unchosen belonging, to a family or a language group or a political system. But this is manifestly damaging and illusory. The Jesus of the gospels is not a human cipher and does not speak to human ciphers: any attempt to pretend otherwise simply means that it is not the whole or the real person who is brought before God. The persons who are involved in the community of the Kingdom are not "new creations" in the sense of having all their relationships and affiliations cancelled. The question thus becomes how existing patterns

14. *Pace* Engberg-Pedersen's explicit distinction between "understanding," which he deems possible for modern readers of Paul's letters, and "appropriation," which he excludes a priori as a "real option" for modern readers (*Paul and the Stoics*, 335).

15. Le Guin, "Bryn Mawr," 149.

of belonging can collaborate with the patterns of the new community, if at all, how the goals and priorities of these existing patterns are to be brought together with the constructive work of the Kingdom, the Body.[16]

Williams speaks here about the relationship between the incarnation and the church, but his comments also illuminate issues involved in the appropriation of Paul's familial metaphors. Such appropriation necessarily involves a complex interface between the conceptual field of the metaphor and the histories — both personal and cultural — of the readers. In other words, there is no simple equivalence between any cultural or individual "mother tongue" and Paul's "mother tongue." The language of the new creation must be learned, and it is learned in the concrete interactions of participants in the new community created by that language.

For this reason, Paul's mode of communication and the character of the community are so tightly fused in the interpretive process that they cannot be separated. Such is the case in Paul's Letter to the Galatians: intensely concerned with his converts' communal character, the apostle employs familial and mimetic appeals to recall them to the personal and cosmic relational matrix they share in Christ. Therefore, in the original and subsequent interpretations of those appeals, the nature of the community in which they are read will render them either nonsensical or deeply nourishing. Insofar as that community fails to hear the mimetic reversal at the heart of Paul's good news, and the transforming and sustaining hope at the heart of his maternal metaphors, it lives at the nexus of the law and merely human effort, forgetful of future judgment and hope, and evading the suffering of the cross. But when its members indeed truly "hear" that mimetic reversal in which God's boundary-crossing love has come into their life together, they may display that love in their mutual interaction, so that it becomes a gracious new family system — a "moving and expanding network of saving relationship" that is conflicted, incomplete, and weak in itself, yet one in which the paradoxical inflections of Paul's "native tongue" may be spoken and heard.

---

16. Rowan Williams, "Incarnation and the Renewal of Community," *On Christian Theology* (Oxford: Blackwell, 2000), 235-36; repr. from *Theology Wales* (Winter 1998): 24-40.

Index of Subjects

Abraham, 12, 13, 16, 46, 48, 53, 55, 128, 130, 131, 134, 136, 137, 139-45, 154, 163, 166, 175, 178; Abraham's seed, 38, 49; call of, 35-36, 40, 185; promise to, 15, 49, 126, 145, 153, 158

Addressable communities, 17

Allegory, 6, 15, 19, 90n.1, 113, 127-34, 139, 144, 161-64, 189

Antinomy, 17, 59-60, 98

Apocalyptic, 3, 14, 16n.36, 19, 20, 29, 33, 45, 48, 60n.92, 61, 65-67, 71, 80, 86-87, 92-93, 98-99, 110-19, 123-26, 127n.1, 147, 149-51, 154, 159, 165, 182

Authority, 10, 17, 45, 82, 84-86, 118, 160, 174, 186, 188

Barrenness, 6, 19, 88, 113, 115-16, 128-30, 133, 140n.43, 141-60, 163, 169, 172, 175-6, 179, 188

Children: of Abraham, 13, 48, 130, 153; of God, 2, 13, 37-8, 49, 51, 153; of promise, 40, 135, 138, 140, 153-55, 158, 160, 163, 170, 175, 189; of the free woman, 38, 40, 127-60, 166, 172, 174-75, 178, 182; of the slave woman, 135, 165, 175

Christ: crucifixion with Christ, 2, 12, 29, 50-50, 56, 66, 70, 73, 84-85, 97, 103-5, 107-8, 110, 123-26, 155, 160, 183; formation of Christ, 14, 60, 95, 117, 126, 162n.2

Circumcision, 4, 6, 12-14, 38, 42, 53-55, 66, 79, 97, 102, 104-5, 109-10, 132, 134, 153, 158-60, 162, 165, 174, 179, 186

Circumcision mission, 13n.32, 134, 186

Continuity, discontinuity: anthropological, 15-18, 185; relational, 12, 57, 59, 125-26, 140-41, 184-85; temporal, 3, 37-39, 41, 56, 125, 184-85; theological, 9, 15-18, 185

Conversion, 10-11, 153, 182

Cosmos, 2, 3n.5, 5, 29, 50-51, 58, 95, 104, 108-9, 112, 116, 125

Covenant, 12, 53-55, 58, 131-32, 134n.28

Elemental spirits; Stoicheia, 2, 6, 30, 34, 38-39, 48-49, 135, 158, 184

Embodiment, 9, 50, 71, 83-84, 86, 105, 108, 110, 119, 123, 182, 193

Eschatology: eschatological community, 116, 120

Eschatological reservation, 85-88, 159, 188, 192; future, 23, 86, 105, 111, 143, 154, 157, 159, 167, 175-78, 189; realized, 159-60, 167

Index of Scripture and Other Ancient Sources

Index of Scripture and Other Ancient Sources